Here A Litt

For additional copies contact:

Here A Little, There A Little
Vol. 2: Commentary
Copyright © 2010
Bryan Huie

DISCLAIMER:

This is not a work of fiction. However, any similarity to any person living or dead, other than explicitly named subjects, is purely coincidental. This publication contains views, opinions and conclusions derived from private research by the author. No assurances are offered, either implicitly or explicitly, that the data is either complete or definitive. All this being said, this book is a true reflection of the beliefs of the author and all research was conducted in a search to find the truth.

Dedication:

Psalm 23:

King James Bible

The LORD is my shepherd; I shall not want.

He maketh me to lie down in green pastures: he leadeth me beside the still waters.

He restoreth my soul: he leadeth me in the paths of righteousness for his name's sake.

Yea, though I walk through the valley of the shadow of death, I will fear no evil: for thou art with me; thy rod and thy staff they comfort me.

Thou preparest a table before me in the presence of mine enemies: thou anointest my head with oil; my cup runneth over.

Surely goodness and mercy shall follow me all the days of my life: and I will dwell in the house of the LORD for ever.

Table of Contents:

Bible Commentary:

The Jerusalem Council	6
Are the Dead Conscious?	18
Biblically Clean Foods	43
Does Grace Nullify God's Law?	54
Galatians Commentary	69
Heaven: Our Eternal Home?	104
The Israelites in Egypt	116
Lazarus and the Rich Man	122
The Mystery of God	136
Pharisees and Sadducees	170
The Resurrection fo Jesus Christ	186
The Role of Women in Church	210
What is Death	225
The Colossian Heresy	247
Synchronizing Calendars	241

Bible Commentary

This is a collection of articles covering a vast variety of biblical topics. The goal of each article is to simply reveal the truth. We look into the Old Testament law, clean foods, parables, freewill, predestination, and death - to name a few.

One of the inherent problems with the New Testament is that the reader does not know the questions asked. We are only provided the response the writer, often Paul, which was sent to the congregation. It is similar to hearing one side of a phone call. We review several Scriptures in great detail to determine exactly what the writer was addressing.

Acts 15:

What Was the Objective of the

Jerusalem Council?

Acts 15 records the decision of the Jerusalem Council regarding the way to handle Gentile believers who were then coming to faith in Yeshua, the Jewish Messiah. The commonly held belief that Gentiles are under a different law or that the Law of Moses is not relevant to them is examined. This article reveals the truth regarding the real intent of the council's very narrow ruling.

Acts 15 is one of the most misunderstood chapters in the Bible. This passage of Scripture describes the decision of the Jerusalem Council regarding the admittance of Gentiles into the Messianic **congregation** (Heb. *qahal*, Gr. *ekklesia*) of Israel. Many scholars use this chapter to claim that the Law given to Moses at Mount Sinai was nullified and no longer applicable to "New Covenant" Gentile believers.

The *Encyclopædia Britannica* reflects this erroneous conclusion, saying that the Jerusalem Council was "a conference of the Christian Apostles in Jerusalem in about AD 50 which decreed that **Gentile Christians did not have to observe the Mosaic Law of the Jews**" ("Jerusalem, Council of").

In this article we're going to thoroughly examine the actual **question** brought before the Jerusalem Council by Paul and Barnabas, and the **solution** that James and the Jerusalem elders arrived at to resolve this issue. Along the way, we'll look closely at what the text of Acts 15 really says.

The 15th chapter of Acts starts by immediately identifying the problem:

ACTS 15:1 And certain men came down from Judea and taught the brethren, "Unless you are **circumcised according to the custom** [ethei] **of Moses**, you cannot be saved." (*NKJV*)

We are told that some men came to the assembly of believers in Antioch, Syria from Judea and started teaching that circumcision "according to the custom of Moses" was a necessary part of salvation. The word "custom" is translated from the Greek noun *ethei* (lit. "custom," "law"). The root word *ethos* is sometimes used in the Bible to denote commands from the Law of Moses (Luke 2:42; Acts 6:14; 21:21). Here is the circumcision command found in the Law of Moses:

LEVITICUS 12:1 Then the LORD spoke to Moses, saying, 2 "Speak to the children of Israel, saying: 'If a woman has conceived, and borne a male child, then she shall be unclean seven days; as in the days of her customary impurity she shall be unclean. 3 And **on the eighth day the flesh of his foreskin shall be circumcised**.' " (*NKJV*)

Instead of this command from the Law of Moses, the messianic Jews from Judea were apparently using the circumcision command for the Passover as the basis for their teaching:

EXODUS 12:43 And the LORD said to Moses and Aaron, "This is the ordinance of the Passover: No foreigner shall eat it. 44 But every man's servant who is bought for money, when you have circumcised him, then he may eat it. 45 A sojourner and a hired servant shall not eat it. 46 In one house it shall be eaten; you shall not carry any of the flesh outside the house, nor shall you break one of its bones. 47 All the congregation of Israel shall keep it. 48 And when a **stranger** [ger] dwells with you and wants to keep the Passover to the LORD, **let all his males be circumcised**, and then let him come near and keep it; and he shall be as a native of the land. For **no uncircumcised person shall eat it**. 49 One law shall be for the native-born and for the **stranger** [ger] who dwells among you." (*NKJV*)

Yeshua was the fulfillment of the Passover (I Cor. 5:7). Apparently, the position of these Jews was that a Gentile who wished to partake of Yeshua's sacrifice was the same as a "stranger" (Heb. *ger*) who anciently dwelled among Israel and desired to observe the Passover. Therefore, these Jews believed that in addition to baptism, adult Gentile males had to be circumcised before they could partake of the true Passover and become part of the covenant people, Israel. Since uncircumcised Gentiles were a part of the Antioch congregation, this message clearly upset the members there.

ACTS 15:2 And when Paul and Barnabas had great dissension and debate with them, the brethren determined that Paul and Barnabas and some others of them should go up to Jerusalem to the apostles and elders concerning this **issue** [zetematos]. (*NASU*)

Paul and Barnabas, who were in Antioch at the time, did not agree with the teaching brought by these Messianic Jews. They vigorously debated this view with the men from Judea. Finally, the members of the congregation decided to send Paul, Barnabas, and others to Jerusalem to request the opinions of the apostles and elders on this matter.

The Greek noun *zetematos*, translated "issue" above, is SINGULAR. This is important to recognize because it tells us that there was **only** ONE issue here – the necessity of circumcision for a Gentile to be saved and receive the covenant promises of Israel. There were **no** other topics being debated.

It is vital to understand that obedience to the entirety of the Mosaic Law was NOT the issue in question at Antioch OR the issue ruled on by the Jerusalem Council! This is a crucial point to comprehend if we are to truly grasp the reason for and the meaning of the decision rendered by James (Acts 15:19-21). Later in this study we will examine the requirements established by the Jerusalem Council for the Gentiles that were accepting Yeshua and see where these requirements originated.

ACTS 15:3 So, being sent on their way by the church, they passed through Phoenicia and Samaria, describing the conversion of the Gentiles; and they caused great joy to all the brethren. (*NKJV*)

As Paul, Barnabas, and the others from Antioch made their way to Jerusalem, they recounted to the groups of believers they met with in Phoenicia and Samaria how God was calling and converting Gentiles. This was a source of great encouragement to these congregations.

ACTS 15:4 And when they had come to Jerusalem, they were received by the church and the apostles and the elders; and they reported all things that God had done with them. (*NKJV*)

Upon reaching Jerusalem, Paul and Barnabas reported all that God had done through them among the Gentiles to the apostles, elders, and the whole congregation (at this point, there obviously had not yet been a division into laity and clergy). They also apparently provided an explanation of the problem that had arisen in Antioch which had necessitated their appearance in Jerusalem.

ACTS 15:5 But some of the sect of the Pharisees who believed rose up, saying, "**It is necessary** [dei] **to circumcise** [peritemnein] **them** [autous], **and to command** *them* [paraggellein te] **to keep** [terein] **the** [ton] **Law** [nomon] **of Moses** [Mouseos]." (*NKJV*)

Paul and Barnabas spoke to the assembly and laid out the matter at hand. Afterward, some of the Pharisees in the congregation rose up to support the teaching about circumcision that had come to Antioch.

The translation above seems to indicate that the Pharisees were not only advocating circumcision, but also the keeping of the entire Law of Moses. However, this impression is due to an inaccurate rendering of their statement from Greek into English. Translating the Greek literally, the Pharisees said, "*dei* [It is necessary] *peritemnein* [to circumcise] *autous* [them], *paraggellein* [to instruct] *te* [and] *terein* [to keep] *ton* [the] *nomon* [Law] *Mouseos* [of Moses]."

What does the statement "It is necessary to circumcise them, to instruct and to keep the Law of Moses" mean? The key to understanding this assertion by the Pharisees is the little Greek particle *te* ("and"). This particle joins the Greek verbs *paraggellein* ("to instruct") and *terein* ("to keep") together. The particle *te* is periphrastic in this verse; that means it is used to connect two verbs that say what could be expressed by a single verb.

Therefore, the meaning of the Pharisees' statement is that it was necessary to circumcise the Gentiles in order to **instruct** AND **keep** the Law of Moses. The Pharisees believed that the act of circumcising the Gentiles would serve a dual purpose; it would educate them on the Law of Moses at the same time they were obeying that Law.

ACTS 15:6 Now the apostles and elders came together to consider this matter. 7 And when there had been much dispute, Peter rose up and said to them: "Men and brethren, you know that a good while ago God chose among us, that by my mouth the Gentiles should hear the word of the gospel and believe." (*NKJV*)

Having had both sides of the issue presented to them, the apostles and church elders assembled together to discuss the matter. Apparently both sides of the argument had supporters. After a heated discussion, the apostle Peter stood up and began to relate how Gentiles had originally been brought into the church.

ACTS 15:8 "So God, who knows the heart, acknowledged them by giving them the Holy Spirit, just as He did to us, 9 and made no distinction between us and them, purifying their hearts by faith. (*NKJV*)

We have to keep in mind that Peter's point here is directly related to the issue at hand – circumcision. Peter's point was that God gave Cornelius and his house the Holy Spirit without requiring them to first be circumcised.

ACTS 15:10 "Now therefore, why do you test God by putting a **yoke** [zugon] on the neck of the disciples which neither our fathers nor we **were able** [ischusamen] **to bear** [bastasai]?" (*NKJV*)

By his question ("why do you test God?"), Peter rebuked those who wanted to require the circumcision of adult Gentile converts in order for them to become part of the covenant people of Israel. Since the ONE issue being discussed here was **circumcision** (NOT the entire Law of Moses), it was **circumcision** that Peter referred to as a "yoke." The word *zugon* ("yoke") literally referred to a piece of wood that fastened on the neck of a beast of burden. But here Peter uses it figuratively to refer to circumcision as something that was burdensome or difficult for the adult Gentile men to endure.

The final two Greek verbs in Peter's statement, *ischusamen bastasai* ("were able to bear"), are both in the aorist tense. In Greek, the aorist tense in all of its moods represents the action denoted by it simply as a **one-time event**. The verb *ischusamen* comes from the root *ischuo*. The ***Theological Dictionary of the New Testament*** says that the primary meaning of this word is: "'to be strong or powerful' physically" (p. 397, vol. III).

Peter's statement to the Council was intended to point out that the Pharisees were trying to lay a burden on the adult Gentiles that none of the Jews themselves would have been **physically strong** enough to endure. The *Tanakh* alludes to how painful it was for an adult male to undergo the ritual of circumcision.

To illustrate this point, let's look at the story of the rape of Jacob's daughter Dinah by Shechem the Hivite. After having sex with Dinah, Shechem and his father Hamor sought to persuade Jacob and her brothers to give her to him in marriage. The brothers were angry about the situation, and concocted a plan to get revenge for their sister. They told them that Dinah would marry Shechem if all their males were circumcised. Since he was captivated by Dinah, Shechem agreed. He and his father then persuaded all the males in their city to be circumcised in order to be able to intermarry with the Israelites. We'll pick up the story in Genesis 34:24:

GENESIS 34:24 And all who went out of the gate of his city heeded Hamor and Shechem his son; every male was circumcised, all who went out of the gate of his city. 25 Now it came to pass **on the third day, when they were in pain**, that two of the sons of Jacob, Simeon and Levi, Dinah's brothers, each took his sword and came boldly upon the city and killed all the males. 26 And they killed Hamor and Shechem his son with the edge of the sword, and took Dinah from Shechem's house, and went out. (*NKJV*)

From this story, it's clear that adult circumcision was traumatic and debilitating to those who underwent the ritual. Peter's question in verse 10 is designed to cause the Jews advocating circumcision to put themselves in the Gentiles' place. Why should they wish to put such a physically burdensome "yoke" on the Gentiles that neither they nor their fathers had needed to bear?

A better translation of Peter's question into English is: "Now therefore, why do you test God by putting a yoke on the neck of the disciples which neither our fathers nor we **would be strong enough to bear**?" **Adult** circumcision was never required of the Jewish disciples of Yeshua because they had been circumcised on the eighth day after their birth in accordance with the Law of Moses (Lev. 12:1-3).

ACTS 15:11 "But we believe that through the grace of the Lord Jesus Christ **we shall be saved in the same manner as they**." (*NKJV*)

Peter ends up by affirming that circumcision is not what saves a believer, but rather the grace of God shown through Yeshua the Messiah. This was an obvious rejection of the position put forth by the Jews who had gone to Antioch (Acts 15:1).

ACTS 15:12 Then all the multitude kept silent and listened to Barnabas and Paul declaring how many miracles and wonders God had worked through them among the Gentiles. (*NKJV*)

Paul and Barnabas followed up Peter's speech by listing the things God had done among the Gentiles through their ministry. The point of mentioning these miracles and wonders was to show that God had accepted the Gentiles without requiring them to first be physically circumcised.

ACTS 15:13 And after they had become silent, James answered, saying, "Men and brethren, listen to me: 14 Simon has declared how **God at the first visited the Gentiles to take out of them a people for His name**. 15 And with this the words of the prophets agree, just as it is written: 16 'After this I will return and will rebuild the tabernacle of David, which has fallen down; I will rebuild its ruins, and I will set it up; 17 so **that the rest of mankind may seek the LORD, even all the Gentiles who are called by My name**, says the LORD who does all these things.' 18 Known to God from eternity are all His works." (*NKJV*)

After Paul and Barnabas finished speaking, James the brother of Yeshua, the leading elder in the Jerusalem congregation, spoke to the group. He confirmed the words of Peter, and then supported them with a quotation from the prophet Amos. In verses 16 and 17, James quotes Amos 9:11-12 from the Greek *Septuagint* translation of the Hebrew Scriptures.

It's interesting to note the context of the passage from Amos that James quotes. Here is the entire prophecy:

AMOS 9:8 Behold, the eyes of the Lord God are upon the kingdom of sinners, and I will cut it off from the face of the earth; only I will not utterly cut off the house of Jacob, saith the Lord. 9 For I will give commandment, and **sift the House of Israel among all the Gentiles**, as corn is sifted in a sieve, and **yet a fragment shall not in any wise fall upon the earth**. 10 All the sinners of my people shall die by the sword, who say, "Calamities shall certainly not draw near, nor come upon us." 11 In that day I will raise up the tabernacle of David that is fallen, and will rebuild the ruins of it, and will set up the parts thereof that have been broken down, and will build it up as in the ancient days: 12 that the remnant of men, and all the Gentiles upon whom my name is called, may earnestly seek me, saith the Lord who does all these things. 13 Behold, the days come, saith the Lord, when the harvest shall overtake the vintage, and the grapes shall ripen at seedtime; and the mountains shall drop sweet wine, and all the hills shall be planted. 14 And I will turn the captivity of my people Israel, and they shall rebuild the ruined cities, and shall inhabit them; and they shall plant vineyards, and shall drink the wine from them; and they shall form gardens, and eat the fruit of them. 15 And I will plant them on their land, and they shall no more be plucked up from the land which I have given them, saith the Lord God Almighty. (*Brenton's LXX*)

This is clearly a messianic prophecy which speaks of the Kingdom of God being established in the Holy Land. James' use of this particular prophecy indicates that he very likely identified those Gentiles coming to faith in Yeshua as the members of the scattered House of Israel ("Ephraim") mentioned in Amos 9:9. For more information on these "Gentiles," see my article on the lost tribes of Israel.

ACTS 15:19 "Therefore I judge that we should not trouble those from among the Gentiles who are turning to God, 20 but that we write to them to **abstain from things polluted by idols, from sexual immorality, from things strangled, and from blood**. (*NKJV*)

Here James announces his judgment on the matter under question. Adult Gentile men would not be required to be circumcised. However, James did expect that these Gentiles would **abstain** from four things in order to become part of messianic Israel:

(1) Eating food sacrificed to idols;
(2) Sexual immorality;
(3) Eating the meat of strangled animals; and
(4) Eating blood.

This decision by James raises several questions in the mind of a modern reader. Why did he choose these four particular requirements? Where did they come from? Was this all that Gentiles had to do? Or were these simply the beginning steps they had to take to enter into the congregation of Israel?

The four requirements James bound upon the Gentiles are *halakah* based on commands found in the Mosaic Law. In Hebrew, *halakah* literally means "the path one walks." Each of these commandments was based on ancient requirements found in the Law of Moses for a "**stranger**" (Heb. *ger*) who desired to live among the tribes of Israel. In fact, all the original commands can be found in the 17th and 18th chapters of Leviticus.

In this matter, James defined the path that the Gentiles should walk in order to be accepted by the Jews. James used a *halakic* interpretation of these commands from the Law of Moses regarding the *ger* to address how first-century Gentile "strangers" could be accepted into the assembly of Israel.

Let's look at these four commands from the *Torah* and see how James interpreted them for the Gentiles of his day:

(1) The precursor requirement to abstain from things contaminated by idols is found in Leviticus 17:3-9. This command requires any ox, lamb or goat sacrificed by an Israelite or a *ger* to be brought to the door of the Tabernacle of Meeting. The reason for this requirement was because these animals were being sacrificed to demons outside the camp instead of to God (Lev. 17:7). Paul tells us that the sacrifices Gentiles made to idols were actually sacrifices to demons (I Cor. 10:19-21). Therefore, James' command based on Leviticus 17:3-9 was designed to remove this demonic influence from the lives of the Gentiles coming into the assembly of Israel.

(2) The command against sexual immorality comes from Leviticus 18:6-

23. This passage is an extensive listing of forbidden sexual practices and relationships. Included in this wide-ranging list are incest, homosexuality, adultery, and bestiality. Leviticus 18:26 states that neither the Israelites nor any *ger* that dwelt among Israel should commit these abominable sins. All of these were detestable practices that had made the Gentiles (Heb. *goyim*) unclean (Lev. 18:24).

(3) The commandment against eating animals that had been strangled was based on Leviticus 17:15-16. This passage states that Israelites or a *ger* living among them would become unclean by eating animals that had died naturally or had been killed by wild beasts (cf. Lev 22:8). This command has its basis in the commandment against eating blood. An animal that has been strangled (or has died naturally or been killed by wild beasts) has not had the blood properly drained from its body. James proclaims that Gentiles coming into the church were to keep from becoming unclean by avoiding such things.

(4) The command to abstain from eating blood is found in Leviticus 17:10-14 (as well as Gen. 9:4; Lev. 3:17; 7:26-27; 19:26; Deu. 12:16, 23; 15:23). Neither the Israelites nor the *ger* dwelling with them were supposed to eat the blood of an animal, because the blood sustains the life of the flesh (Gen. 9:4; Lev. 17:11, 14; Deu. 12:23).

So as we can see, all the underlying commands found in Leviticus 17 and 18 applied to the Israelites as well as the *ger* living with them. James took these ancient commands from the **Torah** and built **halakah** upon them for the Gentiles coming into messianic Israel.

Since the entire Law of Moses was never the focus of this dispute, James' judgment could **not** have abolished the Mosaic Law in favor of the four requirements he put forth for Gentiles. If substitution had been his intention, he certainly left a lot of holes in his "replacement" law code. He failed to cover murder, theft, and many other uncivilized actions prohibited by the Law of Moses and condemned in the New Testament.

Simple logic requires us to admit that James' four requirements for the Gentiles were not all the laws they were expected to follow as believers in Yeshua the Messiah. So why did James only address these four? He tells us in the next verse:

ACTS 15:21 "For Moses has had throughout many generations those who preach him in every city, being read in the synagogues every Sabbath." (*NKJV*)

What does the concluding statement by James mean? This declaration has been widely misunderstood by scholars because of a prevailing antinomian bias in interpretation. However, if we keep in mind that James is explaining here the **reason** for his decision not to require circumcision of adult Gentile males, as well as the reason for the four commands he did bind upon the Gentiles, this verse begins to make sense.

With this statement, James answered the Pharisees' earlier contention that it was necessary to circumcise the Gentiles in order "to instruct and to keep the Law of Moses" (v. 5). Instead of immediate circumcision, he ruled that the same goal of instructing and keeping the Law of Moses could be achieved by the Gentiles attending Sabbath services in the synagogues.

James expected that after being accepted into the congregation of Israel by obeying these four minimal requirements, the Gentiles would attend synagogue services on the Sabbath and LEARN the Law of Moses. If one was truly converted, with this familiarization would come OBEDIENCE. The uncircumcised Gentiles would be taught the command of Leviticus 12:1-3 and would understand that it was required that they circumcise their male children on the eighth day in order to obey the Law.

The Pharisaic *halakah* regarding *gerim* (the plural of *ger*) becoming part of Israel required immediate circumcision of adult Gentile male converts. James disagreed with this interpretation of the Law of Moses, however. He concluded that God had accepted these Gentiles as they were, with only a spiritual circumcision of the heart. So James' *halakic* ruling regarding these *gerim* did not lay the burden of adult circumcision on them, but rather four other requirements based on the Law of Moses. By observing these four commands, the Gentile *gerim* could be accepted into Israel and could attend Sabbath synagogue services with the Jews.

Yet despite his difference of opinion with the Pharisaic believers, James also thought that the circumcision command should ultimately be observed. He believed this would happen as the Gentile converts grew in knowledge of the Law by attending synagogue services on the Sabbath. Although a common misconception is that only Jews attended synagogues, the book of Acts clearly shows that Gentiles also went there (Acts 13:14-32; 14:1; 17:1-4, 10-12, 17; 18:4).

ACTS 15:22 Then it pleased the apostles and elders, with the whole church, to send chosen men of their own company to Antioch with Paul and Barnabas, namely, Judas who was also named Barsabas, and Silas, leading men among the brethren. 23 They wrote this letter by them: The apostles, the elders, and the brethren, to the brethren who are of the Gentiles in Antioch, Syria, and Cilicia: Greetings. (*NKJV*)

James' decision apparently was well accepted by the apostles, elders and the assembly. They decided to write a letter explaining the decision and send it back to Antioch with Paul, Barnabas, and two men from the Jerusalem congregation, Judas and Silas.

ACTS 15:24 Since we have heard that some who went out from us have troubled you with words, unsettling your souls, **saying** [legontes], "*You must* be **circumcised** [peritemnesthai] **and** [kai] **keep** [terein] **the** [ton] **Law** [nomon]" – to whom we gave no *such* commandment – (*NKJV*)

Here in the letter we have a restatement of the original problem; some men went out from Jerusalem and preached that circumcision of adult Gentile men was needed to satisfy the Law of Moses. We know that the men who came to Antioch specifically said, "Unless you are circumcised according to the custom of Moses, you cannot be saved" (Acts 15:1). There was no mention of keeping the entire Law of Moses in the original teaching brought by these men.

The Greek phrase *legontes peritemnesthai kai terein ton nomon* literally reads, "saying to be circumcised and so to keep the Law." The grammar in this verse shows that the last part of the phrase (*terein ton nomon*-"to keep the Law") refers to a one time act – circumcision. The Greek conjunction *kai* ("and so") is used here to emphasize the result of the preceding action *peritemnesthai* ("to be circumcised"). For the Gentiles, "to be circumcised" would enable them "to keep the Law." The Jewish men who had come to Antioch were simply teaching that it was necessary to circumcise the adult Gentile men in order to conform to the Law of Moses. One single issue from the Law, not the whole Law of Moses, was the subject.

ACTS 15:25 It seemed good to us, being assembled with one accord, to send chosen men to you with our beloved Barnabas and Paul, 26 men who have risked their lives for the name of our Lord Jesus Christ. 27 We have therefore sent Judas and Silas, who will also report the same things by word of mouth. (*NKJV*)

Here the letter identifies those who will be bringing the judgment to them, so they may verify that it was sent from Jerusalem. Paul and Barnabas were one witness, Judas and Silas were the second witness, and the letter served as the third witness to the decision arrived at by the Jerusalem Council. "By the mouth of two or three witnesses a matter shall be established" (Deu. 19:15; Matt. 18:16; II Cor. 13:1).

ACTS 15:28 For it seemed good to the Holy Spirit, and to us, to lay upon you no greater burden than these necessary things: 29 that you abstain from things offered to idols, from blood, from things strangled, and from sexual immorality. If you keep yourselves from these, you will do well. Farewell. (*NKJV*)

This was the decision from James and the Jerusalem Council for the Gentiles in Antioch. Since the assembly in Antioch clearly knew that the matter of adult circumcision was what prompted this letter, only the four requirements agreed upon by the apostles and elders were listed.

ACTS 15:30 So when they were sent off, they came to Antioch; and when they had gathered the multitude together, they delivered the letter. 31 When they had read it, they rejoiced over its encouragement. (*NKJV*)

The congregation in Antioch received the letter and rejoiced at the encouragement that the apostles and elders from Jerusalem had sent them. All indications are that they agreed to abide by James' instructions detailed in the letter.

Conclusion:

The **ONE** issue being discussed by the Jerusalem Council was whether adult Gentile men had to be circumcised before they could become part of the congregation of messianic Israel. Some Jews from Judea (probably messianic Pharisees) interpreted the Scriptures to say that they did, and these men went to Antioch to teach that requirement. Meanwhile, Paul and Barnabas disagreed with this Pharisaic *halakic* ruling and went to Jerusalem to see what the consensus of the apostles and elders was regarding this matter. After much discussion, including a speech against adult circumcision by the apostle Peter, James issued an overriding *halakic* decision that adult circumcision was NOT required of Gentiles. However, he did lay down commands that they abstain from food polluted by idols, from sexual immorality, from eating strangled animals, and from eating blood. These four requirements were not a replacement for the Mosaic Law, but rather guidelines on how Gentiles could be accepted into fellowship with Jews in the synagogues on the Sabbath. It was here that James envisioned the Gentiles learning the Law of Moses with the intention of obeying it.

Bryan T. Huie
April 19, 2002

Revised: February 16, 2009

Are the Dead
Conscious or Asleep?

This commentary uncovers many of the lies of our Adversary (Satan) which cloud our understanding of what happens after we die in the flesh. One belief is that we go immediately to heaven to be with our loved ones. Some believe that we are placed in purgatory or a similar area waiting for judgment. Yet another belief is that we enter into "soul sleep", a form of unconsciousness, awaiting the final Day of Judgment. To know the truth, we will review the Scripture to see which view is supported by the word of God.

GENESIS 3:1 Now the serpent was more cunning than any beast of the field which the LORD God had made. And he said to the woman, "Has God indeed said, 'You shall not eat of every tree of the garden'?" 2 And the woman said to the serpent, "We may eat the fruit of the trees of the garden; 3 but of the fruit of the tree which is in the midst of the garden, God has said, 'You shall not eat it, nor shall you touch it, lest you die.' " 4 Then the serpent said to the woman, "**You will NOT surely die.**" (*NKJV*)

That serpent of old, Satan, is the father of lies and there is no truth in him (John 8:44). However, today mainstream Christianity believes and tenaciously clings to Satan's original lie to Eve. The idea that the dead don't really die, but instead remain conscious after death, is one of the fundamental beliefs of most Christian denominations. Funeral services for the religious are routinely filled with platitudes about the dearly departed watching over their still-living loved ones from heaven. Any who dare contradict this belief in the status of the dead are generally vilified and said to be part of a truth-twisting cult.

But we, as believers, should be guided by the Scriptures and not by satanically-inspired human tradition. This article is going to examine what the Bible clearly and repeatedly says about death, the status of the dead, and the only hope for the dead (the resurrection). Additionally, it will address some commonly misunderstood verses used to support the position that the dead are conscious after death.

First, let's understand that humans would have avoided physical death if they had obeyed God from the beginning. If Adam and Eve had followed God's instructions and not partaken of the tree of the knowledge of good and evil, they could have remained in the Garden of Eden. There they would have been able to eat from the tree of life (a tree which was not originally forbidden to them) and they would have lived forever. But when they disobeyed and believed Satan's lie (Gen. 3:4), physical death became part of the human experience.

ROMANS 5:12 Therefore, just as through one man sin entered the world, and death through sin, and thus death spread to all men, because all sinned — (*NKJV*)

The Bible teaches that there are three distinct parts to man: (**1**) body, (**2**) spirit, and (**3**) soul (I The. 5:23). These three are interrelated, but different.

(**1**) The body is the fleshly part of man: skin, bones, and organs. The body is composed of the same physical elements that make up the earth; that's why it is called "dust" (Gen. 2:7). When a person dies, their body eventually decays and reverts back to its component elements (Gen. 3:19). In the Old Testament, the Hebrew noun *basar* is the primary word translated "body" or "flesh," while the Greek words *soma* ("body") and *sarx* ("flesh") are most commonly used in the New Testament.

Through the miracle of resurrection, God brings back to life those who have died. The Bible tells us that the bodies of those resurrected will be of two kinds: renewed **mortal** bodies such as that of Lazarus (John 11:1-45) and the host of Israelites (Eze. 37:1-14), or enhanced **spiritual** bodies such as the one Yeshua received at his resurrection (I Cor. 15:39-54).

The difference in these two types of bodies is one of quality. There are six instances of resurrection recorded in the Bible prior to the raising of Yeshua: the widow's son from Zarephath (I Kings 17:17-23); the Shunammite's son (II Kings 4:17-37); the widow's son from Nain (Luke 7:11-16); the daughter of Jairus (Matt. 9:18-25; Mark 5:22-42; Luke 8:41-55); Lazarus (John 11:1 -45); and the saints raised in Jerusalem when Yeshua died on the cross (Matt. 27:50-53). However, although they all preceded Yeshua, he is called the **firstborn from the dead** (Col. 1:18; Rev. 1:5) and **the firstfruits of those who have fallen asleep** (I Cor. 15:20). This is because he is the only human ever to be brought back to life and given an **immortal** body. This won't occur again until the resurrection of the saints at the last trumpet (I Cor. 15:50-54).

(**2**) The human spirit is the nonphysical part of man. It is the human counterpart to the Holy Spirit, which is God's mind (I Cor. 2:9-16). Combined with the brain, the spirit gives us consciousness. It is referred to in the Scriptures as the "mind" (Deu. 30:1; I Chr. 22:7; Psa. 26:2; 73:21) or "heart" (Gen. 6:5; Job 17:4; Dan. 2:30; Mark 7:21; Heb. 4:12). "Spirit" comes from the Hebrew word *ruach* and the Greek word *pneuma*. These words can also mean "breath" or "wind," things which, like the spirit, can be felt but not seen (John 3:8).

A good way to picture the relationship between the body and the spirit is to draw a comparison to a computer system. The human body is like computer hardware (CPU, motherboard, hard drive, speakers, monitor, etc.) and the human spirit is like computer software (operating system, word processing, spreadsheet, web browser, etc.). Just as computer hardware without software is worthless, computer software can only function when working in combination with the hardware.

So also it is with the human body and spirit. When a person dies, their spirit returns to God who gave it (Ecc. 12:7; Matt. 27:50; John 19:30; Acts 7:59). The body without the spirit is dead (Jam. 2:26). Without a living human body (either mortal or spiritual) to interact with, the human spirit is unconscious, in a state similar to sleep. This is why the Bible so often speaks of death being like sleep. At the time of resurrection, God sends the spirits of the dead back to inhabit their bodies once again (Eze. 37:10; Luke 8:55).

(**3**) The soul is the combination of flesh and spirit. It is the whole person; their character, nature, disposition, temperament, and personality. Man does not **have** a soul, man **IS** a soul, as the Scriptures clearly tell us:

GENESIS 2:7 And the LORD God formed man of the dust of the ground, and breathed into his nostrils the breath of life; and **man became a living soul** [nephesh]. (*RWB*)

I CORINTHIANS 15:45 So also it is written, "**The first MAN, Adam, BE-CAME A LIVING SOUL** [psuchen]." The last Adam became a life-giving spirit. (*NASB*)

The word most commonly translated "soul" in the Old Testament is the Hebrew noun *nephesh* and its variant forms. This word is also often translated "life." The corresponding Greek word *psuche* is translated "soul" in the New Testament.

A soul is not something that can be separated from a person. Man **is** a soul. God creates a human spirit within every man (Zec. 12:1). When God puts a spirit within a person, they become a living soul. When a person dies, that spirit is taken back by God (Ecc. 12:7; Psa. 104:29).

The Bible plainly teaches that souls can die:

EZEKIEL 18:4 "Behold, all souls are Mine; the soul of the father as well as the soul of the son is Mine; **the soul** [nephesh] **who sins shall die**. (*NKJV*)

EZEKIEL 18:20 "**The soul** [nephesh] **who sins shall die**. The son shall not bear the guilt of the father, nor the father bear the guilt of the son. The righteousness of the righteous shall be upon himself, and the wickedness of the wicked shall be upon himself. (*NKJV*)

NUMBERS 31:19 "And as for you, remain outside the camp seven days; whoever has killed any **person** [nephesh], and whoever has touched any slain, purify yourselves and your captives on the third day and on the seventh day." (*NKJV*)

EZEKIEL 13:19 And will ye profane Me among My people for handfuls of barley and for pieces of bread, to **slay the souls** [nephashot] that should not die, and to **save the souls** [nephashot] **alive that should not live**, by your lying to My people that hear your lies? (*RWB*)

I PETER 3:20 . . . When once the Divine longsuffering waited in the days of Noah, while the ark was being prepared, in which a few, that is, eight **souls** [psuchai], **were saved** through water. (*NKJV*)

Most Christians accept the Greek belief that man has a dual nature; spiritual and physical. To these dualists, death is the separation of the immortal soul from the mortal body. However, the Scriptures above and many others clearly show that both the soul and the body are mortal and can die. The soul is extinguished at death, and the body begins to decay. The spirit, which was initially given by God, returns to Him. But since the spirit cannot function without the body, the spirit has no consciousness in death.

Many of those who teach that man remains conscious after death ridicule and mock the doctrine of the dead being unconscious, which they commonly call "soul sleep." They claim that only the body sleeps in death, while the soul is awake in either heaven or hell. A review of their position shows that they generally misunderstand the nature of the three components of humans. They often use soul and spirit interchangeably, even though the Scriptures clearly show there is a difference in the two:

HEBREWS 4:12 For the word of God is living and powerful, and sharper than any two-edged sword, piercing even to **the division of soul and spirit**, and of joints and marrow, and is a discerner of the thoughts and intents of the heart. (*NKJV*)

Now that we are armed with the basic scriptural knowledge of what the body, spirit, and soul are, let's see what the Scriptures really teach about the status of the dead.

Let's begin in the book of Job. Job has quite a lot to say about death. After the physical and material misfortunes brought by Satan befell him, Job cursed the day of his birth and wished that he had died at birth. Here is what he says about the dead, a group that he longs to be among:

JOB 3:11 "Why did I not **die** at birth? Why did I not **perish** when I came from the womb? 12 Why did the knees receive me? Or why the breasts, that I should nurse? 13 **For now I would have lain still and been quiet, I would have been asleep; then I would have been at rest** 14 with kings and counselors of the earth, who built ruins for themselves, 15 or with princes who had gold, who filled their houses with silver; 16 Or why was I not hidden like a stillborn child, like infants who never saw light? 17 **There the wicked cease from troubling**, and **there the weary are at rest.** 18 **There the prisoners rest together; they do not hear the voice of the oppressor.** 19 **The small and great are there**, and **the servant is free from his master.** (*NKJV*)

Job tells us quite distinctly about the status of the dead. He informs us that the dead are asleep, a condition death is compared to numerous times in the Scriptures. Job further discloses to us that ALL the dead, both distinguished and insignificant, are in this state.

JOB 7:21 And why dost Thou not pardon my transgression, and take away my iniquity? For now shall I **sleep in the dust**; and Thou shalt seek me in the morning, but I shall not be. (*RWB*)

Job continues on later with his contemplations on death, but he adds a significant detail:

JOB 14:10 But **man dies and is laid away**; indeed he breathes his last and where is he? 11 As water disappears from the sea, and a river becomes parched and dries up, 12 so **man lies down and does not rise**. Till the heavens are no more, **they will not awake nor be roused from their sleep**. 13 Oh, that You would hide me in the grave, that You would conceal me until Your wrath is past, that You would appoint me a set time, and remember me! 14 **If a man dies, shall he live again?** All the days of my hard service I will wait, **till my change comes**. (*NKJV*)

Here we see that Job had some knowledge of the resurrection. A little further on, he speaks of the resurrection in more detail:

JOB 19:25 For I know that my Redeemer lives, and He shall stand at last on the earth; 26 And **after my skin is destroyed**, this I know, that **in my flesh** I shall see God, 27 whom I shall see for myself, and my eyes shall behold, and not another. How my heart yearns within me! (*NKJV*)

Job knew that even after his body decayed in the grave, he would see God in his flesh. He knew of the resurrection of the dead and was anxiously looking forward to it. Why? Because he understood that the resurrection was mankind's only hope of defeating death. If there were no resurrection, the dead would continue to sleep in their graves forever.

King Solomon shared the same understanding that Job had regarding the fate of those who were dead. Solomon, the wisest man in the world during the time he lived (I Kings 4:29-31), clearly comprehended the finality of death:

ECCLESIASTES 9:2 All share a common destiny — the righteous and the wicked, the good and the bad, the clean and the unclean, those who offer sacrifices and those who do not. As it is with the good man, so with the sinner; as it is with those who take oaths, so with those who are afraid to take them. 3 This is the evil in everything that happens under the sun: **The same destiny overtakes all**. The hearts of men, moreover, are full of evil and there is madness in their hearts while they live, and afterward **they join the dead**. 4 Anyone who is among the living has hope — even a live dog is better off than a dead lion! 5 For the living know that they will die, but **the dead know nothing**; they have no further reward, and even the memory of them is forgotten.

(NIV)

ECCLESIASTES 9:10 Whatever your hand finds to do, do it with all your might, for **in the grave**, where you are going, **there is neither working nor planning nor knowledge nor wisdom**. *(NIV)*

The meaning of these words of Solomon is pretty obvious, if taken at face value. Unfortunately, those who believe and teach that immortal souls consciously continue on after death do not accept these clear comments written by Solomon. Instead, they attack the inspired nature of his words in this passage and claim that Solomon, the wisest man in the world, did not know what he was talking about.

The weight of numerous other plain Scriptures support Solomon's words about the state of the dead, however. Let's look at some passages from the book of Psalms to see if Solomon was speaking contrary to the Scriptures regarding death and the state of the dead:

PSALM 6:5 **No one remembers You when he is dead**. Who praises You from the grave? *(NIV)*

In Psalm 6, David makes the clear statement that no one remembers God when they are dead.

PSALM 13:3 Consider and hear me, O LORD my God; enlighten my eyes, lest **I sleep the sleep of death**; *(NKJV)*

David compares death to sleep in Psalm 13.

PSALM 17:15 As for me, I will see Your face in righteousness; I shall be satisfied when I **awake** in Your likeness. *(NKJV)*

In Psalm 17, David speaks of awaking from death in the likeness of God at the resurrection. This parallels Job's comments about the resurrection (Job 19:26-27).

PSALM 30:2 O LORD my God, I cried out to You, and You healed me. 3 O LORD, You brought my soul up from the grave; You have kept me alive, that I should not go down to the pit. 4 Sing praise to the LORD, You saints of His, and give thanks at the remembrance of His holy name. . . . 9 "**What profit is there in my blood, when I go down to the pit? Will the dust praise You? Will it declare Your truth?** 10 Hear, O LORD, and have mercy on me; LORD, be my helper!" *(NKJV)*

In this song for the dedication of the house of David, the psalmist gives God thanks for saving his life. The questions he asks in verse 9 emphasize that if he were dead, he would not be able to praise God for His works and declare His truth.

PSALM 88:1 O LORD, God of my salvation, I have cried out day and night before You. 2 Let my prayer come before You; incline Your ear to my cry. 3 For my soul is full of troubles, and my life draws near to the grave. 4 I am counted with those who go down to the pit; I am like a man who has no strength, 5 adrift among **the dead, like the slain who lie in the grave, whom You remember no more, and who are cut off from Your hand**. 6 You have laid me in the lowest pit, in darkness, in the depths. 7 Your wrath lies heavy upon me, and You have afflicted me with all Your waves. *Selah* 8 You have put away my acquaintances far from me; You have made me an abomination to them; I am shut up, and I cannot get out; 9 My eye wastes away because of affliction. LORD, I have called daily upon You; I have stretched out my hands to You. 10 **Will You work wonders for the dead? Shall the dead arise and praise You?** *Selah* 11 **Shall Your loving-kindness be declared in the grave? Or Your faithfulness in the place of destruction? 12 Shall Your wonders be known in the dark? And Your righteousness in the land of forgetfulness**? (*NKJV*)

In Psalm 88, Heman the Ezrahite speaks of the affliction he has suffered. He pleads with God to save him before he dies, because he knows that if He doesn't, he has no hope. His rhetorical questions (vv. 10-12) are designed to rouse God to action **before** he dies and all hope is lost.

PSALM 115:17 **The dead do not praise the LORD**, nor do any who go down into silence; (*NASU*)

The psalmist here flatly states that the dead do not praise God. "Silence" here is used to describe the grave, just as it also does in Psalm 94:17.

PSALM 146:3 Do not trust in princes, in mortal man, in whom there is no salvation. 4 **His spirit departs, he returns to the earth; in that very day his thoughts perish**. (*NASU*)

Here the psalmist tells us that a mortal man's thoughts perish on the day that he dies.

As we have just seen, the Psalms are full of insight into the state of the dead. In every case, the dead are portrayed as being asleep in the grave, unconscious and unable to do anything.

God told Moses of his impending death before the Israelites entered the Promised Land, describing it as sleep:

DEUTERONOMY 31:16 And the LORD said to Moses, "Behold, **you are**

about to sleep with your fathers; then this people will rise and play the harlot after the strange gods of the land, where they go to be among them, and they will forsake me and break my covenant which I have made with them. (*RSV*)

The language used to describe the deaths of the kings of Israel and Judah also supports the view that the dead are asleep and at rest in their graves:

II SAMUEL 7:12 And when your [David's] days are over and you **fall asleep with your ancestors**, I shall appoint your heir, your own son to succeed you (and I shall make his sovereignty secure). (*NJB*)

I KINGS 2:10 Then **David slept with his fathers** and was **buried** in the City of David. (*NASU*)

The apostles Peter and Paul confirm this understanding in the book of Acts, going so far as to say that David did not go to heaven when he died:

ACTS 2:29 "Men and brethren, let me speak freely to you of the patriarch **David**, that he **is both dead and buried**, and his tomb is with us to this day. . . . 34 For **David did not ascend into the heavens**" . . . (*NKJV*)

ACTS 13:36 "For David, after he had served his own generation by the will of God, **fell asleep, was buried with his fathers, and saw corruption**;" (*NKJV*)

The phrase "slept with his fathers" is used 36 times in the *Tanakh* to describe the death of the kings of Israel and Judah. It is applied to both the good kings and the wicked kings alike. There is no differentiation between the fate of the kings, whether good or evil. All are said to be sleeping with their forefathers in death.

The New Testament speaks of death as sleep many times also:

JOHN 11:11 These things he said, and after that he said to them, "Our friend Lazarus **sleeps**, but I go that I may wake him up." 12 Then his disciples said, "Lord, if he **sleeps** he will get well." 13 However, **Jesus spoke of his death**, but they thought that he was speaking about taking rest in sleep. 14 Then Jesus said to them plainly, "**Lazarus is dead**." (*NKJV*)

ACTS 7:59 And they stoned Stephen as he was calling on God and saying, "Lord Jesus, receive my spirit." 60 Then he knelt down and cried out with a loud voice, "Lord, do not charge them with this sin." And when he had said this, he **fell asleep**. (*NKJV*)

I CORINTHIANS 11:29 For he who eats and drinks in an unworthy manner eats and drinks judgment to himself, not discerning the Lord's body. 30 For this reason many are weak and sick among you, and many **sleep**. (*NKJV*)

I CORINTHIANS 15:6 After that he was seen by over five hundred brethren at once, of whom the greater part remain to the present, but some have **fallen asleep**. (*NKJV*)

II PETER 3:3 knowing this first: that scoffers will come in the last days, walking according to their own lusts, 4 and saying, "Where is the promise of his coming? For since the fathers **fell asleep**, all things continue as they were from the beginning of creation." (*NKJV*)

The angel who revealed end-time events to Daniel (Dan. 10-12) confirms the scriptural understanding of the status of the dead with his words to him regarding his fate:

DANIEL 12:13 "But you, go your way till the end; for **you shall rest**, and **will arise to your inheritance at the end of the days**." (*NKJV*)

Daniel is told by the angel that he will **rest** in death until the time of the end, and then he will arise in the resurrection to claim his inheritance. This awakening from the sleep of death at the resurrection is spoken of many times in the Bible:

DANIEL 12:2 And many of those who **sleep in the dust of the earth shall awake**, some to everlasting life, some to shame and everlasting contempt. (*NKJV*)

ISAIAH 26:19 **Your dead shall live**; together with my dead body **they shall arise**. **Awake** and sing, **you who dwell in dust**; for your dew is like the dew of herbs, and **the earth shall cast out the dead**. (*NKJV*)

JOHN 5:28 Do not marvel at this; for **the hour is coming when all who are in the tombs will hear his voice** 29 **and come forth**, those who have done good, to the resurrection of life, and those who have done evil, to the resurrection of judgment. (*RSV*)

EPHESIANS 5:13 But all things that are exposed are made manifest by the light, for whatever makes manifest is light. 14 Therefore He says: "**Awake, you who sleep, arise from the dead**, and Christ will give you light." (*NKJV*)

As we have seen over and over, the Bible speaks of death as a condition of unconsciousness similar to sleep. Many quote the apostle Paul's writings (Phi. 1:20-24; II Cor. 5:1-9) to supposedly disprove "soul sleep." However, it is from Paul that we receive the most emphatic declaration of the resurrection from the dead as the **only** hope for those who have died.

Let's examine Paul's comments about the resurrection from the 15th chapter of I Corinthians in detail:

I CORINTHIANS 15:12 Now if Christ is preached that he has been **raised** [egegertai] from the dead, how do some among you say that there is no resurrection of the dead? (*NKJV*)

Here Paul begins to dispute a teaching brought to Corinth that denied the bodily resurrection of the dead. This heresy likely took root among the Corinthian church due to the strong cultural influence exerted by the dualistic Greek view of human nature. The Greek view that the body and soul are separate, and that the soul lives on after the body dies, has influenced Christian doctrine since the 1st century. This view apparently had caused some Corinthian believers to falsely conclude that a resurrection from the dead was not necessary, since the souls of departed believers were already with Christ in heaven.

However, Paul, coming from a Pharisaic Jewish background (Acts 23:6; 26:5; Phi. 3:5), viewed the afterlife in a completely different way. The *Dictionary of Paul and His Letters* (*DPHL*) has this to say about Paul's beliefs regarding the resurrection:

Paul's teaching about the bodily resurrection arises out of a Jewish anthropology in which the "soul" (Heb *nephesh*, Gk *psyche*) is the animating principle of human life. In mainstream Jewish thought human beings do not *have* souls, they *are* souls. . . . Given this background it is perfectly understandable how in Romans 8:23 Paul describes the effects of the resurrection in terms of the ultimate "redemption of our bodies" . . . (p. 810)

As a side note, the Greek word *egegertai* ("raised") found in verse 12 is a form of the Greek verb *egeiro*. The *Exegetical Dictionary of the New Testament* states: "The basic meaning of *egeiro* is (trans.) to *wake* from sleep . . . or (intrans.) *awaken, rise* . . . (p. 372, vol. 1). Literally, Paul's comment could be translated: "He has been **awakened** from the dead . . ."

I CORINTHIANS 15:13 But if there is no resurrection of the dead, then Christ is not **risen** [egegertai]. 14 And if Christ is not **risen** [egegertai], then our preaching is empty and your faith is also empty. 15 Yes, and we are found false witnesses of God, because we have testified of God that He **raised up** [egeiren] Christ, whom He did not **raise up** [egeiren] — if in fact the dead do not **rise** [egeirontai]. (*NKJV*)

Paul attacks the very heart of this false doctrine in verse 13. He firmly links the future resurrection of the dead with the past resurrection of Christ. If the dead aren't going to be awakened from their sleep at the resurrection, then Paul says that neither has Christ been awakened from death. If Christ has not been awakened from death, then their hope is in vain. Additionally, Paul and the other apostles have been spreading a false message!

I CORINTHIANS 15:16 For if the dead do not **rise** [egeirontai], then Christ is not **risen** [egegertai]. 17 And if Christ is not **risen** [egegertai], your faith is futile; you are still in your sins! (*NKJV*)

For emphasis, Paul again states in verse 16 that if the dead are not going to wake up from the sleep of death in the future, then Christ has not already been awakened. If this is the case, Paul tells them that their faith is useless and there has been no forgiveness for their sins.

I CORINTHIANS 15:18 Then also those who have **fallen asleep** in Christ have **perished**. 19 If in this life only we have hope in Christ, we are of all men the most pitiable. (*NKJV*)

Now Paul takes his case a step further. If there is no resurrection, then those believers who have died while believing in Christ have **ceased to exist**! If there is no resurrection, then believers only have hope in Christ during their mortal life on this earth.

There is no ambiguity in Paul's argument. He clearly states that the **only** hope for life after death is the resurrection. Paul's position here totally negates the Hellenistic belief that the disembodied souls of the dead saints are in heaven with Christ.

I CORINTHIANS 15:20 But now Christ is **risen** [egegertai] from the dead, and has become the firstfruits of those who have **fallen asleep**. 21 For since by man came death, by man also came the resurrection of the dead. 22 For as in Adam all die, even so in Christ all shall be made alive. 23 But each one in his own order: Christ the firstfruits, afterward those who are Christ's at his coming. 24 Then comes the end, when he delivers the kingdom to God the Father, when He puts an end to all rule and all authority and power. 25 For he must reign till He has put all enemies under his feet. 26 The last enemy that will be destroyed is death. (*NKJV*)

After laying out the ultimate consequences the rejection of the resurrection had on their theology, Paul goes on to state the facts to the Corinthians. Yeshua had indeed been awakened from the sleep of the dead. When God roused him from the sleep of death to glorious eternal life, Messiah became the firstfruits of all those who will be awakened from death at a later time. Since death originally entered the human race because of Adam's sin, the resurrection of the dead to immortality came by way of a man's perfect obedience. But there is to be an order to the resurrection to immortality: Yeshua the Messiah first, then those messianic believers at the coming of Yeshua. More detail than this we are not given, but Paul does tell us the end result; Messiah will reign until the last enemy, death, is destroyed.

Paul sums up his dissertation on death and the resurrection toward the end of chapter 15:

I CORINTHIANS 15:50 Now this I say, brethren, that flesh and blood cannot inherit the kingdom of God; nor does corruption inherit incorruption. 51 Behold, I tell you a mystery: **We shall not all sleep**, but we shall all be changed — 52 in a moment, in the twinkling of an eye, at the last trumpet. For the trumpet will sound, and **the dead will be raised incorruptible**, and **we shall be changed**. 53 For this corruptible must put on incorruption, and this mortal must put on immortality. 54 So when this corruptible has put on incorruption, and this mortal has put on immortality, then shall be brought to pass the saying that is written: "Death is swallowed up in victory." (*NKJV*)

Paul begins here with a statement that is often overlooked; flesh and blood mortals cannot INHERIT the Kingdom of God. As numerous other Scriptures show, however, they will be **in** the Kingdom of God. He goes on to say that not all believers will die before Messiah Yeshua returns. But when he returns, all believers will be changed instantly at the sounding of the last trumpet (Rev. 11:15-18). At the sounding of this trumpet, the dead saints will awake from their sleep in new, spiritual bodies, and the bodies of those believers then living will be changed to spirit. When this happens, "death is swallowed up in victory!"

Paul spoke of this same event in his first letter to the Thessalonians:

I THESSALONIANS 4:13 But we do not want you to be uninformed, brethren, about **those who are asleep**, so that you will not grieve as do the rest who have no hope. (*NASU*)

In verse 13 he defines for the church at Thessalonica why he is writing; to give them comfort and hope regarding the fate of those believers who had died ("fallen asleep").

I THESSALONIANS 4:14 We believe that Jesus died and rose again and so we believe that God will bring with Jesus those who have **fallen asleep** in him. (*NIV*)

Verse 14 is an affirmation of faith in the resurrection. Paul says that **just as** we believe God raised Yeshua from the dead, so **also** we believe that God will resurrect those who died believing in Christ at his return.

There are those who say this verse teaches that Jesus will bring the conscious souls of the dead believers with him from heaven to be reunited with their resurrected bodies at his coming. However, this interpretation of verse 14 totally misses the point of what Paul is saying. If that understanding of the state of the dead was to be the Thessalonians' consolation and hope, Paul would have had no need to address the resurrection at all. He simply could have stated that the souls of the dead believers were at that time alive and with Christ in heaven. What more consolation would they have needed regarding the fate of their dead brothers and sisters?

But that is not at all the message Paul presents. The hope for the dead, as Paul presents it to the Thessalonians, is the resurrection of Messiah. Just as he told the Corinthians, Paul emphasizes that Yeshua's resurrection is the guarantee of the future resurrection of the "sleeping" saints, who will awake at the time of his return.

I THESSALONIANS 4:15 According to the Lord's own word, we tell you that we who are still alive, who are left till the coming of the Lord, will certainly not precede those who have **fallen asleep**. 16 For the Lord himself will come down from heaven, with a loud command, with the voice of the archangel and with the trumpet call of God, and **the dead in Christ will rise first**. 17 After that, we who are still alive and are left will be caught up together with them in the clouds to meet the Lord in the air. And so we will be with the Lord forever. 18 Therefore encourage each other with these words. (*NIV*)

Paul's consolation to the Thessalonians is the expectation that they will be reunited with their sleeping brethren at the resurrection of the dead. This resurrection will occur when Yeshua comes down from heaven as the last trumpet is blown. The dead will rise from their graves first, and together with them those believers who remain alive will be changed into spirit and will ascend to meet Yeshua in the air (Matt. 24:31). Paul is telling the Thessalonians to have hope in the **resurrection**, not to have hope in being a disembodied, conscious spirit in heaven.

In I Corinthians 15 and I Thessalonians 4, Paul speaks specifically about the resurrection to immortality. But as we mentioned earlier, the Bible also shows a resurrection to mortal life. The widow's son from Zarephath (1 Kings 17:17-23); the Shunammite's son (II Kings 4:17-37); the widow's son from Nain (Luke 7:11-16); the daughter of Jairus (Matt. 9:18-25; Mark 5:22-42; Luke 8:41-55); Lazarus (John 11:1-45); the saints raised in Jerusalem when Yeshua died on the cross (Matt. 27:50-53); Tabitha (Acts 9:36-41); and Eutychus (Acts 20:9-12) all experienced this resurrection back to physical life. The prophet Ezekiel speaks of this type of resurrection for the majority of Israel:

EZEKIEL 37:1 The hand of the LORD came upon me, and He led me out in the spirit of the LORD and set me in the center of the plain, which was now filled with bones. 2 He made me walk among them in every direction so that I saw how many they were on the surface of the plain. How dry they were! 3

He asked me: Son of man, **can these bones come to life**? "Lord GOD," I answered, "you alone know that." 4 Then He said to me: Prophesy over these bones, and say to them: Dry bones, hear the word of the LORD! 5 Thus says the Lord GOD to these bones: See! **I will bring spirit into you, that you may come to life.** 6 I will put sinews upon you, make flesh grow over you, cover you with skin, and **put spirit in you so that you may come to life** and know that I am the LORD. 7 I prophesied as I had been told, and even as I was prophesying I heard a noise; it was a rattling as the bones came together, bone joining bone. 8 I saw the sinews and the flesh come upon them, and the skin cover them, **but there was no spirit in them.** 9 Then He said to me: Prophesy to the spirit, prophesy, son of man, and say to the spirit: Thus says the Lord GOD: **From the four winds come, O spirit, and breathe into these slain that they may come to life.** 10 I prophesied as He told me, and **the spirit came into them; they came alive and stood upright**, a vast army. 11 Then He said to me: Son of man, these bones are the whole house of Israel. They have been saying, "Our bones are dried up, our hope is lost, and we are cut off." 12 Therefore, prophesy and say to them: Thus says the Lord GOD: O my people, **I will open your graves and have you rise from them**, and bring you back to the land of Israel. 13 Then you shall know that I am the LORD, when **I open your graves and have you rise from them**, O my people! 14 I will put my Spirit in you that you may live, and I will settle you upon your land; thus you shall know that I am the LORD. I have promised, and I will do it, says the LORD. (*NAB*)

Just as her spirit returned to Jairus' twelve-year old daughter when Yeshua resurrected her to life (Matt. 9:18-25; Mark 5:22-42; Luke 8:41-55), so also we see here that the spirits of the dead Israelites return to their reconstituted mortal bodies to bring them back to life. These Israelites will live in the land of Israel during the millennial rule of Yeshua. They will be subjects of the Kingdom of God, but unlike resurrected believers, they will not have inheritance in the Kingdom at that time (I Cor. 15:50).

Now that we have thoroughly covered what the Bible says about the state of the dead, I'm going to explain the Scriptures used by those who believe that souls live on after death to support their contention.

Probably the biblical text most used to "prove" that the soul survives death are the words of Yeshua to the thief on the cross:

LUKE 23:42 Then he said to Jesus, "Lord, remember me **when you come into your kingdom.**" 43 And Jesus said to him, "**Assuredly, I say to you, today you will be with me in Paradise.**" (*NKJV*)

"Case closed!" say the conscious soul advocates after quoting this passage. But is it really as cut and dried as appears?

There are several factors that should cause one to pause and reconsider what this passage appears to say. The first is the request made by the thief. He asked Yeshua to remember him WHEN he came into his kingdom. The thief apparently understood the messianic kingdom in the same way most 1st-century Jews did; he knew that it would be a **physical** kingdom ruling on the earth.

When will Yeshua come into his earthly kingdom? When he returns from heaven and rules over all nations from Jerusalem with a rod of iron (Psa. 2:7-9; Rev. 2:26-27; 12: 5; 19:15), as the prophet Isaiah foretold:

ISAIAH 2:1 The word that Isaiah the son of Amoz saw concerning **Judah and Jerusalem**. 2 Now **it shall come to pass in the latter days** that the mountain of the LORD's house shall be established on the top of the mountains, and shall be exalted above the hills; and all nations shall flow to it. 3 Many people shall come and say, "Come, and let us go up to the mountain of the LORD, to the house of the God of Jacob; He will teach us His ways, and we shall walk in His paths." For out of Zion shall go forth the Law, and the word of the LORD from Jerusalem. 4 **He shall judge between the nations, and rebuke many people**; they shall beat their swords into plowshares, and their spears into pruning hooks; nation shall not lift up sword against nation, neither shall they learn war anymore. (*NKJV*)

Since Yeshua has not yet established the Kingdom of God in Jerusalem, he **cannot** yet have granted the thief his request.

Also, for Yeshua's statement to be literally true the way it is presented by the dualists, the thief had to follow Yeshua to "Paradise" the very day they died. As other Scriptures clearly show, Paradise is located in heaven (II Cor. 12:2-4), where the tree of life is (Rev. 2:7). However, we know from Christ's own words that he did **not** go to heaven at his death:

JOHN 20:15 Jesus said to her, "Woman, why are you weeping? Whom are you seeking?" She, supposing him to be the gardener, said to him, "Sir, if you have carried him away, tell me where you have laid him, and I will take him away." 16 Jesus said to her, "Mary!" She turned and said to him, "Rabboni!" (which is to say, Teacher). 17 Jesus said to her, "Do not cling to me, for **I have not yet ascended to my Father**; but go to my brethren and say to them, 'I am ascending to my Father and your Father, and to my God and your God.' " (*NKJV*)

After his resurrection, Yeshua told Mary not to cling to him, because he had NOT YET ascended to heaven to his Father. Instead, he had just spent parts of three days and three nights dead and asleep in the garden tomb (for additional information on the crucifixion and resurrection, see my article "When

<u>Was Christ Resurrected?</u>"). The Scriptures show that he didn't go to heaven until 40 days later (Acts 1:3, 9-11). If Christ didn't ascend to Paradise until 40 days after his resurrection, there's no way the thief could have joined him there that same day they both died on a stake.

If Yeshua and the thief did not ascend to heaven the day of their death, what did Yeshua mean by his statement? There is no punctuation in the original Greek text of this passage. When the King James translators placed a comma before "today," they did so because of their belief (influenced by the traditional teachings of the Roman Catholic Church) in the immortality of the soul. For the same reason, modern translators have followed suit.

Grammatically, this sentence in Greek can also be read as: "Truly I say to you today, you will be with me in Paradise." Since this understanding removes numerous difficulties and apparent scriptural contradictions, it **should** be the preferred rendering. Unfortunately, the traditions of men die hard.

If Yeshua's words to the thief on the cross are most often used to support a conscious existence after death, the parable of Lazarus and the Rich Man runs a very close second:

LUKE 16:19 "There was a certain rich man who was clothed in purple and fine linen and fared sumptuously every day. 20 But there was a certain beggar named Lazarus, full of sores, who was laid at his gate, 21 desiring to be fed with the crumbs which fell from the rich man's table. Moreover the dogs came and licked his sores. 22 So it was that the beggar died, and was carried by the angels to Abraham's bosom. The rich man also died and was buried. 23 And being in torments in Hades, he lifted up his eyes and saw Abraham afar off, and Lazarus in his bosom. 24 Then he cried and said, 'Father Abraham, have mercy on me, and send Lazarus that he may dip the tip of his finger in water and cool my tongue; for I am tormented in this flame.' 25 But Abraham said, 'Son, remember that in your lifetime you received your good things, and likewise Lazarus evil things; but now he is comforted and you are tormented. 26 And besides all this, between us and you there is a great gulf fixed, so that those who want to pass from here to you cannot, nor can those from there pass to us.' 27 Then he said, 'I beg you therefore, father, that you would send him to my father's house, 28 for I have five brothers, that he may testify to them, lest they also come to this place of torment.' 29 Abraham said to him, 'They have Moses and the prophets; let them hear them.' 30 And he said, 'No, father Abraham; but if one goes to them from the dead, they will repent.' 31 But he said to him, 'If they do not hear Moses and the prophets, neither will they be persuaded though one rise from the dead.' " (**NKJV**)

All who cite this narrative as evidence for the existence of consciousness after death staunchly assert that it is a true story. However, a close examination will show that this tale is a parable, not the account of a real occurrence.

But even if we accept the untenable position that the account of Lazarus and the rich man actually happened, this story presents conscious soul advocates with several problems. First, the position of dualists is that all the Scriptures referring to the dead sleeping are actually speaking ONLY of their **bodies**. So dualists believe that the bodies of the dead sleep, while their conscious souls are either in heaven or hell.

If that is the case, then how could the rich man lift up his **eyes** in Hades (which literally means "hidden" in Greek)? Additionally, if this rich man's body was asleep while his soul was being tormented, why did he need Lazarus to put a drop of water on his **tongue** to cool it? Does a disembodied soul have a tongue? Also, would physical flames cause pain to a nonphysical entity? And would the disembodied soul of Lazarus have a **finger** to use to dip the requested water with?

In truth, Yeshua was using a common 1st-century misconception about the afterlife to make a point to the Pharisees he was addressing. For an in-depth analysis of the true spiritual message Yeshua was delivering with this parable, see my article "Lazarus and the Rich Man."

The timing of Lazarus' reward and the rich man's punishment is another serious problem with taking the account literally. In this story, we see that Lazarus obtained his reward and the rich man received his punishment right after their deaths. But the Bible clearly teaches that rewards and punishments will be given after the Messiah's return from heaven:

ISAIAH 40:10 See, the Sovereign LORD comes with power, and his arm rules for him. See, **his reward is with him**, and **his recompense accompanies him**. (*NIV*)

ISAIAH 62:11 The LORD has made proclamation to the ends of the earth: "Say to the Daughter of Zion, 'See, your Savior comes! See, **his reward is with him**, and **his recompense accompanies him**.'" (*NIV*)

MATTHEW 16:27 "For the Son of Man will come in the glory of his Father with his angels, and **then he will reward each according to his works**." (*NKJV*)

I CORINTHIANS 3:11 For no other foundation can anyone lay than that which is laid, which is Jesus Christ. 12 Now if anyone builds on this foundation with gold, silver, precious stones, wood, hay, straw, 13 each one's work will become clear; **for the Day will declare it**, because it will be revealed by fire; and the fire will test each one's work, of what sort it is. 14 **If anyone's work which he has built on it endures, he will receive a reward**. 15 If anyone's work is burned, he will suffer loss; but he himself will be saved, yet so as through fire. (*NKJV*)

REVELATION 11:15 Then the seventh angel sounded: And there were loud voices in heaven, saying, "The kingdoms of this world have become the kingdoms of our Lord and of His Christ, and He shall reign forever and ever!" 16 And the twenty-four elders who sat before God on their thrones fell on their faces and worshiped God, 17 saying: "We give You thanks, O Lord God Almighty, the One who is and who was and who is to come, because You have taken Your great power and reigned. 18 The nations were angry, and Your wrath has come, **and the time of the dead, that they should be judged, and that You should reward Your servants the prophets and the saints**, and those who fear Your name, small and great, and should destroy those who destroy the earth." (*NKJV*)

REVELATION 22:12 "And behold, I am coming quickly, and **my reward is with me**, to give to every one according to his work." (*NKJV*)

Finally, some will argue that Yeshua would certainly **not** have used an untrue story to teach the Pharisees a lesson because it would have amounted to an endorsement of that position. However, Yeshua was referencing a Hellenistic belief about the afterlife that had found its way into Judaism by the 1st century. This belief, despite the fact that it was not scriptural, would have been well known by the Pharisees. Immediately before he told the story of Lazarus and the rich man, Yeshua recounted the parable of the unjust steward (Luke 16:1-12). He clearly did not endorse the specific actions of this unscrupulous manager, but Yeshua was able to use the story to teach a spiritual lesson. So also did he do with the parable of Lazarus and the rich man.

Three Scriptures from Paul are likewise often cited as "proof" that souls live on after the body dies. First, let's look at a passage from Paul's second letter to the Corinthians:

II CORINTHIANS 5:1 For we know that if our earthly house, this tent, is destroyed, we have a building from God, a house not made with hands, eternal in the heavens. 2 For in this we groan, earnestly desiring to be clothed with our habitation which is from heaven, 3 if indeed, having been clothed, we shall not be found naked. 4 **For we who are in this tent groan, being burdened, not because we want to be unclothed, but further clothed, that mortality may be swallowed up by life**. 5 Now He who has prepared us for this very thing is God, who also has given us the Spirit as a guarantee. 6 So we are always confident, knowing that **while we are at home in the body we are absent from the Lord**. 7 For we walk by faith, not by sight. 8 We are confident, yes, well **pleased rather to be absent from the body and to be present with the Lord**. 9 Therefore we make it our aim, whether present or absent, to be well pleasing to Him. (*NKJV*)

If we simply go back to Paul's first letter to the Corinthians, we find that "our earthly house" (v. 1), our physical body, will be "swallowed up by life" (v. 4) at the resurrection (I Cor. 15:50-54). This is the context in which Paul writes here. When Paul says that "while we are at home in the (physical) body we are absent from the Lord," he is simply saying that we can't be with the Lord until we receive our immortal bodies at the resurrection (I Cor. 15:50).

When understood correctly, Paul here **confirms** that it's only at the resurrection that the saints will be alive with Yeshua. When Paul speaks of being "absent from the body to be present with the Lord," he is speaking of the resurrection of the dead, when his mortal body will be replaced by the "building from God" (v. 1).

Biblical scholars have attempted many explanations for Paul's apparently contradictory teaching about the intermediate state of the believer between death and the resurrection. They postulate that Paul came to grasp more about the state of the dead as his eschatological understanding increased. This supposedly explains the difference in views between his earlier writings (I The. 4; I Cor. 15) and those later on (Phi. 1, II Cor. 5). However, some scholars conclude that any perceived deviations are simply due to differences in emphasis caused by the different circumstances under which each letter was written.

In **DPHL**, we find this insightful comment regarding Paul's apparent change in position from I Corinthians to II Corinthians:

. . . Both letters assert a transformation of the believer in Christ; but what of the *timing* of that transformation? F.F. Bruce remarks wisely on this matter: "The tension created by the postulated interval between death and resurrection might be relieved today if it were suggested that in the consciousness of the departed believer there is no interval between dissolution and investiture, however long an interval might be measured by the calendar of earthbound human history." (p. 440)

In other words, a believer whose consciousness ended at death would not be aware of the passage of time on the earth upon awakening in the resurrection. This would allow Paul to say that he would rather be absent from his mortal body and present with the Lord and still not invalidate those things he had earlier written about the dead being in a state of sleep.

Now let's examine a passage from his epistle to the church at Philippi:

PHILIPPIANS 1:21 For to me, to live is Christ, and **to die is gain.** 22 But if I live on in the flesh, this will mean fruit from my labor; yet what I shall choose I cannot tell. 23 For I am hard pressed between the two, **having a desire to**

depart and be with Christ, which is far better. 24 Nevertheless to remain in the flesh is more needful for you. (*NKJV*)

Based on Paul's understanding as presented earlier in I Corinthians 15 and I Thessalonians 4, why would he say that it would be gain for him to die? How would departing allow him to be with Messiah?

Based on Paul's view of the state and resurrection of the dead as outlined in the passages we've already covered, it would be gain for him to die because he would be asleep and would no longer be suffering in the flesh. In the sleep of death, there is no comprehension of the passage of time. The next moment of consciousness for Paul after his death would be at his resurrection, when Yeshua returns for the saints. In view of these considerations, it's easy to see what Paul meant here.

Finally, let's examine another passage from Paul's first epistle to the Thessalonians:

1 THESSALONIANS 5:9 For God did not appoint us to wrath, but to obtain salvation through our Lord Jesus Christ, 10 who died for us, **that whether we wake or sleep, we should live together with him**. (*NKJV*)

The only way to use this text to support the conscious soul theory is to ignore its context. Remember, only a few short verses earlier, Paul is speaking about the awakening of the dead from sleep at the resurrection (I The. 4:13-17). In this verse, Paul is merely saying that whether a believer is awake (alive in the flesh) or asleep (dead in the grave), eventually we will live with Yeshua the Messiah after the resurrection.

Conscious soul advocates prominently use these three passages by Paul to try and substantiate their claim that the righteous dead are alive in heaven with Yeshua. In doing so, they have to discard or explain away many clear Scriptures, from Paul and others, which refute this position. One such obvious Scripture is found in Paul's second letter to Timothy, written just before his death:

II TIMOTHY 4: 6 For I am already being poured out like a drink offering, and **the time has come for my departure**. 7 I have fought the good fight, I have finished the race, I have kept the faith. 8 Now there is in store for me the crown of righteousness, which the Lord, the righteous Judge, will award to me **on that day — and not only to me, but also to all who have longed for his appearing**. (*NIV*)

Here Paul plainly tells Timothy that he is about to die, and his reward won't be received from the Lord until the day of his appearing - the day Yeshua returns from heaven to resurrect the saints. That's about as direct a statement as you will get from the apostle Paul on any topic, and it refutes the belief that the saints are rewarded at death by being consciously present with Christ in heaven.

Now let's examine the account of the transfiguration, which is commonly held up as proof that souls remain conscious after death:

MATTHEW 16:28 "Assuredly, I say to you, **there are some standing here who shall not taste death till they see the Son of Man coming in his kingdom.**" 17:1 Now after six days Jesus took Peter, James, and John his brother, led them up on a high mountain by themselves; 2 and he was transfigured before them. His face shone like the sun, and his clothes became as white as the light. 3 And behold, **Moses and Elijah appeared to them, talking with him**. 4 Then Peter answered and said to Jesus, "Lord, it is good for us to be here; if you wish, let us make here three tabernacles: one for you, one for Moses, and one for Elijah." 5 While he was still speaking, behold, a bright cloud overshadowed them; and suddenly a voice came out of the cloud, saying, "This is My beloved Son, in whom I am well pleased. Hear him!" 6 And when the disciples heard it, they fell on their faces and were greatly afraid. 7 But Jesus came and touched them and said, "Arise, and do not be afraid." 8 When they had lifted up their eyes, they saw no one but Jesus only. 9 Now as they came down from the mountain, Jesus commanded them, saying, "Tell the **vision** [horama] to no one until the Son of Man is risen from the dead." (***NKJV***)

Dualists claim that the only way Moses and Elijah could have appeared on the mountain with Yeshua is if they were alive in heaven and came down from there. Unfortunately, that claim is not substantiated by the Scripture. In fact, the Greek text of verse 9 literally invalidates that belief.

First, we must understand that this event took place to fulfill Yeshua's promise that some of the apostles would "not taste death until they saw the Kingdom of God after it had come with power" (Mark 9:1; Matt. 16:28). It has been nearly 2,000 years since Yeshua walked the earth as a man, and the Kingdom of God still has not come in power. It will not come in power until the Messiah returns from heaven to rule the nations with a rod of iron. So how could any of the twelve apostles see that event before they died?

The key to properly understanding this passage is to realize that what Peter, James and John saw was a **supernatural vision** of the future, not a present reality. The word translated "vision" in Matthew 17:9 is the Greek noun ***horama***. Regarding the meaning of this word, ***Friberg's Analytical Lexicon of the Greek New Testament*** says: "in the NT, [***horama*** is] a supernatural *vision*, given as a means of divine communication . . ."

This same word (*horama*) is used to describe Peter's vision of the great sheet filled with all kinds of four-footed animals of the earth, wild beasts, creeping things, and birds of the air (Acts 10:9-17) and Paul's vision of the Macedonian man pleading for the gospel to be preached to them (Acts 16:9-10). Additionally, in the *Septuagint* Greek translation of the Old Testament, *horama* is used to describe the supernatural visions of the future given to Daniel (Dan. 7:1; 8:13; 10:1), as well as others.

Clearly the transfiguration on the mountain was a vision of the future Kingdom, given to Peter, James and John to fulfill Yeshua's pledge. They were granted a glimpse of the Messiah in his glory, with two of the saints who will be there with him in the Kingdom (Moses and Elijah). Scripturally, it's very difficult to make a convincing case that Moses and Elijah had to be alive at that very time in order to be seen in a vision of the future.

Next, let's examine Yeshua's claim that the God of Abraham, Isaac, and Jacob is not the God of the dead but of the living. Some proponents of the conscious soul theory claim that this statement is proof that Abraham, Isaac, and Jacob were alive at the time Yeshua said this.

First, we need to realize that the premise for Yeshua's statement was to disprove the Sadducees contention that there is no resurrection. With the understanding of why Yeshua said this, let's look at what the Scriptures really say:

MATTHEW 22:31 "But **concerning the resurrection of the dead**, have you not read what was spoken to you by God, saying, 32 'I am the God of Abraham, the God of Isaac, and the God of Jacob'? God is not the God of the dead, but of the living." (*NKJV*)

MARK 12:26 "But **concerning the dead, that they rise**, have you not read in the book of Moses, in the burning bush passage, how God spoke to him, saying, 'I am the God of Abraham, the God of Isaac, and the God of Jacob'? 27 "He is not the God of the dead, but the God of the living. You are therefore greatly mistaken." (*NKJV*)

LUKE 20:37 "But even Moses showed in the burning bush passage that **the dead are raised**, when he called the Lord 'the God of Abraham, the God of Isaac, and the God of Jacob.' 38 For He is not the God of the dead but of the living, for all live to Him." (*NKJV*)

Clearly, Yeshua was pointing out to the disbelieving Sadducees the reality of the resurrection in these parallel passages. Even though Abraham, Isaac and Jacob were dead at the time Yeshua made this statement, God had promised to resurrect them. God gives life to the dead and calls those things which do not exist as though they did (Rom. 4:17). Therefore Yeshua could confidently state that Abraham, Isaac, and Jacob were alive, because he knew that God would keep His promise to resurrect them.

The book of Hebrews twice clearly tells us that these three (as well as all the other Old Testament saints) are dead, awaiting their perfection and reward at the resurrection of the righteous:

HEBREWS 11:13 **These all** [including Abraham-v. 8, Isaac-v. 9, Jacob-v. 9] **died in faith, not having received the promises**, but having seen them afar off were assured of them, embraced them and confessed that they were strangers and pilgrims on the earth. (*NKJV*)

HEBREWS 11:39 And **all these** [including Abraham-vv. 17-19, Isaac-v. 20, Jacob-v. 21], having obtained a good testimony through faith, **did not receive the promise**, 40 God having provided something better for us, **that they should not be made perfect apart from us**. (*NKJV*)

Some try to use the words of the "souls under the altar" in Revelation 6 to support their belief in conscious souls in heaven:

REVELATION 6:9 When he opened the **fifth seal**, I saw under the altar the **souls** of those who had been slain for the word of God and for the testimony which they held. 10 And **they cried with a loud voice**, saying, "How long, O Lord, holy and true, until you judge and avenge our blood on those who dwell on the earth?" 11 Then a white robe was given to each of them; and it was said to them that **they should rest a little while longer**, until both the number of their fellow servants and their brethren, who would be killed as they were, was completed. (*NKJV*)

First and foremost, we have to realize that the book of Revelation was written in **symbolic** language. No scholar that I know of expects four horsemen to literally ride throughout the world at the time of the end, wreaking havoc when the first four seals are opened (Rev. 6:1-8). These horsemen and their mounts are understood to be allegorical representations of events that will take place. So why would we interpret the fifth seal in a strictly literal sense when the first four are clearly symbolic?

The altar is the place where sacrifices are presented. Its appearance here is representative of those martyrs who sacrificed their lives in the service of God. The question asked by these "souls" is used to symbolically introduce the final great martyrdom of believers at the end of this age.

Even this illustrative event shows the true status of the dead. These slain saints are told to REST a while longer, until the last massive slaughter of believers is finished. They are to return to resting in the sleep of death until the resurrection of all believers occurs at the seventh trumpet (Rev. 11:15-18).

Lastly, let's examine the account of Saul conjuring up the spirit of Samuel. Saul was facing the Philistine army, and because of his disobedience, God had forsaken him. Since he was afraid of the Philistine army and God would not answer his inquiries about the coming battle, Saul resorted to the use of a medium to contact the dead prophet Samuel. The account is found in I Samuel 28:

I SAMUEL 28:11 The woman asked, 'Whom shall I conjure up for you?' He replied, 'Conjure up Samuel.' 12 The woman then saw Samuel and, giving a great cry, she said to Saul, 'Why have you deceived me? You are Saul!' 13 The king said, 'Do not be afraid! What do you see?' The woman replied to Saul, 'I see a **ghost** [Heb. *'elohim*, lit. "god"] rising from the earth.' 14 'What is he like?' he asked. She replied, 'It is an old man coming up; he is wrapped in a cloak.' Saul then knew that it was Samuel and, bowing to the ground, prostrated himself. 15 Samuel said to Saul, '**Why have you disturbed my rest by conjuring me up?**' Saul replied, 'I am in great distress; the Philistines are waging war on me, and God has abandoned me and no longer answers me either by prophet or by dream; and so I have summoned you to tell me what I ought to do.' 16 Samuel said, 'Why consult me, when Yahweh has abandoned you and has become your enemy?' 17 Yahweh has treated you as he foretold through me; he has snatched the sovereignty from your hand and given it to your neighbour, David, 18 because you disobeyed Yahweh's voice and did not execute his fierce anger against Amalek. That is why Yahweh is treating you like this today. 19 What is more, Yahweh will deliver Israel and you too, into the power of the Philistines. **Tomorrow you and your sons will be with me**; and Yahweh will hand over the army of Israel into the power of the Philistines.' (*NJB*)

Those who believe that souls continue to live after the body dies sometimes use this passage to try and prove their point. However, if they really considered what "Samuel" says here, they might choose to ignore it.

One school of thought holds that this appearance by "Samuel" was only a demon disguised as the dead prophet. However, since the text seems to treat the *'elohim* which appeared as the actual Samuel, we will analyze the passage in that light.

Notice the very first thing Samuel says to Saul through the medium: "Why have you **disturbed** my **rest** by conjuring me up?" (v. 15). It certainly sounds like the dead Samuel was **asleep** in death, and wasn't too happy about being bothered by Saul and his medium.

From the Scriptures, we know that Samuel was a righteous man, a servant of God who judged Israel all his life. We also know that Saul was originally selected by God to be the king of Israel, but was later rejected by Him because of rebellion and disobedience (I Sam. 15:23).

Biblically Clean Foods

This commentary reviews what the New Testament teaches regarding clean and unclean animals, which animals are considered food, and how food may become unclean. Old Testament references are reviewed, along with Peter's vision recorded in the book of Acts, Paul's words to Timothy and the Romans, and the words of Yeshua (Jesus) the Messiah on this topic

In Leviticus 11 and Deuteronomy 14 God gives us a list of animals that are not to be eaten as food. Included in this list declared "unclean" are some of man's favorites: swine, shrimp, lobster, crab, catfish, as well as squid, rabbit, squirrel, etc. However, there are several places in the New Testament where God seems to indicate that He has changed His mind on these things:

MARK 7:18 And he said to them, "Are you so lacking in understanding also? Do you not understand that whatever goes into the man from outside cannot **defile** him, 19 because it does not go into his heart, but into his stomach, and is eliminated?" (***Thus he* declared all foods clean.**) (*NASU*)

ROMANS 14:14 As one who is in the Lord Jesus, I am fully convinced that **no food is unclean in itself**. But if anyone regards something as **unclean**, then for him it is **unclean**. (*NIV*)

ACTS 10:10 He became hungry and wanted something to eat, and while the meal was being prepared, he fell into a trance. 11 He saw heaven opened and something like a large sheet being let down to earth by its four corners. 12 It contained **all kinds of four-footed animals, as well as reptiles of the earth and birds of the air**. 13 Then a voice told him, "Get up, Peter. Kill and eat." 14 "Surely not, Lord!" Peter replied. "I have never eaten anything **impure** or **unclean**." 15 The voice spoke to him a second time, "**Do not call anything impure that God has made clean**." (*NIV*)

On the surface, it looks pretty clear, doesn't it? Go ahead and eat what you want, God has given you the green light. But has God really changed his mind? Are these animals listed in Leviticus 11 and Deuteronomy 14 now OK to eat?

In Malachi 3:6, God declares that He does NOT change. This would seem to indicate the opposite of what's stated above. In order to determine if God has really changed His position on the issue of clean and unclean foods (considered important enough to be included in the *Torah* twice), let's look at the passages above (and a few others) in more detail. You may be surprised at what the Scriptures **really** say on this topic.

Let's begin in the seventh chapter of Mark. In order to fully understand Yeshua's words, we'll start at the first of the chapter and get the context:

MARK 7:1 Then the Pharisees and some of the scribes came together to him, having come from Jerusalem. 2 Now when they saw some of his disciples eat bread with **defiled** [koinais], that is, with **unwashed** hands, they found fault. 3 For the Pharisees and all the Jews do not eat unless they wash their hands in a special way, holding the tradition of the elders. 4 When they come from the marketplace, they do not eat unless they wash. And there are many other things which they have received and hold, like the washing of cups, pitchers, copper vessels, and couches. 5 Then the Pharisees and scribes asked him, "Why do your disciples not walk according to the tradition of the elders, but eat bread with unwashed hands?" (*NKJV*)

This passage is the background context for what Yeshua states afterward. As the Scripture shows, the problem that arose was related to Messiah's disciples not washing their hands in the traditional way. The reason for this specialized washing was for **ceremonial** purity, not cleanliness.

The word translated "defiled" in verse 2 is a form of the Greek adjective *koinos*. Like many words, this word and the related verb *koinoo* (along with their variations) can be used positively or negatively. In the positive sense, these related words mean "common," such as in Acts 2:44 and 4:32, where the disciples of Messiah were said to have had "all things **in common**." In a negative context, these words are used to contrast the "holy" with that which is "common," "defiled," or "profane." This is the sense in which *koinais* is used in Mark 7:2.

Yeshua uses the Pharisees' criticism of his disciples over a non-biblical ritual to launch a scathing attack on their use of human traditions to override the scriptural commandments of God. He then spoke a parable to the crowd to illustrate the true cause of spiritual defilement:

MARK 7:14 When he had called all the multitude to himself, he said to them, "Hear me, everyone, and understand: 15 There is nothing that enters a man from outside which can **defile** [koinosai] him; but the things which come out of him, those are the things that **defile** [koinounta] a man. 16 If anyone has ears to hear, let him hear!"(*NKJV*)

As with most parables Yeshua used, this one was not readily understood (Matt. 13:10-15). The disciples asked Yeshua for a further explanation of what he meant:

MARK 7:17 When he had entered a house away from the crowd, his disciples asked him concerning the parable. 18 So he said to them, "Are you thus without understanding also? Do you not perceive that whatever enters a man from outside cannot **defile** [koinosai] him, 19 because **it does not enter his heart but his stomach, and is eliminated, thus purifying all foods**?" 20 And he said, "What comes out of a man, that **defiles** [koinoi] a man. 21 For from within, out of the heart of men, proceed evil thoughts, adulteries, fornications, murders, 22 thefts, covetousness, wickedness, deceit, lewdness, an evil eye, blasphemy, pride, foolishness. 23 All these evil things come from within and **defile** [koinoi] a man." (**NKJV**)

Yeshua explained to his disciples that those things which go into a man's body from the outside (such as dirt from unwashed hands) do **not** keep a man from being holy. Instead, the evil things that come out of a man's heart and lead him to commit sin are the things that prevent him from being holy.

Now let's look more closely at verse 19. The **New King James Version** renders this verse differently than does the **New American Standard Bible** 1995 update cited at the beginning of this article. The **NASU** (and most other modern translations) ends Yeshua's quotation after "eliminated" (**ekporeuetai**) and sets off the final phrase as an explanatory comment by Mark. According to this interpretation, Yeshua was using the parable to declare all animals to be edible, in contradiction to Leviticus 11 and Deuteronomy 14. However, the **NKJV** considers this entire verse to be the words of Yeshua.

Why is there a difference between the two?

The reason for the differing translations is a **ONE** letter variation between the Greek manuscript base used by the **NKJV** translators and the manuscript base used by the translators of other modern versions (such as the **NASU**). The vast majority of the Greek manuscripts of Mark end verse 19 with the conclusion to Yeshua's statement being ". . . *thus* cleansing all foods" (Gr. **katharizon panta ta bromata**). The "o" in **katharizon** (καθαριζον, "cleansing") is the Greek letter **omicron** (o). However, a very few Greek manuscripts instead have **katharizon** (καθαριζων) spelled with the "o" being the Greek letter **omega** (ω) instead of **omicron**. The **omega** changes the word's gender from neuter to masculine, allowing for the difference in translation.

Without getting into a technical debate regarding Greek grammar or the pros and cons of each manuscript base, the overwhelming textual evidence supports the **NKJV** rendering of verse 19 over the **NASU** translation.

Most Greek manuscripts of Mark 7:19 literally read: "Because it does not enter into his heart, but into the stomach, and into the toilet passes, cleansing all foods." It is clear that Yeshua is not declaring all foods "clean" here, because the cleansing process he refers to is digestion, which ultimately leads to defecation. Yeshua' point here appears obvious: Breaking God's law defiles a man, not non-adherence to man-made traditions. This parable has nothing to say about eating unclean animals.

Next, let's look at the experience of Peter recorded in Acts 10 to see if it supports eating unclean animals. As we did with Mark 7, let's start at the beginning to get the proper context:

ACTS 10:1 There was a certain man in Caesarea called Cornelius, a centurion of what was called the Italian Regiment, 2 a devout man and one who feared God with all his household, who gave alms generously to the people, and prayed to God always. 3 About the ninth hour of the day he saw clearly in a vision an angel of God coming in and saying to him, "Cornelius!" 4 And when he observed him, he was afraid, and said, "What is it, lord?" So he said to him, "Your prayers and your alms have come up for a memorial before God. 5 Now send men to Joppa, and send for Simon whose surname is Peter. 6 He is lodging with Simon, a tanner, whose house is by the sea. He will tell you what you must do." 7 And when the angel who spoke to him had departed, Cornelius called two of his household servants and a devout soldier from among those who waited on him continually. 8 So when he had explained all these things to them, he sent them to Joppa. (*NKJV*)

Here we see that Cornelius, a God-fearing Roman centurion, was given a vision of a holy angel. In the vision, the angel told him to send for Simon Peter and have him come to his house in Caesarea. In obedience to the words of the angel, Cornelius sent **THREE** men (two of his household servants and one of his soldiers) to get Peter. That particular number will be important a little later in the story:

ACTS 10:9 The next day, as they went on their journey and drew near the city, Peter went up on the housetop to pray, about the sixth hour. 10 Then he became very hungry and wanted to eat; but while they made ready, he fell into a trance 11 and saw heaven opened and an object like a great sheet bound at the four corners, descending to him and let down to the earth. 12 In it were all kinds of four-footed animals of the earth, wild beasts, creeping things, and birds of the air. 13 And a voice came to him, "Rise, Peter; kill and eat." 14 But Peter said, "Not so, Lord! For I have never eaten anything **common** [koinon] or **unclean** [akatharton]." 15 And a voice spoke to him again the second time, "What God **has cleansed** [ekatharisen] you must not call **common** [koinou]." 16 **This was done three times**. And the object was taken up into heaven again. (*NKJV*)

Notice the situation; Peter went to the rooftop about noon to pray at the same time the three men from Cornelius were drawing near. After he had finished praying, he became very hungry. While those in the house were preparing the noon meal, Peter (still on the roof) fell into a trance and had a vision. In this vision, he saw a sheet being let down from above with all kinds of animals in it, both clean and unclean.

When a supernatural voice told him to rise, kill and eat, Peter responded the way any good *Torah*-observant Jew of the 1st century would have. He refused, saying that he had **NEVER** eaten anything "common" (*koinon*) or "unclean" (*akatharton*). That statement by itself is interesting, considering that it had probably been at least ten years since the resurrection of Messiah at that time. Clearly, Peter did not take Yeshua's words recorded in Mark 7 (examined above) to mean that any animal could legally be eaten.

Why did Peter differentiate between "common" ("defiled") and "unclean" in his reply? The Greek word *akatharton* specifically refers to those animals prohibited from being eaten in Leviticus 11 and Deuteronomy 14, as an examination of the Greek *Septuagint* translation of the Old Testament clearly shows. But "common" referred to a different group of animals altogether. Only clean animals designated as food sources in the *Torah* could become "common" or "defiled" in such a way that they became inedible.

Peter was saying here that he had never eaten any "unclean" animals or any clean animals that had been "defiled" ceremonially. The angel's answer to Peter is interesting; it conclusively shows that **food** is not the subject of this vision at all. The angel told Peter not to call "common" that which God **had cleansed** (*ekatharisen*). There is no mention of the "unclean" here at all by the angel. This statement was repeated **three** times before the vision ended.

ACTS 10:17 Now while **Peter wondered within himself what this vision which he had seen meant**, behold, the men who had been sent from Cornelius had made inquiry for Simon's house, and stood before the gate. 18 And they called and asked whether Simon, whose surname was Peter, was lodging there. 19 While Peter thought about the vision, the Spirit said to him, "Behold, **three men** are seeking you. 20 Arise therefore, go down and go with them, doubting nothing; for I have sent them." (*NKJV*)

Notice that Peter did not immediately understand the vision. As he sat on the roof contemplating what the vision meant, the three men from Cornelius arrived. God's Spirit let Peter know that he was to go down and go with the men. At this point Peter likely began to understand the vision and the reason that the angel had repeated his message **three** times (once for each of the Gentiles sent by Cornelius to fetch him):

ACTS 10:21 Then Peter went down to the men who had been sent to him from Cornelius, and said, "Yes, I am he whom you seek. For what reason have you come?" 22 And they said, "Cornelius the centurion, a just man, one who fears God and has a good reputation among all the nation of the Jews, was divinely instructed by a holy angel to summon you to his house, and to hear words from you." 23 Then he invited them in and lodged them. On the next day Peter went away with them, and some brethren from Joppa accompanied him. 24 And the following day they entered Caesarea. Now Cornelius was waiting for them, and had called together his relatives and close friends. 25 As Peter was coming in, Cornelius met him and fell down at his feet and worshiped him. 26 But Peter lifted him up, saying, "Stand up; I myself am also a man." 27 And as he talked with him, he went in and found many who had come together. 28 Then he said to them, "**You know how unlawful it is for a Jewish man to keep company with or go to one of another nation. But God has shown me that I should not call any man COMMON** [koinon] **or UNCLEAN** [akatharton]. 29 Therefore I came without objection as soon as I was sent for. . . ." (*NKJV*)

By the time Peter arrived at Cornelius' house, he fully understood the purpose of the vision given to him on the rooftop. It was **not** meant to allow the consumption of prohibited animals as food, but rather it was designed to show Peter (and the rest of the messianic Jews) that God was now calling people that they considered to be defiled into His family. No longer could the messianic Jews justify not keeping company with or going to a Gentile (a tenet of the oral law, not the written *Torah*). Instead, God showed Peter (and through him the rest of the messianic Jews) that he must accept these people as part of His chosen nation Israel.

Peter was told by the angel in Acts 10:15 that what God **had cleansed** (*ekatharisen*) he was not to call "defiled." A review of the usage of the Greek root word *katharizo* ("cleanse") in the Gospels illustrates the point God was making more fully. This word and its variants are used several times to describe the cleansing of leprosy by Yeshua and his disciples (Matt. 8:2-3; 10:8; 11:5; Mark 1:40-42; Luke 4:27; 5:12-13; 7:22; 17:12-19). Just as Yeshua physically **cleansed** many lepers of their disease, God was showing Peter that He was spiritually cleansing the Gentiles of their impurities (Acts 15:9; Eph. 5:26; Titus 2:14; Heb. 9:14, 22-23; I John 1:7-9) through the blood of Messiah. When properly understood, this passage of Scripture has absolutely nothing to say about the consumption of unclean animals.

Now let's look at Romans 14 in detail. In his letter to the Romans, Paul is addressing a congregation composed of both Jews and Gentiles. Although Paul had never been to Rome to meet with the assembly there (Rom. 1:10-15), he had apparently heard of some problems between the two factions which motivated him to write them. His letter to the Romans is a compilation of instructions and explanations to help these two groups coexist as one unified body.

The entire chapter deals with food customs that were dividing the Roman congregation. From the beginning of Romans 14 to the end, food and drink are mentioned 16 times. There were **two specific problems related to eating and drinking** that Paul addresses in this chapter:

(1) WHAT to eat or not eat, and

(2) WHEN to eat or not eat.

Both of these issues are introduced by Paul in this chapter, along with his solutions to the difficulties they were causing the Roman assembly.

The first problem is mentioned by Paul in Romans 14:2:

ROMANS 14:1 Accept him whose faith is weak, without passing judgment on disputable matters. 2 **One man's faith allows him to eat everything, but another man, whose faith is weak, eats only vegetables.** 3 The man who eats everything must not look down on him who does not, and the man who does not eat everything must not condemn the man who does, for God has accepted him. 4 Who are you to judge someone else's servant? To his own master he stands or falls. And he will stand, for the Lord is able to make him stand. (*NIV*)

Paul begins this chapter by telling the Romans not to pass judgment on one another in regards to differences of opinion. He then defines one of the areas where the Roman believers were judging each other (eating meat versus eating only vegetables).

Why would this issue present a problem for the Roman congregation? Romans 14:14 holds the key to answering that question:

ROMANS 14:14 I know and am convinced by the Lord Jesus that there is nothing **unclean** [koinon] of itself; but to him who considers anything to be **unclean** [koinon], to him it is **unclean** [koinon]. (*NKJV*)

The underlying Greek word translated "unclean" is *koinon*. As it is in the passages we've already looked at from Mark 7 and Acts 10, this word would be better translated "common" or "defiled."

Verse 14, when translated properly, should read: "I know and am convinced by the Lord Yeshua that there is nothing **defiled** of itself; but to him who considers anything to be **defiled**, to him it is **defiled**."

This verse is really the key to understanding why some in the Roman assembly would not eat meat. There were those in the congregation that considered the meat sold in the meat markets to be ceremonially "defiled" (*koinon*).

But what was it that caused some in the Roman congregation to view the meat this way? The most likely reason was that they assumed most of the meat sold in the local market was defiled because it had been offered in sacrifice to idols.

Paul had addressed a similar situation which arose in Corinth (I Cor. 10:18-28). His answer to the Corinthians' concerns over this issue was that they should eat whatever is sold in the meat market without raising questions of conscience about whether the meat had been sacrificed to an idol (I Cor. 10:25). But if they knew for certain that meat had been sacrificed to an idol, they were to avoid eating it (I Cor. 10:28).

Paul's advice to the Romans was very comparable. He said he was convinced that nothing was defiled of itself. In other words, he told the Roman believers not to automatically assume that meat sold in the marketplace had been sacrificed to idols. However, he went on, if someone in the congregation could not in good conscience eat such meat (because they could not be certain it had not been sacrificed to an idol), then to him it was defiled and he shouldn't eat it.

Obviously, Romans 14:14 has nothing to do with eating unclean meats.

In Romans 14:5, Paul addresses the second "eating" problem:

ROMANS 14:5 **One person esteems one day above another; another esteems every day alike**. Let each be fully convinced in his own mind. 6 He who observes the day, observes it to the Lord; and he who does not observe the day, to the Lord he does not observe it. He who eats, eats to the Lord, for he gives God thanks; and he who does not eat, to the Lord he does not eat, and gives God thanks. (*NKJV*)

What is Paul talking about here? In the first problem, he clearly explains the dispute. But here, the problem is not quite as evident. In verse 6, Paul mentions "he who eats" and contrasts him with "he who does not eat."

The second area of contention over eating in the Roman assembly was a question about when it was proper (or expected) that congregation members would fast. It is in this context that Paul speaks of "one who esteems one day above another" (Rom. 14:5).

The very issue of setting aside particular days for fasting was a contentious one in the early church. *The Didache* (also known as *The Teaching of The Twelve Apostles*), written sometime between 80-150 A.D., addresses this exact controversy:

DIDACHE 8:1 Be careful not to schedule your fasts at the times when the hypocrites fast. They fast on the second (Monday) and fifth (Thursday) day of the week, therefore make your fast on the fourth (Wednesday) day and the Preparation day (Friday, the day of preparation for the Sabbath-Saturday). (The Didache, 1998 translation by Ivan Lewis)

"The hypocrites" mentioned here is a reference to the Pharisees. The author of *The Didache* urged believers in Yeshua to fast on days other than those chosen by the Pharisees. In agreement with *The Didache*, the *Mishnah* indicates in tract *Taanit* that the Pharisees fasted on Monday and Thursday. This is also alluded to in Luke's Gospel:

LUKE 18:11 "The Pharisee stood and prayed thus with himself, 'God, I thank You that I am not like other men – extortioners, unjust, adulterers, or even as this tax collector. 12 **I fast twice a week**; I give tithes of all that I possess.' (*NKJV*)

Paul's point in this passage (Rom. 14:5-6) is that no particular days of the week had been sanctioned by God for fasting. Those who chose to fast regularly on days such as Monday and Thursday (or Wednesday and Friday) would be accepted if they did it to honor God. Likewise, those who didn't view any particular day as mandatory for fasting would be accepted if they ate in the proper spirit and gave thanks to God.

Paul goes on in the rest of chapter 14 to urge the believers in Rome not to judge one another and not to cause their brethren to stumble in these matters. Paul succinctly sums up both problems in the final verse of chapter 14:

ROMANS 14:23 But **he who doubts is condemned if he eats**, because he does not eat from faith; for whatever is not from faith is sin. (*NKJV*)

From our examination of the Scriptures, it is clear that God did **not** nullify Leviticus 11 or Deuteronomy 14 in Mark 7, Acts 10, and Romans 14. But there is one other Scripture that appears to show that any animal may now be eaten by believers:

I TIMOTHY 4:1 Now the Spirit expressly says that in latter times some will depart from the faith, giving heed to deceiving spirits and doctrines of demons, 2 speaking lies in hypocrisy, having their own conscience seared with a hot iron, 3 forbidding to marry, and commanding to abstain from foods which God created to be received with thanksgiving by those who believe and know the truth. 4 **For every creature of God is good, and nothing is to be refused if it is received with thanksgiving**; 5 for it is SANCTIFIED [hagiazetai] by the word of God and prayer. (*NKJV*)

This passage by Paul appears very plainly to show that every creature on earth is now edible. However, one very important limiting factor is usually over-looked by those who use this passage to teach that doctrine.

Paul tells us that "every creature of God is good," and is not "to be refused if it is received with thanksgiving" (I Tim. 4:4). But he qualifies that statement in verse 5 by saying that these creatures are "sanctified by the word of God" (I Tim. 4:5).

The Greek word translated "sanctified" in verse 5 is *hagiazetai*; it literally means "set apart." What creatures of God have been "set apart" **by the word of God** for use as food? Leviticus 11 and Deuteronomy 14 conclusively list those creatures of God which are to be eaten and the ones which are **not** to be eaten. Instead of contradicting the *Torah*'s prohibition on eating unclean animals, Paul is actually supporting it in this Scripture.

Nowhere in the New Testament can it be found where all foods are conclusively declared clean and fit for human consumption. But is there a passage of Scripture that shows that this prohibition will remain in force past the time of Messiah's first coming? Yes, there is!

In the final chapter of the book of Isaiah, we find a prophecy which speaks of the return of Messiah to pour out God's anger, fury and wrath on those who rebel against Him. A description of some of the identifying activities of this group is revealing:

ISAIAH 66:15 For behold, the LORD will come with fire and with His chari-ots, like a whirlwind, to render His anger with fury, and His rebuke with flames of fire. 16 For by fire and by His sword the LORD will judge all flesh; and the slain of the LORD shall be many. 17 "Those who sanctify themselves and purify themselves, to go to the gardens after an idol in the midst, **eating swine's flesh and the abomination and the mouse**, shall be consumed to-gether," says the LORD. 18 For I know their works and their thoughts. It shall be that I will gather all nations and tongues; and they shall come and see My glory. (*NKJV*)

God does not change. The prohibition He placed on which animals His people can use for food still exists. As the prophecy from Isaiah 66 shows, those who do not acknowledge these commands will be among those God pours His an-ger out upon at the time of the Messiah's return. Don't be counted among this rebellious group destined for punishment.

<u>Does Grace Nullify God's Law?</u>

This study examines what the Scriptures really teach about God's grace and its relationship to His Law. Is God's grace intended to replace the Law or does His grace compliment the Law? What is the "curse of the Law" and what does it mean to be "under the Law"?

The grace of God and its relationship to His Law is one of the most misunder-stood topics in the Bible. Many Christians today have been taught and firmly believe that God's grace is the opposite of the Law. They believe that God's grace alone is enough for a believer. In fact, some so-called "ministers" go so far as to state that anyone who seeks to obey God's Law has rejected the sal-vation found in the Messiah. In this warped view of Christianity, obedience to the Law is attacked and declared to be "legalism."

How did this sad, unscriptural state of affairs come about? Many cite the epis-tles of Paul when addressing this topic, using his writings to justify nullifying the Law. Here are some of the "proof texts" commonly used to support the idea that obedience to the Law is no longer required (or even forbidden) for believers in Messiah:

EPHESIANS 2:8 For by grace you have been saved through faith, and that not of yourselves; it is the gift of God, 9 not of works, lest anyone should boast. (*NKJV*)

ROMANS 6:14 For sin shall not have dominion over you, for **you are not under Law but under grace**. (*NKJV*)

ROMANS 7:6 But now **we have been released from the Law**, having died to that by which we were bound, so that we serve in newness of the Spirit and not in oldness of the letter. (*NASU*)

GALATIANS 2:21 I do not nullify the grace of God, for **if justification were through the Law, then Christ died for no purpose**. (*ESV*)

GALATIANS 3:10 **All who rely on observing the Law are under a curse**, for it is written: "Cursed is everyone who does not continue to do everything written in the Book of the Law." 11 Clearly **no one is justified before God by the Law**, because, "The righteous will live by faith." 12 The Law is not based on faith; on the contrary, "The man who does these things will live by them." 13 Christ redeemed us from **the curse of the Law** by becoming a curse for us, for it is written: "Cursed is everyone who is hung on a tree." (*NIV*)

GALATIANS 3:23 Now before faith came, **we were held captive under the Law**, imprisoned until the coming faith would be revealed. 24 So then, **the Law was our guardian until Christ came**, in order that we might be justified by faith. 25 But now that faith has come, **we are no longer under a guardi-an**, 26 for in Christ Jesus you are all sons of God, through faith. (*ESV*)

GALATIANS 5:4 You have become estranged from Christ, **you who attempt to be justified by Law; you have fallen from grace**. (*NKJV*)

On the surface, the passages above **seem** to teach that those who have re-ceived God's grace don't need to (in fact, should NOT) keep the Law. But did Paul truly believe and teach that God's grace trumped the Law and made it invalid? Many have taken these comments from Paul to mean just that. To these "Antinomians" (Greek *anti*-"against," *nomos*-"law"), God's grace, as manifested in the sacrifice of Messiah, is like a "Get Out of Jail Free" card in the game Monopoly. They believe they can teach and practice disobedience to God's Law in this present age (Matt. 5:19) and still be **justified** ("reckoned as righteous") at the judgment seat of Christ (Rom. 14:10; II Cor. 5:10).

Some, however, cannot reconcile these verses with other Scriptures that show obedience to God's Law is a necessary part of a believer's life. As a result, they have taken the extreme position of rejecting the writings of Paul altogether. These "Anti-Paulinians" conclude that Paul wasn't a true apostle of the Messiah Yeshua. Therefore, they believe his epistles should not be considered Scripture and his teachings should be discarded.

In this article, we are going to look at the proper relationship between the Law of God and His grace. In the process, we'll examine the words of Paul to see what he was really saying about this vital topic.

Since the "grace only" doctrine is derived from the writings of Paul, let's start with the comments of the apostle Peter on that topic:

II PETER 3:15 And count the patience of our Lord as salvation, just as **our beloved brother Paul** also wrote to you according to the wisdom given him, 16 as he does in all his letters when he speaks in them of these matters. **There are some things in them that are hard to understand, which the ignorant and unstable twist to their own destruction, as they do the other Scriptures.** 17 You therefore, beloved, knowing this beforehand, **take care that you are not carried away with the error of lawless people** and lose your own stability. (*ESV*)

First, we must notice in verse 16 that Peter acknowledges that Paul's writings are on a par with "the other Scriptures." Peter clearly considered Paul's epistles to be inspired and authoritative. But he also plainly warns believers that Paul's writings were "hard to understand" and that some people were twisting what Paul had said "to their own destruction." He concludes with a warning to believers not to be fooled into making the same errors as the LAWLESS people who had misused Paul's teachings. Even in the days of the early church, it seems that some who called themselves Christians were using Paul's epistles to do away with God's Law.

Before we can do an accurate analysis of what the Scriptures teach on this topic, we have to define some of the terms we'll be using. These include (1) grace, (2) justification, (3) lasciviousness, (4) lawlessness and (5) legalism.

1. GRACE - In the New Testament, the Greek word generally translated "grace" is *charis*. The *Greek-English Lexicon of the New Testament and Other Early Christian Literature* (*BDAG*) gives the following definitions for *charis*:

1. a winning quality or attractiveness that invites a favorable reaction, *graciousness, attractiveness, charm, winsomeness* . . . 2. a beneficent disposition toward someone, *favor, grace, gracious care/help, goodwill* . . . 3. practical application of goodwill, (*a sign of*) *favor, gracious deed/gift, benefaction* . . . 4. exceptional effect produced by generosity, *favor.* . . . 5. response to gener-

osity or beneficence, *thanks, gratitude* . . .

As you can see, this word has several related meanings. But when referring to God's grace given to sinning humans, it is defined as God's benevolent attitude toward mankind. This attitude results in favor being granted by God to man. God's grace is wholly undeserved by mankind; it has not been (and cannot be) earned.

2. JUSTIFICATION - This English word comes from the Greek nouns *dikaioma* and *dikaiosis*. Additionally the verbal forms, "justify," "justifies," and "justified" all come from the related verb *dikaioo*.

There is a subtle difference of meaning between *dikaioma* and *dikaiosis*. According to **BDAG**, *dikaioma* refers to "a regulation relating to just or right action, *regulation, requirement, commandment*" and "an action that meets expectations as to what is right or just, *righteous deed* . . ." Implicit within this word is the concept of being made right with God by keeping His commandments.

Friberg's *Analytical Lexicon to the Greek New Testament (ALGNT)* states that *dikaiosis* means "strictly, an act of *making right* or *just*; hence *justification, acquittal, vindication* (RO 4.25) . . . *righteous act that sets free and gives life* (RO 5.18)." So we see that the first of these words refers to being made righteous by our own acts, while the second means to receive imputed righteousness by being acquitted of our transgressions.

3. LASCIVIOUSNESS - This archaic English word, also translated "lewdness" and "licentiousness" in modern translations, comes from the Greek noun *aselgeia*. *ALGNT* states that this word means "as living without any moral restraint *licentiousness, sensuality, lustful indulgence* (2C 12.21); especially as indecent and outrageous sexual behavior *debauchery, indecency, flagrant immorality* (RO 13.13)."

4. LAWLESSNESS - *Anomia* is the Greek word underlying "lawlessness." *Thayer's Greek-English Lexicon of the New Testament* (*Thayer*) says that *anomia* is "properly, *the condition of one without law – either because ignorant of it, or because violating it. . . . contempt and violation of law, iniquity, wickedness*" (p. 48).

I John 3:4 defines SIN as lawlessness; therefore, sin is biblically defined as the violation of God's Law. Those who break God's Law because of their contempt for its value to a believer are practicing lawlessness (Matt. 7:23; 13:41). In II Corinthians 6:14, Paul rhetorically asks "what fellowship has RIGHTEOUSNESS (Gr. *dikaiosune*) with LAWLESSNESS (*anomia*)?" The implied answer is NONE.

5. LEGALISM - This final term is not found in the Bible. The *Webster Comprehensive Dictionary, Encyclopedic Edition* gives two theological definitions for legalism: "The doctrine of salvation by works, as distinguished from that by grace," and "the tendency to observe the letter rather than the spirit of the law" (p. 728, vol. 1).

Scripturally speaking, the first of these definitions best fits what will be addressed in this article. However, in practice "legalism" has become the principal term of choice for "grace only" advocates to describe the belief that obeying the Law of God is required of believers. It is frequently redefined by those who use it, but "legalism" is generally meant to slander, disparage, and cast doubt upon the beliefs so labeled. Due to the negative connotation of the word, those tagged as "legalists" are immediately put on the defensive regarding their beliefs.

All of these terms are important in understanding what the Bible truly teaches about the grace of God and its relationship to the Law. But before we delve extensively into the Scriptures on this matter, I want to use an analogy to illustrate the folly of the "grace only" position regarding grace versus Law.

Let's assume that we have a man who was caught selling sensitive information to a foreign government. He was legally tried and convicted of treason against the United States. Even though the man realized he had made a terrible mistake and was sorry for what he had done, the severity of the crime required a death sentence be given to him based on the laws of the United States. This prisoner is on death row awaiting execution. But in a spirit of forgiveness and grace (unmerited favor), the President of the United States grants the man a full and unconditional pardon and has him released from prison.

Does this pardon received by the prisoner now nullify the legal code of the United States? Would the man be able to break any and all US laws with impunity after his release? Would he be able to quit paying income tax to the IRS, traffic in illegal drugs, distribute child pornography, or even murder another US citizen, without having to worry about the consequences of his actions?

Just using human reasoning, it's easy to see that the pardoned man would NOT be free to break the laws of the United States after his pardon. In fact, it's reasonable to expect that the man would be so thankful for his undeserved reprieve from death that he would become a model, law-abiding citizen. How do you think the man would react to someone who advocated that he actively set out to disobey US law? I imagine that he would reject such advice, and have nothing to do with the one giving it.

Through His grace, God has provided a way for us to be pardoned from the death sentence we've earned by breaking His Law. Why, then, would someone assume that this pardon negates the Law of God? Why would someone repay the unmerited favor shown to them by God with a rebellious disregard for His commandments? Why would someone think that an eternal, unchanging God would contradict Himself by requiring believers to disobey His own Law in order to maintain His divine favor?

First, let's address the "grace only" proof texts cited at the beginning of this article. In his writings, Paul states that all mankind has sinned and fallen short of the glory of God (Rom. 3:9, 23; 5:12; Gal. 3:22). James tells us that breaking any one law makes us guilty of the whole Law (Jam. 2:10). Therefore, we cannot be saved by our works, because our works are imperfect. We are in need of God's grace for our salvation. This is the context of Paul's statement found in Ephesians 2:

EPHESIANS 2:8 For **by grace** [chariti] **you have been saved through faith**, and that not of yourselves; it is the gift of God, 9 **not of works**, lest anyone should boast. (*NKJV*)

In our previous analogy, the man convicted of treason could never be declared innocent based on his own actions. Even if he never broke another law in his life, his prior transgression would forever brand him as a criminal. He could never be JUSTIFIED or made right by his own power or actions after committing his crime. It is in this light that we should view Paul's statements regarding justification in Galatians 2:

GALATIANS 2:21 I do not nullify the **grace** [charin] of God; for if **justification** [dikaiosune] comes through the Law, then Christ died for nothing. (*NRSV*)

The Greek noun *dikaiosune*, translated "justification" in this verse, is closely related to *dikaioma*. Some translations alternately render this word as "righteousness." *ALGNT* defines *dikaiosune* as "(1) *righteousness, uprightness*, generally denoting the characteristics of δικιος (*righteous, just*) (MT 5.6); (2) legally *justice, uprightness, righteousness* (PH 3.6); (3) as an attribute of God *righteousness, integrity* (RO 3.5); (4) of the right behavior that God requires of persons *righteousness, good behavior, uprightness* (MT 5.20), opposite αδικια (unrighteousness, wrongdoing); (5) in Pauline thought of the divine action by which God puts a person right with himself and which then becomes a dynamic power in the believer's life *making right(eous); state of having been made righteous* (RO 1.17)." In this Scripture, it literally means to be "justified" or "righteous" in the sight of God.

If one can eventually keep the Law good enough to override prior sins, then the sacrifice of Yeshua was needless. But just as the convicted man can never afterward keep the Law perfectly enough to erase his conviction, we cannot remove our prior sins by subsequently keeping God's Law. Forgiveness requires faithfully accepting the sacrifice of the Messiah for the removal of our sins.

Paul's point in Galatians 2:21 is that those who think that they can earn their salvation by Law-keeping are effectively nullifying God's grace. Does this mean that keeping God's Law is wrong? By no means! It all boils down to the REASON for keeping the Law. There is no scriptural condemnation of those who obey God's Law in order to emulate the Messiah's example and honor their heavenly Father. But those who do so as a means of accumulating enough brownie points with God to be saved are misguided and in error, as Paul points out.

Now let's examine another passage from Paul's letter to the Galatians dealing with justification:

GALATIANS 3:10 For **all who rely on works of the Law are under a curse**; for it is written, "Cursed be everyone who does not abide by all things written in the Book of the Law, and do them." 11 Now it is evident that **no one is justified** [dikaioutai] **before God by the Law**, for "The **righteous** [dikaios] shall live by faith." 12 But the Law is not of faith, rather "**The one who does them shall live by them**." 13 Christ redeemed us from **the curse of the Law** by becoming a curse for us-for it is written, "Cursed is everyone who is hanged on a tree"- (*NIV*)

Paul speaks of those "who rely on the works of the Law" being "under a curse" (v. 10). His implication is that some of the people in Galatia were relying on keeping the Law to be justified before God. The "curse of the Law" (v. 13) is not the Law itself, but rather the penalty for disobedience to that Law (i.e., death). To avoid the curse of death, one had to keep the Law perfectly (v. 12). But since Paul understood that the whole world had transgressed the Law, he recognized that no one could be justified in the sight of God by keeping the Law. It was only through Christ's sacrificial death on the wooden stake that the curse brought about by Law-breaking could pass from us, that we might be made right with God.

GALATIANS 5:4 You who are trying to be **justified** [dikaiousthe] **by Law** have been alienated from Christ; you have fallen away from **grace** [charitos]. (*NIV*)

When one begins to think that they can be justified in God's sight by Law-keeping, they have in fact separated themselves from the Messiah. Again, Paul is not disparaging the Law here. He is simply finding fault with the Galatians' motives for keeping it. It is possible for someone to do the RIGHT thing for the WRONG reason.

You might have noticed that I initially skipped the verses where Paul speaks about believers not being "under the Law." This phrase (Gr. *hupo nomon*) is used by Paul ten times in eight verses, and he uses it in slightly different ways, depending on the point he's trying to make.

The first way Paul uses this phrase is to designate those who have been given God's Law, i.e., the Jews. An example of this usage is found in 1 Corinthians 9:

I CORINTHIANS 9:20 And to the Jews I became as a Jew, that I might win Jews; to those who are **under the Law** [hupo nomon], as **under the Law** [hupo nomon], that I might win those who are **under the Law** [hupo nomon]; 21 to those who are without Law, as without Law (not being without Law toward God, but **under Law** [ennomos] toward Christ), that I might win those who are without Law; (*NKJV*)

In this passage, we see that Paul differentiates between Jews who had been given the Law and were under its requirements, and Gentiles who did not have the Law. The Greek word translated "under Law" in verse 21 is *ennomos*, an adjective that *ALGNT* defines as "strictly *within law*; hence *lawful, legal, according to law* (AC 19.39); as a personal characteristic *committed to law, obedient to law* (1C 9.21)". Paul essentially said here that even when interacting with the Gentiles who didn't know or have the Law, he was still obedient to the Law for Messiah's sake.

So in Paul's writings, being "under the Law" can refer to those who had received the Law and were required to keep it (I Cor. 9:20; Gal. 4:4-5, 21).

However, Paul also uses the phrase ***hupo nomon*** to refer specifically to being subject to the PENALTY for disobedience to the Law (i.e., death). This usage can clearly be seen in Romans 6:

ROMANS 6:11 In the same way, count yourselves dead to sin but alive to God in Christ Jesus. 12 Therefore do not let sin reign in your mortal body so that you obey its evil desires. 13 Do not offer the parts of your body to sin, as instruments of wickedness, but rather **offer yourselves to God, as those who have been brought from death to life**; and offer the parts of your body to him as instruments of **righteousness** [dikaiosunes]. 14 For sin shall not be your master, because you are not **under Law** [hupo nomon], but under **grace** [charin]. 15 What then? Shall we sin because we are not **under Law** [hupo nomon] but under **grace** [charin]? **By no means!** 16 Don't you know that when you offer yourselves to someone to obey him as slaves, you are slaves to the one whom you obey-- whether you are slaves to sin, which leads to death, or to obedience, which leads to **righteousness** [dikaiosunen]? 17 But thanks be to God that, though you used to be slaves to sin, you wholeheartedly obeyed the form of teaching to which you were entrusted. 18 You have been set free from sin and have become slaves to righteousness. (*NIV*)

Paul states that believers are "not under Law but under grace" (v. 14). By this, he means that they are not under the death penalty for sin imposed by the Law. Instead, they have been given life by God's grace. But Paul goes on to state that this grace does NOT allow them to continue in sin (v. 15). To continue sinning, Paul states, would lead them back to death (v. 16). However, Paul says that obedience leads to righteousness (v. 16). Although he states that the Roman believers used to be slaves to sin (v. 17), their obedience to the teaching brought to them has freed them from sin. Now they are to be slaves to righteousness (v. 18).

By definition, a slave has to work for his master. When sin was their master, the Romans had to serve it by indulging the lusts of the flesh. Now that they had been saved from the punishment required for their Law-breaking, Paul expected them to serve their new master, righteousness. This master required that they be obedient to the Law.

GALATIANS 3:21 **Is the Law then contrary to the promises of God? Certainly not! For if a Law had been given that could give life, then righteousness would indeed be by the Law.** 22 But the Scripture imprisoned everything under sin, so that the promise by faith in Jesus Christ might be given to those who believe. 23 Now before faith came, we were held captive under the Law, imprisoned until the coming faith would be revealed. 24 So then, the

Law was our **guardian** [paidagogos] until Christ came, in order that we might be justified by faith. 25 But now that faith has come, we are no longer under a **guardian** [paidagogon], 26 for in Christ Jesus you are all sons of God, through faith. (*ESV*)

Paul starts this passage of Scripture by stating that the Law is NOT opposed to the promises of God. In fact, he extols the value of the Law, stating that if **any** Law would have been able to give life, it would have been God's Law. But his implied point is that life CANNOT be gained through the Law (any law). This passage by Paul is generally misunderstood because of wrong understanding of the function of the *paidagogos* in ancient society. This Greek word, translated "guardian" above, is translated "schoolmaster" and "tutor" in some versions. However, the key to understanding Paul's point is to truly understand the role of the *paidagogos*. Here is what *BDAG* states about the function of a *paidagogos*:

. . . Orig[inally] 'boy-leader', the man, usu[ally] a slave (Plut., Mor. 4ab), whose duty it was to conduct a boy or youth (Plut., Mor. 439f) to and from school and to superintend his conduct gener[ally]; he was not a 'teacher' . . . When the young man became of age, the [*paidagogos*] was no longer needed . . .

As you can see from the definition above, Paul is NOT speaking of the Law as a teacher. Instead, the context indicates that the Law functioned as a **guardian** for those convicted of sin (which was all mankind-Rom. 5:12). When forgiveness came through faith in the sacrifice of Yeshua, we were no longer under the guardianship of the Law; we were no longer under its penalty for disobedience. This does not mean that the Law's function as God's standard of right conduct has been voided.

Paul addresses the Law and the way to true righteousness in the 5th chapter of Romans:

ROMANS 5:12 Therefore, just as sin came into the world through one man, and death through sin, and so **death spread to all men because all sinned** - 13 for sin indeed was in the world before the Law was given, but sin is not counted where there is no Law. 14 Yet death reigned from Adam to Moses, even over those whose sinning was not like the transgression of Adam, who was a type of the one who was to come. 15 But the free gift is not like the trespass. For if many died through one man's trespass, much more have the grace of God and the free gift by the grace of that one man Jesus Christ abounded for many. 16 And the free gift is not like the result of that one man's sin. For the judgment following one trespass brought condemnation, but the free gift following many trespasses brought **justification** [dikaioma]. 17 If, because of one man's trespass, death reigned through that one man, much more will those who receive the abundance of **grace** [charitos] and the free gift of **righteousness** [dikaiosunes] reign in life through the one man Jesus Christ. 18 Therefore, as one trespass led to condemnation for all men, so one act of **righteousness** [dikaiomatos] leads to **justification** [dikaiosin] and life for all men. 19 For as by the one man's disobedience the many were made sinners, so by the one man's obedience the many will be made **righteous** [dikaioi]. 20 Now the Law came in to increase the trespass, but where sin increased, **grace** [charis] abounded all the more, 21 so that, as sin reigned in death, **grace** [charis] also might reign through **righteousness** [dikaiosunes] leading to eternal life through Jesus Christ our Lord. (*ESV*)

In his own particular way, Paul shows in this passage of Scripture that God's Law has existed since at least the time of Adam. He begins by saying that sin entered the world when Adam disobeyed God's command not to eat of the tree of knowledge. Because of this disobedience, Paul tells us, death came to all men, because all who lived after Adam sinned also.

To emphasize that God's Law has always existed, Paul tells us that sin is not counted when no law is present. If the Law had not existed from the time of Adam to Moses, then God could not legitimately inflict the penalty for sin on mankind. However, by telling us that death reigned during this time period because all sinned, Paul is showing that the Law DID exist, and that the penalty for breaking it was enforced. The Law is not relative, but is an eternal standard of righteous conduct.

BDAG says that in Romans 5:16, *dikaioma* is used as an equivalent to ***dikaiosis*** "to clear someone of a violation." This demonstrates that Paul considered Messiah's obedience to God to have been transferred to believers, acquitting them in the sight of God and making them righteous.

Because God does not change (Mal. 3:6), He will not nullify or set aside His Law. Disobedience to the Law has to be punished. Paul tells us that the wages of SIN is **death** (Rom. 6:23). All men are sinners and have fallen short of the perfect standard of God's Law (Rom. 3:23). But since it is God's nature to be gracious, He allows a way for sinful mankind to escape the death penalty required by the Law.

However, God's grace is not something that can be earned. Through Yeshua, God justifies ("acquits") the ungodly sinner who accepts his sacrifice on the cross (Rom. 8:32-34). The Father does this because of His grace ("favor") toward mankind.

Earlier in the letter to the Romans, Paul defines the function of the Law:
ROMANS 3:19 Now we know that whatever the Law says, it says to **those who are under the Law**, that **every mouth** may be stopped, and **all the world may become guilty before God**. 20 Therefore by the deeds of the Law no flesh will be justified in His sight, for **by the Law is the knowledge of sin**. (*NKJV*)

Here, Paul shows that the Law is not for justification, but rather for us to know right from wrong. Incidentally, Paul shows here that the Law is not just for the Jews, but for all mankind. Notice that it's not just Jews that become guilty by breaking the Law, but "all the world."

Paul explains how living by the Spirit removes one from the penalty of Law-breaking in the 5th chapter of Galatians:

GALATIANS 5:16 I say then: Walk in the Spirit, and you shall not fulfill the lust of the flesh. 17 For the flesh lusts against the Spirit, and the Spirit against the flesh; and these are contrary to one another, so that you do not do the things that you wish. 18 But **if you are led by the Spirit, you are not under the Law**. 19 Now the works of the flesh are evident, which are: adultery, fornication, uncleanness, lewdness, 20 idolatry, sorcery, hatred, contentions, jealousies, outbursts of wrath, selfish ambitions, dissensions, heresies, 21 envy, murders, drunkenness, revelries, and the like; of which I tell you beforehand, just as I also told you in time past, that those who practice such things will not inherit the kingdom of God. 22 But **the fruit of the Spirit is love, joy, peace, longsuffering, kindness, goodness, faithfulness, 23 gentleness, self-control. Against such there is no law**. 24 And those who are Christ's have crucified the flesh with its passions and desires. 25 If we live in the Spirit, let us also walk in the Spirit. (*NKJV*)

There is no law against the fruits of the Spirit; these actions fulfill God's Law. However, if one does the works of the flesh, they have sinned and will come under the penalty of the Law. Paul clearly states that those who sin in such a manner will NOT inherit the kingdom of God.

God's grace doesn't nullify the Law, but rather it voids the penalty we deserve for breaking the Law:

TITUS 3:4 But when the kindness and the love of God our Savior toward man appeared, 5 **not by works of righteousness which we have done, but according to His mercy He saved us**, through the washing of regeneration and renewing of the Holy Spirit, 6 whom He poured out on us abundantly through Jesus Christ our Savior, 7 that having been **justified** [dikaiothentes] **by His grace** [chariti] we should become heirs according to the hope of eternal life. 8 This is a faithful saying, and these things I want you to affirm constantly, that **those who have believed in God should be careful to maintain good works. These things are good and profitable to men**. (*NKJV*)

Paul here encourages Titus to teach believers that, because of the grace God had shown them through Messiah, they should be sure to do good works. What were those "good works"? Paul tells us in his first letter to the Corinthians:

I CORINTHIANS 7:19 Circumcision means nothing, and uncircumcision means nothing; **what matters is keeping God's commandments**. (*NAB*)

Now that we've examined what the Scriptures really teach about God's grace, let's see some of the problems that arose in the early church due to misusing the concept of grace. We'll start in the epistle of Jude:

JUDE 3 Beloved, while I was very diligent to write to you concerning our common salvation, I found it necessary to write to you exhorting you to contend earnestly for the faith which was once for all delivered to the saints. 4

For certain men have crept in unnoticed, who long ago were marked out for this condemnation, ungodly men, who turn the grace of our God into **lewdness** [aselgeian] and deny the only Lord God and our Lord Jesus Christ. (*NKJV*)

Jude clearly shows that there were so-called "Christians" in the 1st century who were already perverting God's grace, claiming that it allowed them to live an immoral lifestyle. These people were practicing "laciviousness" (*aselgeia*) disguised as liberty from the Law.

In his ensuing comments, Jude makes the character and fate of these people very clear. He calls them "dreamers" in verse 8, because they promoted false teachings they had dreamed up. These dreamers defile their flesh because they reject the authority of God's Law in their lives. Jude tells us in verse 13 that "the blackness of darkness" (cf. Matt. 8:12; 22:13; 25:30) is their reward "in the age" (Gr. *eis aiona*).

In his letter to Titus, Paul speaks of those believers who, by their works, show themselves to actually be "unbelievers":

TITUS 1:15 To the pure all things are pure, but to those who are defiled and unbelieving nothing is pure; but even their mind and conscience are defiled. 16 **They profess to know God, but in works they deny Him**, being abominable, **disobedient**, and disqualified for every good work. (*NKJV*)

Yeshua also spoke of those who proclaimed themselves to be his followers, but didn't keep God's Law:

MATTHEW 7:15 "Beware of false prophets, who come to you in sheep's clothing, but inwardly they are ravenous wolves. 16 **You will know them by their fruits**. Do men gather grapes from thornbushes or figs from thistles? 17 Even so, every good tree bears good fruit, but **a bad tree bears bad fruit**. 18 A good tree cannot bear bad fruit, nor can a bad tree bear good fruit. 19 Every tree that does not bear good fruit is cut down and thrown into the fire. 20 Therefore **by their fruits you will know them**. 21 Not everyone who says to me, 'Lord, Lord,' shall enter the kingdom of heaven, but **he who does the will of my Father in heaven**. 22 Many will say to me in that day, 'Lord, Lord, have we not prophesied in your name, cast out demons in your name, and done many wonders in your name?' 23 "And then I will declare to them, 'I never knew you; depart from me, you who practice **lawlessness** [anomian]!' " (*NKJV*)

The parable of the wheat and tares speaks of this very situation:

MATTHEW 13:24 He put another parable before them, saying, "The kingdom of heaven may be compared to a man who sowed good seed in his field, 25 but while his men were sleeping, his enemy came and sowed weed among the wheat and went away. 26 So when the plants came up and bore grain, then the weeds appeared also. 27 And the servants of the master of the house came and said to him, 'Master, did you not sow good seed in your field? How then does it have weeds?' 28 He said to them, 'An enemy has done this.' So the servants said to him, 'Then do you want us to go and gather them?' 29 But he said, 'No, lest in gathering the weeds you root up the wheat along with them. 30 Let both grow together until the harvest, and at harvest time I will tell the reapers, Gather the weeds first and bind them in bundles to be burned, but gather the wheat into my barn.'" (*ESV*)

Yeshua afterward explained the meaning of this parable to his disciples: MATTHEW 13:36 Then Jesus sent the multitude away and went into the house. And his disciples came to him, saying, "Explain to us the parable of the tares of the field." 37 He answered and said to them: "He who sows the good seed is the Son of Man. 38 The field is the world, the good seeds are the sons of the kingdom, but the tares are the sons of the wicked one. 39 The enemy who sowed them is the devil, the harvest is the end of the age, and the reapers are the angels. 40 Therefore as the tares are gathered and burned in the fire, so it will be at the end of this age. 41 The Son of Man will send out his angels, and they will gather out of his kingdom all things that offend, and **those who practice lawlessness** [anomian], 42 and will cast them into the furnace of fire. There will be wailing and gnashing of teeth. 43 Then the righteous will shine forth as the sun in the kingdom of their Father. He who has ears to hear, let him hear!" (*NKJV*)

Yeshua likens these false, Law-breaking Christians to tares growing among his wheat crop. *Faussett's Bible Dictionary* has this to say about the nature of tares:
. . . Mt. 13:24-30. *Zizanion*, Arabic, zowan, Hebrew *zowniyn*; *zan* means "nausea." Not our vetch, but darnel; at first impossible to distinguish from wheat or barley, until the wheat's ear is developed, when the thin fruitless ear of the darnel is detected. Its root too so intertwines with that of the wheat that the farmer cannot separate them, without plucking up both, "till the time of harvest." The seed is like wheat, but smaller and black, and when mixed with wheat flour causes dizziness, intoxication, and paralysis; Lolium temulentum, bearded darnel, the only deleterious grain among all the numerous grasses. . . . ("Tares")

Although tares look like wheat at first, the fruit of tares is "bad." Yeshua tells us that one of the primary spiritual fruits of tares is "lawlessness." One of the first acts that Yeshua will initiate when his kingdom is established is the removal of these spiritual tares.

Conclusion

God's grace and His Law are two sides of the same coin. The Law defines our expected behavior, and God's grace provides forgiveness when we don't live up to that standard. Grace doesn't nullify the Law, it compliments it. Clearly, those who think they can be part of God's people without obedience to His Law are deceived. Yeshua himself stated this clearly:
MATTHEW 5:17 "Do not think that I came to destroy the Law or the Prophets. I did not come to destroy but to fulfill. 18 For assuredly, I say to you, till

heaven and earth pass away, one jot or one tittle will by no means pass from the Law till all is fulfilled. 19 **Whoever therefore breaks one of the least of these commandments, and teaches men so, shall be called least in the kingdom of heaven**; but whoever does and teaches them, he shall be called great in the kingdom of heaven." (*NKJV*)

Bryan T. Huie
June 14, 2003
Revised: April 18, 2009

Galatians Commentary

This commentary on Galatians explains Paul's position on the Law (Torah) and shows why he was NOT invalidating the Law of God. This article helps to explain many of Paul's apparently contradictory statements regarding the Law. As you will see, Paul was preaching against a legalistic form of Judaism, not against the Law of Moses itself.

GALATIANS - WAS PAUL TEACHING AGAINST THE LAW?

Paul's letter to the Galatians is the Scripture most often used to try and prove that *YHVH's* Law has been done away. Many theologians cite passages from Galatians to establish that the so-called "Mosaic Law" (i.e., *Torah*) given at Mount Sinai has no validity for "new covenant" believers. But is this position correct? Did Yeshua remove the Law that God gave the Israelites at Sinai and replace it with a different law?

The key to understanding anything in the Bible is an awareness of the CONTEXT of the Scripture you're reading. Paul's epistle to the Galatians is no exception. We have to remember that this text is a letter that Paul wrote to try and correct a problem that was occurring in Galatia. However, we only have ONE side of the discussion. We don't know what questions or statements Paul had received from the Galatians. In effect, reading this letter is like listening to a telephone conversation we're not directly involved with. We can't hear what the other party is saying, so we have to try and determine what was said through the answers given by the one we *can* hear.

To fully grasp what Paul is saying in this pivotal New Testament epistle, we must become aware of the specific problems that had arisen in Galatia. We must also try to discern who was causing those problems. Our goal in this article is to compare Paul's comments to the Galatians with teachings that existed in 1st-century Judaism. By doing this, we will attempt to identify the group of "Judaizers" who were disturbing Paul's converts in Galatia. In the process, we will look extensively at some of the documents uncovered during the 20th century in the Dead Sea scrolls found at Qumran.

Now let's begin our journey through the book of Galatians with Paul's introduction and greeting to the Galatians:

GALATIANS 1:1 Paul, an apostle (not from men nor through man, but through Jesus Christ and God the Father who raised him from the dead), 2 and all the brethren who are with me, to the churches of Galatia: 3 Grace to you and peace from God the Father and our Lord Jesus Christ, 4 who gave himself for our sins, that he might deliver us from this present evil age, according to the will of our God and Father, 5 to whom be glory forever and ever. Amen. (*NKJV*)

After his short greeting, Paul quickly launches into the problem occurring in Galatia:

GALATIANS 1:6 I marvel that you are turning away so soon from Him who called you in the grace of Christ, to a **different gospel**, 7 which is not another; but there are some who trouble you and want to **pervert the gospel of Christ**. 8 But even if we, or an angel from heaven, preach any other gospel to you than what we have preached to you, let him be accursed. 9

As we have said before, so now I say again, if anyone preaches any other gospel to you than what you have received, let him be accursed. (**NKJV**)

Some person or group was attempting to deceive the Galatians with a "different gospel." At this point in his letter, we don't yet know what this other **gospel** ("good news") is that Paul refers to here. As we delve more deeply into his epistle, Paul will give us some vital clues about how the good news proclaimed by Messiah had been perverted. To emphasize the depth of his displeasure at this development, Paul pronounces a double curse on the person(s) attempting to convert the Galatians to this heretical religious view.

GALATIANS 1:10 For do I now persuade men, or God? Or do I seek to please men? For if I still pleased men, I would not be a bondservant of Christ. 11 But I make known to you, brethren, that the gospel which was preached by me is not according to man. 12 For I neither received it from man, nor was I taught it, but it came through the revelation of Jesus Christ. (**NKJV**)

Here Paul emphasizes the divine nature of his teaching. He claims that Yeshua the Messiah himself revealed the truth to him. This claim is designed to differentiate the gospel that Paul initially brought to the Galatians from the gospel they later accepted.

GALATIANS 1:13 For you have heard of my former conduct in Judaism, how I persecuted the church of God beyond measure and tried to destroy it. 14 And I advanced in Judaism beyond many of my contemporaries in my own nation, being more exceedingly zealous for the **traditions of my fathers**. (**NKJV**)

In the Second Temple period, Pharisees, Sadducees, Essenes, Qumran sectarians, Nazarenes, etc. all considered themselves to be Jews. Judaism is a useful term insofar as it indicates that one worships the God of Abraham, Isaac, and Jacob. However, the different Jewish sects differed widely in belief and practice in the 1st century.

We know from the New Testament that Paul was a member of the sect of the Pharisees (Acts 23:6; 26:5; Phi. 3:5). The "traditions of the fathers" he mentions in verse 14 is a reference to the Oral Law of the Pharisees. The Pharisees (and later their successors, rabbinic Judaism) believed that Moses was given oral laws as well as the written Law while on Mount Sinai for 40 days. According to Jewish tradition, these oral laws were handed down through the generations from father to son to explain how the written Law was to be kept. Many of these oral laws were later recorded by the rabbis in the *Mishnah* and the *Talmud*.

Paul does not just mention the "traditions of the fathers" in passing here. His comment is intended to set up what he will write to the Galatians later in his letter about the teachings of the "false brethren."

GALATIANS 1:15 But when it pleased God, who separated me from my mother's womb and called me through His grace, 16 to reveal His Son in me, that I might preach him among the Gentiles, I did not immediately confer with flesh and blood, 17 nor did I go up to Jerusalem to those who were apostles before me; but I went to Arabia, and returned again to Damascus. (*NKJV*)

Unlike many who would have sought human validation for the supernatural instruction he had just received, Paul did not go to Jerusalem to consult with the disciples who had been with Yeshua. Instead, he went to Arabia and then Damascus for a total of three years (v. 18).

GALATIANS 1:18 Then after three years I went up to Jerusalem to see Peter, and remained with him fifteen days. 19 But I saw none of the other apostles except James, the Lord's brother. 20 (Now concerning the things which I write to you, indeed, before God, I do not lie.) 21 Afterward I went into the regions of Syria and Cilicia. 22 And I was unknown by face to the churches of Judea which were in Christ. 23 But they were hearing only, "He who formerly persecuted us now preaches the faith which he once tried to destroy." 24 And they glorified God in me. (*NKJV*)

At the end of chapter 1, Paul speaks of his trip to Jerusalem three years after his experience on the road to Damascus. While there, he conferred with the apostle Peter for 15 days.

GALATIANS 2:1 Then after fourteen years I went up again to Jerusalem with Barnabas, and also took Titus with me. 2 And I went up by revelation, and communicated to them that gospel which I preach among the Gentiles, but privately to those who were of reputation, lest by any means I might run, or had run, in vain. 3 Yet not even Titus who was with me, being a Greek, was **compelled to be circumcised.** (*NKJV*)

Paul tells of another trip he took to Jerusalem after 14 more years, this time accompanied by Barnabas and Titus. He states that he was told to go "by revelation." The purpose of his trip was to confirm that he was preaching the same message to the Gentiles that the original apostles were preaching to the Jews.

Paul's statement regarding Titus not being compelled to be circumcised (v. 3) is another clue regarding the problems that had arisen in Galatia. Indications from the text are that **coerced circumcision** was one of the primary false teachings being brought to the Galatians.

The different Jewish sects taught different meanings for circumcision. Despite the common misconception of most Christians, Paul was not opposed to circumcision per se. In fact, he required circumcision of his co-worker Timothy (Acts 16:1-4), and he stated that "the sign of circumcision" is "a seal of the righteousness of the faith" (Rom. 4:11). But Paul's adversaries in Galatia wanted circumcision not to be simply a sign that showed faith, but rather part of the method through which righteousness was attained.

GALATIANS 2:4 But because of false believers secretly brought in, who slipped in to spy on the freedom we have in Christ Jesus, so that they might enslave us – 5 we did not submit to them even for a moment, so that the truth of the gospel might always remain with you. (*NRSV*)

Verses 4 and 5 seem somewhat out of place because these verses are an inset equating the "false brethren" bothering the Galatians with other false believers the apostle Paul had met during his ministry. They are mentioned at this point in Paul's letter because their actions and attitudes were the opposite of those Paul visited while in Jerusalem. Paul's contrast between Titus not being required to be circumcised by the apostles when they visited Jerusalem (v. 3) and the mention of "false brethren" (v. 4) shows that forced circumcision based on the teaching of the "false brethren" was one of the central issues Paul was concerned about in Galatia.

GALATIANS 2:6 But from those who seemed to be something – whatever they were, it makes no difference to me; God shows personal favoritism to no man – for those who seemed to be something added nothing to me. 7 But on the contrary, when they saw that the gospel for the uncircumcised had been committed to me, as the gospel for the circumcised was to Peter 8 (for He who worked effectively in Peter for the apostleship to the circumcised also worked effectively in me toward the Gentiles), 9 and when James, Cephas, and John, who seemed to be pillars, perceived the grace that had been given to me, they gave me and Barnabas the right hand of fellowship, that we should go to the Gentiles and they to the circumcised. 10 They desired only that we should remember the poor, the very thing which I also was eager to do. (*NKJV*)

After the two inset verses, Paul continues discussing his trip to Jerusalem. He shows that Peter was the leader of the apostles who had been with Yeshua. This passage is designed to show the Galatians that Paul was preaching the same good news to the Gentiles that the original apostles let by Peter were preaching to the Jews.

In the next story Paul relates about Peter, he sets up his main point against the false brethren in Galatia:

GALATIANS 2:11 Now when Peter had come to Antioch, I withstood him to his face, because he was to be blamed; 12 for before certain men came from James, he would eat with the Gentiles; but when they came, he withdrew and separated himself, fearing those who were of the circumcision. 13 And the rest of the Jews also played the hypocrite with him, so that even Barnabas was carried away with their hypocrisy. (*NKJV*)

Apparently Peter later made a reciprocal visit to Paul at Antioch. Initially, he ate meals with the Gentile converts there. But when some Jewish men sent by James showed up later, he discontinued eating with the Gentiles.

The reason Peter ceased eating with the Gentiles when the Jewish men from Jerusalem arrived was due to requirements found in the Oral Law. The eating Paul speaks of here had nothing to do with unclean food. Peter himself confirms this tenet of the Oral Law in his visit to Cornelius:

ACTS 10:28 He said to them: "You are well aware that **it is against our law for a Jew to associate with a Gentile or visit him.** But God has shown me that I should not call any man impure or unclean." (*NIV*)

This prohibition is NOT found in the *Torah*, but rather was part of the Oral Law. According to strict Jewish tradition, it was not permitted to eat with an un-circumcised Gentile even if he worshiped the God of Israel and served clean food. This was because it was automatically assumed that the house was ritually unclean, and that the Gentiles in it were also unclean. According to the Oral Law, this uncleanness would make the Jew entering into the house unclean also.

The tradition of separating from the Gentiles to maintain ritual purity was contrary to the truth of the Gospel. There is no law in the *Torah* which forbids Israelites from eating with Gentiles. Paul's commission was to preach the good news to as many Gentiles as were willing to hear it. Jews refusing to eat with Gentile believers would have made this task very difficult, if not impossible.

GALATIANS 2:14 But when I saw that they were not straightforward about the truth of the gospel, I said to Peter before them all, "If you, being a **Jew** [Ioudaios], live in the manner of Gentiles and not as the **Jews** [Ioudaikos], why do you compel Gentiles to live as **Jews** [Ioudaizein]?" (*NKJV*)

Paul called Peter's hand on this practice in front of all the Jews, including those from Jerusalem, because he knew Peter's true feelings on this issue. Paul's words to Peter are hard for us to understand today, as Peter himself later commented about many of Paul's writings (2 Pet. 3:16). However, a careful analysis of them will reveal the true point that Paul was making to Peter.

In the New Testament, the word "Jew" (from the Greek root word *Ioudaios*) has basically three meanings. It either refers to (1) one who is descended from the House of Judah, (2) someone from the land of Judea, or (3) someone who practiced the religion of Israel. At times, these designations overlapped.

In Paul's case, his rebuke of Peter was designed to call attention to the hypocrisy he showed when the religious Jews arrived from Judea. Paul chastised Peter for trying to adhere to ritual purity customs based on the Oral Law which were kept by the strict Jews in Judea. However, these traditions were not normally required of the Gentile brethren outside of Judea. A Jewish evangelist who followed these traditional customs while in other nations would have had a tough time converting the Gentiles.

Below is a literal translation of verse 14 that better illustrates Paul's point:

GALATIANS 2:14 But when I saw that they were not straightforward about the truth of the gospel, I said to Peter before them all, "If you, being a **Jew** [Ioudaios], live in the manner of Gentiles and not as the **Judeans** [Ioudaikos], why do you compel Gentiles to live as **Judeans** [Ioudaizein]?" (*literal*)

Paul asked Peter a simple but biting question: "Peter, although you are a Jew, while dwelling among the Gentiles you don't normally seek to be ritually pure like the Jews in Judea. So why are you now trying to force the Gentiles to adhere to the purity traditions just as if they were in Judea?" Paul said Peter did not normally follow the oral tradition that he was advocating by his actions, and that made him a hypocrite.

In the context of Paul's argument, to "live as Jews," or "Judeans" was synonymous with following the oral customs regarding contact with Gentiles that those in Judea followed. The issue here was not compliance with the written Law, but remaining ritually pure according to the Oral Law. The Judeans from Jerusalem were apparently concerned about maintaining their ritual purity. Peter, who was not adhering to those customs when he first arrived in Antioch, returned to the stricter Judean practice of maintaining ritual purity when the Jews from Jerusalem arrived. His hypocrisy was evident to Paul because he knew that Peter did not believe the Oral Law's ritual purity requirements regarding eating with Gentiles were valid (Acts 10:28).

Paul's use of the example of Peter here in his letter was intended to lead in to the problem of the "false gospel" being promoted in Galatia by his opponents. It is within Paul's next statement that we see the crux of the problem in Galatia first addressed by Paul:

GALATIANS 2:15 "We who are Jews by nature, and not sinners of the Gentiles, 16 knowing that a man is not justified by the **works of the law** [ergon nomou] but by faith in Jesus Christ, even we have believed in Christ Jesus, that we might be justified by faith in Christ and not by the **works of the law** [ergon nomou]; for by the **works of the law** [ergon nomou] no flesh shall be justified. (*NKJV*)

Here we are introduced to the phrase "works of the law" for the first time in the letter to the Galatians. This phrase has been the foundation for much Christian doctrine and theological understanding. Most Christians believe that "works of the law" is a reference to observing the Law of Moses. They interpret Paul's words here to mean that obedience to the *Torah* is no longer required. In fact, some take Paul's statement to mean that obedience to the Law demonstrates a lack of faith.

However, this interpretation is unjustified based on Paul's prior comments to Peter. Peter was NOT following the Law of Moses when he separated himself from the Gentiles. Rather, he was adhering to traditions found in the Oral Law. Could it be that Paul's use of the phrase "works of the law" was intended to refer to something other than the Law of Moses?

Due to the discovery of the Dead Sea Scrolls in 1947, new light has been shed on the heresy that Paul was combating in Galatia. In the fourth cave excavated at Qumran, a manuscript named **Miqsat Ma'ase haTorah** (4QMMT) was found. It was only translated and released to the public in 1994.

In the November/December 1994 issue of **Biblical Archaeological Review**, scholar Martin Abegg commented on the importance of this document to understanding Paul's letter to the Galatians:

MMT . . . stands for *Miqsat Ma'ase Ha-Torah*, which Strugnell and Qimron translate "Some Precepts of the Torah." This translation unfortunately obscures MMT's relationship to Paul's letters.

In this case, *miqsat* does not mean simply "some." The same word is used in Genesis 47:2, where Joseph presents five of his brothers to Pharaoh. Here the word could be understood to mean the most important of the brothers or perhaps the choice or select. In other words, when the word is used in MMT, it does not refer just to some random laws; these laws are important to the writer. A similar understanding of the meaning of the word can be gleaned from its use in the Talmud. Thus we might translate the word more accurately as "some important" or "pertinent."

More significant for our purposes, however, are the other two words, *ma'ase ha-torah*. Strugnell and Qimron translate this phrase as "precepts of Torah," while Lawrence Schiffman offers "legal rulings of Torah." These translations are accurate enough, but they nonetheless cloud the Paul connection.

A few minutes with a concordance of the Septuagint, the Greek translation of the Hebrew Bible, leaves little doubt that the Greek equivalent of *ma'ase ha-torah* is likely *ergon nomou. Ergon nomou* is commonly translated in English versions of the New Testament as "works of the law." This well-known Pauline phrase is found in Romans 3:20,28 and in Galatians 2:16; 3:2,5,10.

. . . *Ma'ase ha-torah* is equivalent to what we know in English from Paul's letters as "works of the law." This Dead Sea Scroll and Paul use the very same phrase. The connection is emphasized by the fact that this phrase appears *nowhere* in rabbinic literature of the first and second centuries A.D.—*only* in Paul and in MMT. (pp. 52-53, "Paul, 'Works of the Law,' and MMT," *Biblical Archaeological Review*, November/December 1994)

This ancient document is of great importance in understanding the heresy that Paul was combating at Galatia. As we will see by another of Paul's statements later (Gal. 4:10), the evidence is overwhelming that his opponents there were adherents to some of the same doctrines that those in Qumran held.

Several books have addressed this particular Dead Sea Scroll since it was first published. In a more recent work, Abegg speaks further about the significance of 4QMMT (which he calls *A Sectarian Manifesto*):

In all of antiquity, only the *Manifesto* and Paul's Letters to the Galatians and Romans discuss the connection between works and righteousness. For that reason alone this writing is of immense interest and importance. But the *Manifesto* has additional significance. While the sectarian documents found in the caves at Qumran fairly bristle with legal discussions on a variety of issues, only this work, commonly known as 4QMMT (an acronym from the Hebrew words meaning "some of the works of the Law"), directly challenges the position of another religious group.

. . . The *Manifesto* presents a well-reasoned argument couched in a homily, complete with applications, illustrations, and exhortations. Following a thesis statement that identifies the central problem—the impure are being allowed to mix with the pure (the profane with the holy)—the author lists some two dozen examples to prove his point . . . The addressee (and secondarily, the reader) is then encouraged to follow the author: separate from those who practice such things. . . . (p. 358, *Dead Sea Scrolls: A New Translation*)

Abegg's translation of the 4QMMT author's concluding statements shows that the Qumran sectarians were advocating obedience to their particular interpretation of the *Tanakh*:

[Indeed,] we [have written] to you so that you might understand the book of Moses, the book[s of the Pr]ophets, and Davi[d] . . . (p. 363, *Dead Sea Scrolls: A New Translation*)

Here is Abegg's translation of the final exhortation found in 4QMMT:

Now, we have written to you some of the **works of the Law**, those which we determined would be beneficial for you and your people, because we have seen [that] you possess insight and knowledge of the Law. Understand all these things and beseech Him to set your counsel straight and so keep you away from evil thoughts and the counsel of Belial. Then you shall rejoice at the end time when you find the essence of our words to be true. And **it will be reckoned to you as righteousness**, in that you have done what is right and good before Him, to your own benefit and to that of Israel. (p. 364, *Dead Sea Scrolls: A New Translation*)

Abegg succinctly summarizes the author's intention for a reader of 4QMMT:

. . . The final exhortation presses home the author's true point: to be accounted righteous, one must obey the Law as interpreted in the *Manifesto*.

This final exhortation is of great importance for a fuller understanding of statements the apostle Paul makes about works and righteousness in his Letter to the Galatians. The author of the *Manifesto*, probably thinking of Psalm 106:30-31 (where the *works* of Phinehas were "reckoned to him as righteousness"), is engaged, as it were, in a rhetorical duel with the ideas of the apostle. Paul appeals to Genesis 15:6 to show that it was the *faith* of Abraham that was "reckoned to him as righteousness" (Gal. 3:6) and goes on to state categorically that "by the works of the law shall no flesh be justified" (Gal. 2:16). Probably the "false brethren" (Gal. 2:4) that Paul opposed held a doctrine on justification much like that of the present writing (i.e., 4QMMT). (p. 359, *Dead Sea Scrolls: A New Translation*)

In his essay "The Dead Sea Scrolls and the Historical Jesus," James H. Charlesworth speaks of the emphasis the Qumran Essenes placed on purity:

As we know from an unpublished letter ("Some of the Precepts of the Torah") . . . the Qumran group held to rules for purification that differed from other Jews (4QMMT). The Qumranic penal code, which included the death penalty, was closely aligned with the rules for purity. In terms of the concept of purity Jesus was categorically different from the Essenes. (p. 25, *Jesus And The Dead Sea Srolls*)

It was the issue of ritual purity as defined by the Oral Law that caused Peter to separate from Gentiles in Antioch. The relationship between the cause for Peter's hypocrisy and the "different gospel" being brought to Galatia by the "false brethren" is why Paul chose to use the story of Peter to launch his attack on his opponents there. Regarding the nature of the teachings found at Qumran, Charlesworth writes:

. . . The Essenes originated as a separate group because of their interpretation of legal issues (4QMMT). Many of the Dead Sea Scrolls are legalistic . . . (p. 32, *Jesus And The Dead Sea Srolls*)

The Essenes at Qumran were a subgroup of the majority of Essenes:

. . . The Essenes of Josephus cannot be simply equated with the Qumranites. The history of the Qumranites is long, covering three centuries, and there is considerable development at Qumran. Likewise the lifestyle of the "Qumran Essenes" would be more strict than those living, for example, in Jerusalem. There were at least two distinct types of Essenes in Palestine. (p. 42, *Jesus And The Dead Sea Scrolls*)

As these quotations show, the teaching brought to Galatia by the sectarians went far above and beyond the requirements of the written *Torah*.

GALATIANS 2:17 "If, while we seek to be justified in Christ, it becomes evident that we ourselves are sinners, does that mean that Christ promotes sin? Absolutely not! 18 If I rebuild what I destroyed, I prove that I am a **lawbreaker**. (*NIV*)

Now Paul, in an effort to head off any counter argument that he was opposed to obeying the **written Law of Moses**, goes on the offensive against lawlessness (I John 3:4). He states that justification through the sacrifice of the Messiah does not give us license to sin.

GALATIANS 2:19 For I through the Law died to the Law that I might live to God. 20 I have been crucified with Christ; it is no longer I who live, but Christ lives in me; and the life which I now live in the flesh I live by faith in the Son of God, who loved me and gave himself for me. (*NKJV*)

The penalty for sin is death, as Paul states in his epistle to the Romans (Rom. 6:23). Therefore, those who have broken **any** of God's laws are under this penalty (cf. Jam. 2:10). Because of this requirement of the Law, Paul had to die. But instead of physically dying, Paul was able to substitute the Messiah's sacrificial death for his own. However, in order not to become a lawbreaker again after having been cleansed of his sins, Paul had to subject his will to that of Messiah Yeshua. He had to become a living sacrifice, living his life in obedience to God instead of obeying his own fleshly lusts.

GALATIANS 2:21 I do not set aside the grace of God; for if **righteousness comes through the Law**, then Christ died in vain." (*NKJV*)

Here Paul finishes his opening remarks and establishes the premise for his attack on the teachings of the "false brethren" in Galatia that follows in chapter 3. Paul's position is that legalistic observance of the Law (whether according to the sectarians' "Works of the Law," the Oral Law of the Pharisees, etc.) **for the purpose of establishing one's own righteousness** is worthless in the sight of God.

In his letter to the Galatians, Paul contrasts the two ways for gaining righteousness: (1) Legalistic obedience to the Law *versus* (2) obedience to the Law due to faith in the Messiah. To understand Paul's comments about the Law in Galatians, we must realize his position about the PURPOSE of the Law. He speaks of this extensively in his letter to the Romans:

ROMANS 3:19 Now we know that **whatever the Law says it speaks to those who are under the Law** [hupo nomon], so that **every mouth** may be stopped, and **the whole world** may be held accountable to God. 20 For by **works of the law** [ergon nomou] no human being will be justified in His sight, since **through the Law comes knowledge of sin.** 21 But **now the righteousness of God has been manifested apart from the Law**, although the Law and the Prophets bear witness to it - 22 **the righteousness of God through faith in Jesus Christ for all who believe.** For there is no distinction: 23 for all have sinned and fall short of the glory of God, 24 and are justified by His grace as a gift, through the redemption that is in Christ Jesus, (**ESV**)

Taken in context, Paul's words here show his true understanding of the purpose of the Law. The Law was intended to show the conduct God expected from mankind. Any deviation from that specified conduct was sin. As the apostle John tells us explicitly in the New Testament, "sin is lawlessness" (I John 3:4).

The Law speaks to those who are "under the Law" (Gr. *hupo nomon*). Here this phrase refers to the judging function of the Law. Paul is speaking of those who, because they have sinned, are **under the PENALTY for breaking the Law** (Rom. 6:14-15; Gal. 3:23; 5:18). This penalty is DEATH (Rom. 6:23). Lest anyone think that only the Jews are subject to this judgment, Paul tells us that through the Law the **whole world** will be held accountable to God (Rom. 3:19).

ROMANS 3:28 For we maintain that a **man is justified by faith** apart from **works of the law** [ergon nomou]. (**NASU**)

By "works of the law" (legalistic observance of the Law to gain God's favor), no one will be justified in God's sight. The reason why this is so is because "all have sinned" (Rom. 3:23). However, God has provided a way for our justification other than through perfect observance of the Law. That way is through FAITH, by accepting the sacrifice of Messiah Yeshua (Rom. 3:20, 28).

ROMANS 3:31 Do we then **overthrow** [katargoumen] **the Law** BY THIS FAITH? **By no means** [me genoito]! On the contrary, **we uphold** [histomen] **the Law.** (**ESV**)

Finally, to ensure that the Romans did not misunderstand his stance on the Law, Paul summed up the relationship of faith to the Law. Paul first asks if our FAITH **overthrows** (Gr. *katargoumen* - "nullifies," "makes void," "destroys") the Law. Answering his own rhetorical question, Paul emphatically states "NO WAY!" using a strong negative Greek phrase (*me genoito*). Paul finishes by stating that instead of our faith nullifying the Law, it should motivate us to **uphold** (Gr. *histomen* - "establish," "make valid," "confirm") the Law. It's amazing that anyone could misconstrue the plain meaning of these words. But unfortunately, most of the Christian world has done just that.

Later in the book of Romans, Paul speaks about HOW the Jews who did not accept Yeshua as the Messiah had gotten off track:

ROMANS 9:30 What shall we say then? That Gentiles, who did not pursue righteousness, have attained to righteousness, even **the righteousness of faith**; 31 but Israel, pursuing **the law of righteousness**, has not attained to the **the law of righteousness**. 32 Why? Because they did not seek it by faith, but as it were, by the **works of the law** [ergon nomou]. For they stumbled at that stumbling stone. (**NKJV**)

Refusing to accept God's grace and the imputed righteousness provided by the sacrifice of His Son, the Jews had sought to establish their own righteousness through scrupulous keeping of the Law. In Romans 10, Paul continued his explanation of this Jewish error:

ROMANS 10:1 Brethren, my heart's desire and prayer to God for Israel is that they may be saved. 2 For I bear them witness that they have a zeal for God, but not according to knowledge. 3 For they being ignorant of **God's righteousness**, and **seeking to establish their own righteousness**, have not submitted to the **righteousness of God**. 4 For **Christ is the end of the Law** for righteousness **to everyone who believes**. (**NKJV**)

Too many read that the "Messiah is the end of the Law" without acknowledging the remainder of Paul's statement. Messiah was NOT the end of the Law; he was only the end of the Law **as a means of righteousness** for those who had FAITH in his atoning sacrifice.

Did this shift in the way righteousness was obtained mean that the Law was no longer valid? No, as Paul himself states elsewhere (Rom. 3:31; Gal. 3:21). Paul was simply showing that the MOTIVATION for keeping the Law changed when one through faith accepted the Messiah's sacrifice.

Paul speaks in his letter to the Philippians about the differences between the "righteousness of the Law" and the righteousness obtained through faith:

PHILIPPIANS 3:4 Though I also might have confidence in the flesh. If anyone else thinks he may have confidence in the flesh, I more so: 5 circumcised the eighth day, of the stock of Israel, of the tribe of Benjamin, a Hebrew of the Hebrews; concerning the Law, a Pharisee; 6 concerning zeal, persecuting the church; **concerning the righteousness which is in the Law, blameless**. 7 But what things were gain to me, these I have counted loss for Christ. 8 Yet indeed I also count all things loss for the excellence of the knowledge of Christ Jesus my Lord, for whom I have suffered the loss of all things, and count them as rubbish, that I may gain Christ 9 and be found in him, **not having my own righteousness, which is from the Law**, but **that which is through faith in Christ, the righteousness which is from God by faith**; (*NKJV*)

Paul shows here that, according to his legalistic observance of the Law before his conversion, he was considered righteous and blameless. However, this righteousness was based on Paul's **fleshly** ability to conform to the Law. The righteousness which is from God through faith in Yeshua is based on the power of the **Holy Spirit** to enable a person to be obedient. As we shall see later, Paul speaks of this allegorically in Galatians 4:22-31.

Armed with this view of Paul's understanding of the Law's purpose, let's now examine his specific comments about the Law in Galatians 3:

GALATIANS 3:1 O foolish Galatians! Who has bewitched you that you should not obey the truth, before whose eyes Jesus Christ was clearly portrayed among you as crucified? 2 This only I want to learn from you: Did you receive the Spirit by the **works of the law** [ergon nomou], or by the hearing of faith? (*NKJV*)

Now Paul begins to attack the premise underlying the sectarian teaching in earnest. He asks the Galatians if keeping the *Torah* perfectly (or in this case, according to the sectarians' "Works of the Law") was what had initially allowed them to receive God's Spirit, or whether it was hearing the gospel he had proclaimed and believing it in faith. Clearly, his implication is that they were first accounted righteous through faithful acceptance of Yeshua's sacrifice, not by legalistic observance of the Law.

GALATIANS 3:3 Are you so foolish? Having begun in the Spirit, are you now being made perfect by the flesh? 4 Have you suffered so many things in vain – if indeed it was in vain? 5 Therefore He who supplies the Spirit to you and works miracles among you, does He do it by the **works of the law** [ergon nomou], or by the hearing of faith? – (*NKJV*)

Here Paul reemphasizes his previous point: It was through faith that the Galatians had obtained the Spirit, not through perfect observance of the *Torah* such as that encouraged by the sectarians.

GALATIANS 3:6 Just as Abraham "believed God, and it was accounted to him for righteousness." 7 Therefore know that only those who are of faith are sons of Abraham. 8 And the Scripture, foreseeing that God would justify the Gentiles by faith, preached the gospel to Abraham beforehand, saying, "In you all the nations shall be blessed." 9 So then those who are of faith are blessed with believing Abraham. (*NKJV*)

Many think that Paul here (quoting in v. 6 from Genesis 15:6) is stating that all one has to do is believe in faith, and that faith somehow substitutes for keeping the commandments of God. But let's examine the example of Abraham more closely. The Bible clearly shows that **his faith led to obedience**, as Hebrews 11 (the "faith chapter") records:

HEBREWS 11:8 **By faith Abraham obeyed** when he was called to go out to the place which he would receive as an inheritance. And **he went out**, not knowing where he was going. (**NKJV**)

HEBREWS 11:17 **By faith Abraham**, when he was tested, **offered up Isaac**, and he who had received the promises offered up his only begotten son, (**NKJV**)

The author of Hebrews clearly shows that Abraham's faith was confirmed by his OBEDIENCE to God. Faith is **not** a substitute for obedience. True faith leads to obedience, because the one who obeys believes that God "is a **rewarder** of those who diligently seek him" (Heb. 11:6). This is affirmed in God's confirmation to Isaac of the promises made to Abraham:

GENESIS 26:2 Then the LORD appeared to him [Isaac] and said: "Do not go down to Egypt; live in the land of which I shall tell you. 3 Dwell in this land, and I will be with you and bless you; for to you and your descendants I give all these lands, and I will perform the oath which I swore to Abraham your father. 4 And I will make your descendants multiply as the stars of heaven; I will give to your descendants all these lands; and in your seed all the nations of the earth shall be blessed; 5 **because Abraham obeyed My voice and kept My charge, My commandments, My statutes, and My laws**." (**NKJV**)

Paul's statement in verse 6, when understood properly, perfectly compliments the words of James regarding Abraham's faith:

JAMES 2:21 **Was not Abraham our father justified by works when he offered Isaac his son on the altar?** 22 Do you see that faith was working together with his works, and **by works faith was made perfect?** 23 And the Scripture was fulfilled which says, "Abraham believed God, and it was accounted to him for righteousness." And he was called the friend of God. 24 You see then that **a man is justified by works, and not by faith only**. (**NKJV**)

These Scriptures do not contradict each other; Paul and James were making the same point regarding Abraham's faith. But Abraham's faithful obedience and the Galatian's legalistic obedience were two different things. The former showed faith in God's imputed righteousness, while the latter indicated reliance on one's own actions and abilities to become righteous.

GALATIANS 3:10 For as many as are of the **works of the law** [ergon nomou] are under the curse; for it is written, "Cursed is everyone who does not continue in all things which are written in the Book of the Law, to do them." (**NKJV**)

When the Galatians began to seek their own righteousness by observing the *Torah* according to the sectarians' "Works of the Law," they had ceased depending on the sacrifice of the Messiah to make them righteous. At that point, in order to remain righteous, they had to keep the Law perfectly. This is the reason for Paul's warning here. He wanted to make them understand that their choice had left them no room for error.

GALATIANS 3:11 But that **no one is justified by the Law in the sight of God** is evident, for "the just shall live by faith." 12 Yet **the Law is not of faith**, but "the man who does them shall live by them." (**NKJV**)

What did Paul mean by his declaration that "the Law is not of faith"? Many take this to mean that observance of the Law is not required after the death and resurrection of Messiah. Some go so far as to say that those who seek to do what God has commanded are under a curse. That certainly was not Paul's view. To him, observing the "works of the law" represented a legalistic mindset that sought to earn righteousness. Paul is not disparaging the Law itself, but rather the attitude represented by the sectarian teachings that had come to Galatia.

To better understand Paul's comments about the relationship of God's commandments to a believer, let's examine a scenario put forth by the Messiah himself:

LUKE 17:7 "And which of you, having a servant plowing or tending sheep, will say to him when he has come in from the field, 'Come at once and sit down to eat'? 8 But will he not rather say to him, 'Prepare something for my supper, and gird yourself and serve me till I have eaten and drunk, and afterward you will eat and drink'? 9 **Does he thank that servant because he did the things that were commanded him? I think not.** 10 So likewise you, **when you have done all those things which you are commanded**, say, 'We are unprofitable servants. **We have done what was our duty to do.**' " (**NKJV**)

According to Yeshua, doing what God has commanded is not optional; it is our duty as His people. Those who anticipate earning a reward for obeying God's commandments will be disappointed. As his example clearly shows, obedience to the Law is expected of believers; it is a prerequisite to being considered a true follower of Yeshua the Messiah (Matt. 7:21-23).

GALATIANS 3:13 Christ has redeemed us from **the curse of the Law**, having become a curse for us (for it is written, "Cursed is everyone who hangs on a tree"), 14 that the blessing of Abraham might come upon the

Gentiles in Christ Jesus, that we might receive the promise of the Spirit through faith. (*NKJV*)

Here Paul quotes from the *Torah* regarding the penalty for a capital crime under the Mosaic Law:

DEUTERONOMY 21:22 "If a man has committed a sin deserving of death, and he is put to death, and you hang him on a tree, 23 his body shall not remain overnight on the tree, but you shall surely bury him that day, so that you do not defile the land which the LORD your God is giving you as an inheritance; for **he who is hanged is accursed of God**. (*NKJV*)

Paul told the Romans that by committing sin, one earns the death penalty (Rom. 6:23). James stated that even if a person kept the majority of the Law and just stumbled in one point of it, he was guilty of breaking it all (Jam. 2:10). Therefore, rather than the commonly held assumption that "the curse of the Law" is having to obey the Law, we see that "the curse of the Law" is the DEATH PENALTY required for **not** obeying the Law.

By living a sinless life (II Cor. 5:21; Heb. 4:15), Yeshua was not under this death penalty. But even though he was not subject to the "curse of the Law," Yeshua gave his life to redeem those who **were** under that judgment. Faithful acceptance of his sacrifice will save us from the "curse of the Law," which is God's wrath against unrepentant sinners:

ROMANS 5:8 But God demonstrates His own love toward us, in that **while we were still sinners, Christ died for us**. 9 Much more then, having now been justified by his blood, **we shall be saved from wrath through him**. (*NKJV*)

To further make his point, Paul next addresses the covenant God made with Abraham:

GALATIANS 3:15 Brethren, I speak in the manner of men: Though it is only a man's covenant, yet if it is confirmed, no one annuls or adds to it. 16 Now to Abraham and his Seed were the promises made. He does not say, "And to seeds," as of many, but as of one, "And to your Seed," who is Christ. 17 And this I say, that the Law, which was four hundred and thirty years later, cannot annul the covenant that was confirmed before by God in Christ, that it should make the promise of no effect. 18 For if the inheritance is of the Law, it is no longer of promise; but God gave it to Abraham by promise. (*NKJV*)

Now Paul goes into the promises and blessings given to Abraham. God gave Abraham the promise of a multitude of descendants, but He also promised him one SPECIFIC descendant:

GENESIS 22:18 "In your **seed** [zar'akha] all the nations of the earth shall be blessed, **because you have obeyed My voice**." (**NKJV**)

The Hebrew word *zar'akha* (root word *zera*, "seed") is **singular** (as is the Greek word *spermati* used in the **Septuagint**). This verse is the source of Paul's reference to ONE seed, the Messiah. Although Abraham certainly has a multitude of physical descendants, he has even more "offspring" through the work being performed by the Messiah.

Paul's point here is that legalistic obedience to the Law, which came 430 years after God made the promises to Abraham, does not nullify God's covenant with Abraham. This covenant promises God's salvation to all mankind through the work of the Messiah. However, this salvation does not negate the importance of obedience. The promises were given to Abraham based on his **faithful** obedience. Abraham BELIEVED what God told him, and he DID what God said. This included obeying God's laws, statutes and commandments, as God told Isaac (Gen. 26:5).

But here is the most important point: Abraham believed FIRST, and then OBEYED. The sectarian approach was just the opposite of Abraham's actions. They required perfect obedience to the Law FIRST as a qualification for the promised inheritance. In their view, faith was not the primary reason for observing the Law; ensuring one's place as an inheritor of the promises of Abraham was.

GALATIANS 3:19 Why then the Law? It was added because of transgressions, until the Offspring would come to whom the promise had been made; and it was ordained through angels by a mediator. (**NRSV**)

To correctly understand this verse, we must remember Paul's position on the Law. It was not a tool to enable righteousness, but rather a way to know what God expects of us. Paul addresses this point more fully in verse 21.

The mediator mentioned in verse 19 is Moses, who stood between the people of Israel and Israel's *'elohim*, the preincarnate Messiah. Paul mentions this to set up his next point:

GALATIANS 3:20 Now a mediator does not mediate for one only, but God is one. (**NKJV**)

The covenant between *'elohim* and Abraham had no mediator; *'elohim* and Abraham spoke face to face. Here Paul is again emphasizing the preeminence of God's covenant with Abraham over the covenant made with Abraham's descendants at Mount Sinai.

GALATIANS 3:21 Is the Law then against the promises of God? Certainly not [me genoito]! For if there had been a law given which could have given **life**, truly **righteousness** would have been by the Law. (**NKJV**)

Paul, realizing that some might take his previous comments to be AGAINST the Law, now seeks to dispel any such notion in verse 21. He states without reservation that the Law is not, in any way, contrary to God's promises to Abraham. In the last part of the verse, Paul equates LIFE with RIGHTEOUSNESS (and by implication, DEATH with UNRIGHTEOUSNESS / SIN). He goes so far as to say that if it were possible for ANY law to give life, then the Law given through Moses would have been the one to do so. But it could not, because that was not the function of the Law.

Why could the Law not provide life?

GALATIANS 3:22 But **the Scripture has confined all under sin**, that the promise by faith in Jesus Christ might be given to those who believe. (**NKJV**)

The Law could not provide life because of the flawed nature of human beings, not because of some defect in the Law:

ROMANS 8:3 What the Law could not do **because of the weakness of human nature**, God did, sending His own Son in the same human nature as any sinner to be a sacrifice for sin, and condemning sin in that human nature. (**NJB**)

Going back to Paul's understanding of the PURPOSE of the Law discussed earlier, we see he recognized that it provided a guide for conduct and penalties for disobedience. But because of the sin nature of mankind, the Law was not a means for achieving righteousness. Paul tells us that **all** have broken the Law (cf. Rom. 3:9, 23). Therefore, all have incurred the resulting penalty, which is DEATH.

GALATIANS 3:23 Now before faith came, we were held captive **under the Law** [hupo nomon], imprisoned until the coming faith would be revealed. 24 So then, the Law was our **guardian** [paidagogos] until Christ came, in order that we might be justified by faith. 25 But now that faith has come, we are no longer under a **guardian** [paidagogon], (**ESV**)

Paul's point here is generally misunderstood because of a wrong view of the function of the *paidagogos* in ancient Greek society. This Greek word, translated "guardian" above, is translated "schoolmaster" and "tutor" in some versions. However, the key to comprehending Paul's point is to truly understand the responsibilities of the *paidagogos*. Here is what the *Greek-English Lexicon of the New Testament and Other Early Christian Literature* states about the function of a *paidagogos*:

. . . Orig[inally] 'boy-leader', the man, usu[ally] a slave (Plut., Mor. 4ab), whose duty it was to conduct a boy or youth (Plut., Mor. 439f) to and from school and to superintend his conduct gener[ally]; **he was not a 'teacher'** . . . When the young man became of age, the [*paidagogos*] was no longer needed . . .

As you can see from the definition above, Paul is NOT referring to the Law as a teacher. Instead, he is again speaking of the judgment function of the Law. The context indicates that the Law functioned as a **guardian** for those convicted of sin. Since all have sinned (Gal. 3:22), this was all of humanity.

When forgiveness came through faith in the atoning sacrifice of Yeshua, we were no longer subject to the guardianship of the Law; we were no longer under its penalty for disobedience. However, this does not mean that the Law's role as God's standard of right conduct has been voided.

GALATIANS 3:26 For **you are all sons of God through faith in Christ Jesus.** 27 For as many of you as were baptized into Christ have put on Christ. 28 There is neither Jew nor Greek, there is neither slave nor free, there is neither male nor female; for you are all one in Christ Jesus. 29 And **if you are Christ's, then you are Abraham's seed, and heirs according to the promise.** (*NKJV*)

This passage is often used to try and show that no physical or racial differences should exist within the body of Messiah. That was not Paul's point. He gives us three pairs: (1) Jew/Greek; (2) slave/free; and (3) male/female. Obviously differences still existed between all these groups in Paul's day. Instead, Paul was saying that each has equal access to **Yah**'s salvation. As children of God, each is an heir, along with Messiah, of the promises made to Abraham.

GALATIANS 4:1 My point is this: heirs, as long as they are minors, are no better than slaves, though they are the owners of all the property; 2 but they remain under guardians and trustees until the date set by the father. 3 So with us; while we were minors, we were enslaved to **the elemental spirits of the world** [ta stoicheia tou kosmou]. (*NRSV*)

Paul states his point using the analogy of human children. Even though we are children of God, until we come to spiritual maturity, we are no better than slaves. Just as the Galatians were under the judgment of the Law until they accepted the Messiah's sacrifice, Paul says that they were subject to "the elemental spirits of the world" (Gr. *ta stoicheia tou kosmou*). Regarding the meaning of this Greek phrase, *The New International Dictionary of New Testament Theology* states:

In the case of Gal. 4:3, 9 and Col. 2:8, 20 it is a disputed question whether or not the *stoicheia tou kosmou*, the "elements of the world", are angels, demons, gods . . . Most commentators hold this to be the case . . . (p. 452, vol. 2)

In his *Jewish New Testament Commentary*, David Stern agrees with this understanding of *ta stoicheia tou kosmou* in Galatians. He writes:

Elemental spirits of the universe . . . both Jews and Gentiles, **were slaves** to them. Gentiles served these demonic spirits as gods. Jews, though knowing the one true God, were sometimes led astray by demonic spirits . . ." (p. 556)

Paul's point here is the same thing that he stated in his letter to the Ephesians:

EPHESIANS 6:12 For our struggle is not with flesh and blood but with **the principalities**, with **the powers**, with **the world rulers of this present darkness**, with **the evil spirits in the heavens**. (*NAB*)

As Paul states a little further on in his letter to the Galatians (Gal. 4:8-9), it is these evil spiritual forces that lead a person from faithful obedience into legalistic observance of the Law.

GALATIANS 4:4 But when **the time had fully come** [to pleroma tou chronou], God sent his Son, born of a woman, born **under Law** [hupo nomon], 5 to redeem those **under Law** [hupo nomon], that we might receive the full rights of sons. (*NIV*)

When "the fullness of the time" (*to pleroma tou chronou*) had come, when it was the exact moment planned out before the foundation of the world (Rev. 13:8), Paul tells us that God sent His divine Son to this earth as a human being. This was done to provide a way for mankind to overcome the "curse of the Law" and become fellow heirs of God with Messiah (Rom. 8:17).

GALATIANS 4:6 And because you are sons, God has sent forth the Spirit of His Son into your hearts, crying out, "Abba, Father!" 7 Therefore you are no longer a slave but a son, and if a son, then an heir of God through Christ. (*NKJV*)

Through the Holy Spirit, God had provided the Galatians with the very mind of Messiah (Phi. 2:5). Having been released from the penalty for breaking the Law, they had become heirs of God instead of slaves to sin (Rom. 6:16).

GALATIANS 4:8 Formerly, when you did not know God, you were in bondage to **beings that by nature are no gods**; (*RSV*)

The "elemental spirits" Paul referred to earlier (Gal. 4:3) were the false gods the Galatians had ignorantly worshiped before their conversion. As Paul clearly explained in his first letter to the Corinthian church, idol worship is actually the worship of demons (I Cor. 10:19-20).

GALATIANS 4:9 Now, however, that you have come to know God, or rather to be known by God, how can you turn back again to the **weak and beggarly elemental spirits**? How can you want to be enslaved to them again? (*NRSV*)

The "weak and worthless elemental spirits" which had shackled the Galatians in sin prior to their conversion were evil spirits (i.e., fallen angels and de-mons"). Paul now equates the doctrines being taught by the sectarians with the pagan demon worship the Galatians had previously abandoned. The comparison between paganism and the (legalistic) observance of the Law must have shocked the Galatians, who undoubtedly thought that they were growing spiritually rather than regressing.

The next verse has been widely misunderstood. Yet in regard to identifying Paul's opponents, it is one of the most important verses in the letter to the Galatians:

GALATIANS 4:10 You observe **days** and **months** and **seasons** and **years**. (*NKJV*)

The long-standing position of traditional Christian scholars is that Paul is criticiz-ing the Galatians here for keeping the Sabbath and Holy Days given to Israel in the *Torah*. However, this position requires the assumption that Paul equates the observance of God's Holy Days with slavery to/worship of evil spirit beings.

This view ignores Paul's command to the Corinthians to observe the Feast of Un-leavened Bread (I Cor. 5:8), as well as his background and training as a *Torah*-observant Pharisee. In fact, it implies that Paul held the **Gnostic** position that the god of the Old Testament was an evil angelic being ("demiurge").

Clearly, the sectarians proselytizing at Galatia were trying to get the congregation to observe some type of Jewish "days and months and seasons and years." But were these the same "days and months and seasons and years" that normative Ju-daism kept?

If you remember from our earlier discussion, Paul's use of the phrase "Works of the Law" indicates that he was speaking specifically against beliefs held by the Qumran Essene sectarians, as defined in 4QMMT. According to Martin Abegg, another Qumran document (4Q327) was connected to 4QMMT:

4Q327 . . . plots the Sabbaths and festivals for one complete solar year . . . This is one of the few calendars that designates the extrabiblical Festival of Oil, which fell on the twenty-second day of the sixth month. The structure of the work makes it likely that two more extrabiblical festivals were originally listed as well: the Wine Festival and the Festival of Wood Offering. . . .

Some scholars believe that 4Q327 was not actually a separate and distinct work. They argue that instead it originally attached to the beginning of one copy of *A Sectarian Manifesto* (text 84). In favor of this suggestion is the handwriting: the same scribe wrote both 4Q327 and the copy of the *Mani-festo*. . . . (p. 319, *Dead Sea Scrolls: A New Translation*)

As shown by 4Q327, another core belief of the Qumran Essene group was their calendar. It was a solar calendar consisting of 364 days per year which included the Essene version of God's commanded Holy Days (Lev. 23), as well as extrabiblical observances. Here is a copy of this calendar:

A recent article in the **Biblical Archaeological Review** gives us some specific information about this calendar and how it differed from the calendar used by the majority of Jews:

Even the Essene calendar was different. The Temple authorities maintained a lunar calendar; the Essenes followed a solar calendar, which consisted of exactly 52 weeks per year, that is, 364 days. According to this calendar, festivals always fell on the same day of the week. Thus, Rosh Hashanah (the Feast of Trumpets), Passover and the first day of Sukkot (the Feast of Tabernacles) always occurred on a Wednesday. The Essenes considered the solar calendar used by the Hasmoneans in the Temple, tied as it was to a 354-day lunar calendar, to be adulterated with Babylonian elements. For example, the names of the months - Nisan, Shevet, Adar, Tishri - were Babylonian. **The difference in calendars created a terrible discrepancy in holiday observance, with the Temple authorities and the Essenes celebrating festivals on different days**. This naturally created a sharp rift between the two groups. (p. 64, "Jerusalem's Essene Gateway," **Biblical Archaeological Review**, May/June 1997)

The Essene calendar was a rival to the traditional Jewish calendar endorsed by the Pharisees. Paul, trained as a Pharisee (Acts 23:6; 26:5; Phi. 3:5), would have followed the traditional calendar sanctioned by the Temple authorities. Yeshua himself endorsed this calendar indirectly (Matt. 23:1-3).

The Essene calendar (and consequently, their new year) always began on a Wednesday because the sun, moon, and stars were created on this day (Gen. 1:14-19). The first of the month was called "A Day of Remembrance"; however, the Essene months generally did **not** start with a new moon. The Qumran sectarians, following the Essene calendar, had substituted different feast days and different months for the true calendar observed by the majority of Jews. Because of the seasonal drift caused by the structure of their calendar, the Essene seasons were also off. Finally, as another document from Qumran (4Q319, "Calendar of the Heavenly Signs") shows, the Essenes had a different system of sabbatical and Jubilee years.

It is easy to understand why Paul would have viewed this calendar and its different holy "days," "months" which did not start on the new moon, out-of-sync "seasons," and variant sabbatical "years" as demonically inspired. These "days and months and seasons and years" were just as much satanic counterfeits as the pagan observances the Galatians had kept before their conversion.

GALATIANS 4:11 I am afraid for you, lest I have labored for you in vain. 12 Brethren, I urge you to become like me, for I became like you. You have not injured me at all. 13 You know that because of physical infirmity I preached the gospel to you at the first. 14 And my trial which was in my flesh you did not despise or reject, but you received me as an angel of God, even as Christ Jesus. 15 What then was the blessing you enjoyed? For I bear you witness that, if possible, you would have plucked out your own eyes and given them to me. 16 Have I therefore become your enemy because I tell you the truth? (**NKJV**)

Here Paul shows his exasperation with the Galatians' acceptance of the Essene heresy. He recounts how he originally came to Galatia and how he was overwhelmingly accepted by them. Now, he asks, had he become their enemy by pointing out their errors to them?

GALATIANS 4:17 Those people are zealous to win you over, but for no good. What they want is to alienate you from us, so that you may be zealous for them. 18 It is fine to be zealous, provided the purpose is good, and to be so always and not just when I am with you. 19 My dear children, for whom I am again in the pains of childbirth until Christ is formed in you, 20 how I wish I could be with you now and change my tone, because I am perplexed about you! (**NIV**)

Paul continues his chiding of the Galatians. He tells the Galatian congregation that the sectarians desire was to win them for themselves and separate them from Paul and the truth he had brought.

GALATIANS 4:21 Tell me, you who want to be **under Law** [hupo nomon], do you not listen to the **Law**? (**NASU**)

Paul uses the term "Law" in two different ways in this verse. First, "under Law" refers to legalistic observance of the Law for the purpose of establishing one's own righteousness. As Paul stated earlier (Gal. 3:10), this attitude subjects a person to the "curse of the Law" (i.e., "death") if it is not kept perfectly.

The second usage of "Law" by Paul specifically refers to the book of Genesis. Here he introduces the allegorical story of Hagar/Ishmael and Sarah/Isaac:

GALATIANS 4:22 For it is written that Abraham had two sons: the one by a bondwoman, the other by a freewoman. 23 But he who was of the bondwoman was born according to the flesh, and he of the freewoman through promise, 24 which things are symbolic. For these are the two covenants: the one from Mount Sinai which gives birth to bondage, which is Hagar – 25 for this Hagar is Mount Sinai in Arabia, and corresponds to Jerusalem which now is, and is in bondage with her children – 26 but the

Jerusalem above is free, which is the mother of us all. (*NKJV*)

In this parable, Paul uses Hagar and her son Ishmael to symbolically represent the covenant made at Mount Sinai. Conversely, Sarah and her son Isaac represent the new covenant promised to Israel and Judah (Jer. 31:33; Heb. 8:10). This also must have stunned the Galatians, who surely thought that their zeal to observe some "Works of the Law" would ensure that they were counted as righteous, just like their father Abraham.

To fully understand Paul's point with this comparison, let's examine the difference between the two covenants:

EXODUS 24:12 The LORD said to Moses, "Come up to me on the mountain and stay here, and I will give you **the tablets of stone, with the law and commands I have written** for their instruction." (*NIV*)

JEREMIAH 31:33 "This is the covenant I will make with the house of Israel after that time," declares the LORD. "**I will put My Law in their minds and write it on their hearts**. I will be their God, and they will be My people." (*NIV*)

The Law implemented at the first covenant was written on stone, but the Law of the new covenant will be written on the hearts of the people. The prophet Ezekiel also highlights the contrast between the first covenant and that "new covenant" which would come:

EZEKIEL 36:26 "**I will give you a new heart and put a new spirit within you**; I will take the heart of stone out of your flesh and give you a heart of flesh. 27 I will put My Spirit within you and cause you to walk in My statutes, and you will keep My judgments and do them. 28 Then you shall dwell in the land that I gave to your fathers; you shall be My people, and I will be your God. (*NKJV*)

Most misunderstand why there is a need for a "new" covenant. The Law was NOT the problem! Remember, Paul earlier told the Galatians that if any law could have given life, the Law of Moses would have given it (Gal. 3:21). Yes, there was something wrong with the first covenant, but it wasn't the Law, as the author of Hebrews states:

HEBREWS 8:7 For if that first covenant had been faultless, then no place would have been sought for a second. 8 Because **finding fault with them**, He says: "Behold, the days are coming, says the LORD, when I will make a new covenant with the house of Israel and with the house of Judah – 9 not according to the covenant that I made with their fathers in the day when I took them by the hand to lead them out of the land of Egypt; because **they did not continue in My covenant**, and I disregarded them, says the LORD." (**NKJV**)

The problem with the covenant made at Mount Sinai was not the Law; it was the PEOPLE. They could not keep the covenant because human nature made them weak through their flesh:

ROMANS 8:3 For what **the Law** could not do in that it **was weak through the flesh**, God did by sending His own Son in the likeness of sinful flesh, on account of sin: He condemned sin in the flesh, (**NKJV**)

The Law governing the first covenant was written on tablets of stone and obedience depended upon the flesh. But due to human nature, the Israelites were weak; they couldn't keep the covenant. Under the promised new covenant, the Law is to be written on the hearts of the Israelites, and it is to be kept through the power of God's Spirit.

In Paul's story, Hagar and Ishmael represented the efforts of the flesh. God had promised Abram that he would have a physical son who would be his heir (Gen. 15:1-5). But although Abram believed God (Gen. 15:6), his wife Sarai decided to help in the fulfillment of the divine promise. Considering her barrenness and advancing age, Sarai convinced Abram to take her Egyptian maid, Hagar, as a secondary wife for the purpose of bearing him a child (Gen. 16:1-2).

Abram did have a son by Hagar (Gen. 16:15); he was named Ishmael ("God hears"). But Ishmael was NOT the son God had promised Abram. Ishmael was born by the will and efforts of the flesh, not by the power of God's Spirit.

GALATIANS 4:27 For it is written: "Rejoice, O barren, You who do not bear! Break forth and shout, you who are not in labor! For the desolate has many more children than she who has a husband." 28 Now we, brethren, as Isaac was, are children of promise. 29 But, as he who was born according to the flesh then persecuted him who was born according to the Spirit, even so it is now. 30 Nevertheless what does the Scripture say? "Cast out the bondwoman and her son, for the son of the bondwoman shall not be heir with the son of the freewoman." 31 So then, brethren, we are not children of the bondwoman but of the free. (**NKJV**)

Soon after the birth of Ishmael, God reiterated the promise to Abram ("exalted father") and changed his name to Abraham ("father of a multitude"), telling him that He would make him the father of many nations (Gen. 17:4-5). When Abraham was 100 years old, Sarah (then 90 years old) bore him the son of promise, Isaac, through divine intervention (Gen. 21:1-7). It was through this son that God intended to fulfill His promises to Abraham.

On the day Isaac was weaned, Abraham made a great feast for him (Gen. 21:8). Probably because of jealousy, Ishmael mocked Isaac and scoffed at him (Gen. 21:9). Sarah saw Ishmael making fun of her son and insisted that Abraham send him and his mother away (Gen. 21:10). Abraham didn't want to do this, but God told him to listen to Sarah, because it was Isaac that was the son of promise (Gen. 21:11-12).

Using the backdrop of Ishmael and Isaac, we are able to see Paul's point with this allegory. Paul is not disparaging the Law, because as we saw earlier, the Law is a part of both the first covenant and the new covenant. Rather, Paul is again contrasting those who seek to keep the Law through the efforts of the flesh (legalism) and those who seek to observe the Law by the Spirit (faith).

GALATIANS 5:1 Stand fast therefore in the liberty by which Christ has made us free, and do not be entangled again with a **yoke of bondage.** (*NKJV*)

In this chapter, Paul focuses on the freedom believers have in Messiah. But he begins by speaking of the opposite of freedom. The "yoke of bondage" referenced here by Paul is the enslavement to the "elemental spirits of the world" he had mentioned earlier (Gal. 4:3, 9).

In the context of the Galatian problem, this slavery was typified by LEGALISTIC observance of the Law as a means of establishing one's own righteousness. When viewed properly, the letter to the Galatians shows that Paul did NOT consider the Law itself a "yoke of bondage."

GALATIANS 5:2 Indeed I, Paul, say to you that **if you become circumcised, Christ will profit you nothing.** 3 And I testify again to every man who becomes circumcised that he is a debtor to keep the whole Law. (*NKJV*)

Once again, we see that the false brethren troubling the Galatians were seeking to have them circumcised. Circumcision itself was not the principal issue. The meaning being assigned to circumcision was what Paul opposed. This ritual was being promoted by the sectarians for the purpose of making the Galatians righteous.

Paul reiterates that once they began depending on their own fleshly ability to keep the Law, the Galatians would have to keep ALL the Law **perfectly** to be considered righteous. The sacrifice of Messiah would be of no further benefit to them because they had ceased depending on his blood to cleanse them of sin.

GALATIANS 5:4 You have become estranged from Christ, you who attempt to be **justified by Law**; you have fallen from grace. (*NKJV*)

Because "all have sinned and have fallen short of the glory of God" (Rom. 3:23), justification CANNOT come through the flesh. It only comes through God's grace, which leads us to repentance (Rom. 2:4) and faith in the sacrifice of the Messiah (Rom. 3:24-26).

However, the sectarians had nullified God's grace, which had provided a way for the Galatians to be justified through Yeshua's sacrifice. In its place, they had brought them a doctrine of legalism, teaching them that through the efforts of their flesh, they could achieve righteousness by the Law. Of course, Paul knew this effort was ultimately doomed to fail.

GALATIANS 5:5 For we through the Spirit **eagerly WAIT for the hope of righteousness by faith.** (*NKJV*)

Again, Paul highlights the true way to righteousness - faith in the sacrifice of Yeshua. Notice, Paul stated that believers were eagerly WAITING for the hope of righteousness by faith. Apparently, they had not YET attained that righteousness.

GALATIANS 5:6 For in Christ Jesus neither circumcision nor uncircumcision avails anything, but **faith working through love.** (*NKJV*)

Paul states that it is only "faith working through love" that brings this righteousness. As Paul told the Romans, physical circumcision ALONE does **not** make a person righteous:

ROMANS 2:25 **For circumcision indeed is of value if you obey the Law, but if you break the Law, your circumcision becomes uncircumcision.** 26 So, if a man who is uncircumcised keeps the precepts of the Law, will not his uncircumcision be regarded as circumcision? 27 Then he who is physically uncircumcised but keeps the Law will condemn you who have the written code and circumcision but break the Law. (*ESV*)

Paul told the Romans that when the physically circumcised break the Law, they become spiritually uncircumcised. Conversely, one who is physically uncircumcised will be considered spiritually circumcised if he obeys the Law. Whether physically circumcised or not, "faith working through love" inspires one to be obedient to God, as the apostle John shows:

I JOHN 5:3 **This is love for God: to obey His commands.** And His commands are not burdensome, (*NIV*)

"Faith working through love" does not nullify the Law. Instead, it motivates one to obedience in order to fulfill the two greatest commandments:

MATTHEW 22:36 "Teacher, which is the great commandment in the Law?" 37 Jesus said to him, " 'You shall love the LORD your God with all your heart, with all your soul, and with all your mind.' 38 This is the first and great commandment. 39 And the second is like it: 'You shall love your neighbor as yourself.' 40 **On these two commandments hang all the Law and the Prophets.**" (*NKJV*)

Here, Yeshua breaks the 10 Commandments given at Mount Sinai down into two groups: (1) those that show us how to love God (Exo. 20:1-11), and (2) those that show us how to love our neighbor as ourself (Exo. 20:12-17). According to Ye-shua, these two principles form the basis for everything written in the Old Testament.

GALATIANS 5:7 You were running well; who hindered you from obeying the truth? 8 This persuasion did not come from Him who calls you. 9 A little leaven leavens the whole lump of dough. 10 I have confidence in you in the Lord that you will adopt no other view; but the one who is disturbing you will bear his judgment, whoever he is. 11 But I, brethren, if I still preach circumcision, why am I still persecuted? Then the stumbling block of the cross has been abolished. 12 I wish that those who are troubling you would even mutilate themselves. (**NASU**)

Here, Paul wonders who it was that had come to Galatia and gotten them off course. He states that these sectarians certainly were not from God. Paul compares them with yeast, which, even in minute amounts, will eventually work its way throughout an entire lump of dough and leaven it. He allows his exasperation with the Galatians to show through again, stating that he wished those teaching righteousness by circumcision would go the whole way and emasculate themselves.

Paul's statement in verse 11 shows that he no longer believed or taught that righteousness comes by circumcision (in contrast to the sectarians). He now taught that righteousness came through the sacrifice of Yeshua the Messiah on the cross. This teaching was a stumbling block to most Jews and foolishness to most Greeks (I Cor. 1:23).

GALATIANS 5:13 For you, brethren, have been called to liberty; only do not use liberty as an opportunity for the flesh, but through love serve one another. 14 For **all the Law is fulfilled in one word**, even in this: "You shall **love** your neighbor as yourself." (**NKJV**)

The Galatians had been called to be free through Messiah. But this liberty was a freedom from their slavery to sin (John 8:34-36). In Romans, Paul states that those freed from sin must become God's slaves (Rom. 6:22). Love is the summation of God's Law, because God is love (I John 4:8).

In a passage that deals with the same topic, James the brother of Yeshua speaks of the "Law of liberty":

JAMES 2:8 If you really fulfill the Royal Law according to the Scripture, **"You shall love your neighbor as yourself,"** you do well; 9 but if you show partiality, you commit sin, and are convicted by the Law as transgressors. 10 For whoever shall keep the whole Law, and yet stumble in one point, he is guilty of all. 11 For He who said, "Do not commit adultery," also said, "Do not murder." Now if you do not commit adultery, but you do murder, you have become a transgressor of the Law. 12 So speak and so do as those who will be judged by the Law of liberty. (**NKJV**)

James references the "Royal Law according to the Scripture" and then cites two commands from that Law: "Do not commit adultery" (Exo. 20:14) and "Do not murder" (Exo. 20:13). Clearly, the Law he is referring to is that which was given to Moses and the Israelites on Mount Sinai. James states that it is this "Royal Law" from Scripture that sums up the command to "love your neighbor as yourself" (Lev. 19:18). Although speaking to believers, James stated that they should refrain from transgression of this Law because they would be **judged** by it if they broke it.

In his letter to the Romans, Paul also defines love of one's neighbor:

ROMANS 13:8 Owe no one anything except to love one another, for **he who loves another has fulfilled the Law**. 9 For the commandments, "You shall not commit adultery," "You shall not murder," "You shall not steal," "You shall not bear false witness," "You shall not covet," and if there is any other commandment, are all summed up in this saying, namely, "You shall love your neighbor as yourself." 10 **Love does no harm to a neighbor; therefore love is the fulfillment of the Law**. (**NKJV**)

Is the "love" spoken of here by Paul simply an emotional feeling? No. This scriptural love begins with concrete actions such as NOT committing adultery with your neighbor's wife (Exo. 20:14), NOT murdering him (Exo. 20:13), NOT stealing from him (Exo. 20:15), NOT bearing false witness against him (Exo. 20:16), and NOT coveting his possessions (Exo. 20:17). Paul also includes the other commandments from the Law dealing with human relationships in his definition of love of neighbor. Far from doing away with these commandments, Paul told the Romans that obedience to them was "love."

In the words of Paul and James, we are not seeing some new doctrine or teaching. The Messiah himself defined obedience to the Law as "love of neighbor":

MATTHEW 19:16 Now behold, one came and said to him, "Good Teacher, what good thing shall I do that I may have eternal life?" 17 So he said to him, "Why do you call me good? No one is good but One, that is, God. But **if you want to enter into life, keep the commandments**." 18 He said to him, "Which ones?" Jesus said, " 'You shall not murder,' 'You shall not commit adultery,' 'You shall not steal,' 'You shall not bear false witness,' 19 'Honor your father and your mother,' and, 'You shall love your neighbor as yourself.' " (**NKJV**)

Yeshua told the ruler who came to him that these commandments showed love to his neighbor. But he went even further, stating that obedience to these commandments was necessary for eternal life.

The Law shows us how God expects us to love Him (Exo. 20:1-11; cf. Matt. 22:37-38; Mark 12:28-30), and also how we are to love our neighbor as ourself (Exo. 20:12-17; cf. Matt. 22:39-40; Mark 12:31).

However, the apostle John tells us that obedience to the two great commandments does not progress as one would normally expect. It must begin with the second, not the first:

I JOHN 4:20 If someone says, "I love God," and hates his brother, he is a liar; for **he who does not love his brother whom he has seen, how can he love God whom he has not seen?** 21 And this commandment we have from Him: that **he who loves God must love his brother also.** (**NKJV**)

It's ironic that we cannot fulfill the greatest commandment (love of God) until we are first able to keep the second commandment (love of neighbor).

GALATIANS 5:15 But if you bite and devour one another, beware lest you be consumed by one another! (**NKJV**)

Apparently, the legalistic teaching of the sectarians had caused friction in the Galatian congregation. Paul contrasts this attitude with love, which is the true motivation for keeping the Law.

GALATIANS 5:16 But I say, walk by the Spirit, and you will not gratify the desires of the flesh. 17 For the desires of the flesh are against the Spirit, and the desires of the Spirit are against the flesh, for these are opposed to each other, to keep you from doing the things you want to do. 18 But if you are led by the Spirit, you are not **under the Law** [hupo nomon]. (**ESV**)

Why is one led by the Spirit not under the Law? Because those who walk by the Spirit do NOT live to satisfy the desires of the flesh, but are slaves to God. Therefore, they will not be subject to the judgment of the Law. Paul speaks of this extensively in Romans 8:

ROMANS 8:5 For those who live according to the flesh set their minds on the things of the flesh, but those who live according to the Spirit, the things of the Spirit. 6 For **to be carnally minded is death**, but to be spiritually minded is life and peace. 7 Because **the carnal mind is enmity against God; for it is not subject to the Law of God, nor indeed can be**. 8 So then, those who are in the flesh cannot please God. 9 But you are not in the flesh but in the Spirit, if indeed the Spirit of God dwells in you. Now if anyone does not have the Spirit of Christ, he is not His. (**NKJV**)

The Spirit of God is the key to being able to keep the Law in an attitude of love. The flesh seeks its own way, which leads to death. But the Holy Spirit helps us to rise above our flawed human nature and live our lives in obedience to

God.

Paul next defines the works of the flesh in his epistle to the Galatians:

GALATIANS 5:19 Now the works of the flesh are evident, which are: adultery, fornication, uncleanness, lewdness, 20 idolatry, sorcery, hatred, contentions, jealousies, outbursts of wrath, selfish ambitions, dissensions, heresies, 21 envy, murders, drunkenness, revelries, and the like; of which I tell you beforehand, just as I also told you in time past, that those who practice such things will not inherit the kingdom of God. (*NKJV*)

This is not a detailed, comprehensive list of sin. Instead, Paul provides a broad synopsis of the weaknesses of our carnal nature and the areas where men fall short of God's perfect standard of love.

GALATIANS 5:22 But the fruit of the Spirit is love, joy, peace, longsuffering, kindness, goodness, faithfulness, 23 gentleness, self-control. Against such there is no law. 24 And those who are Christ's have crucified the flesh with its passions and desires. (*NKJV*)

After listing the bad fruit produced by man's imperfect carnal nature, Paul lists the good fruit produced by God's Spirit dwelling in a believer. There are no commands in the Law against these attitudes and actions, and those who are truly following the Messiah will have quit practicing the "works of the flesh" listed in verses 19-21.

GALATIANS 5:25 If we live in the Spirit, let us also walk in the Spirit. 26 Let us not become conceited, provoking one another, envying one another. (*NKJV*)

Now Paul finishes this line of thought with an exhortation to the Galatian believers to allow God's Spirit to enable them to exhibit the "fruits of the Spirit." Apparently, the fruit produced by the sectarian doctrine was noticably bad. It seems to have brought out conceit, anger, and envy among the congregation.

GALATIANS 6:1 Brothers, if someone is caught in a sin, you who are spiritual should restore him gently. But watch yourself, or you also may be tempted. 2 Carry each other's burdens, and in this way you will fulfill the **law of Christ**. (*NIV*)

Paul here asks that, instead of a legalistic approach to Law-keeping, the Galatians practice forgiving and helping one found to be engaged in sin. However, he also warns them not to be enticed into the sinner's error themselves.

Many believe Paul teaches that the Law of God given to Moses at Mount Sinai has been abolished and replaced with the "law of Christ" for new covenant believers. We've already seen that Messiah upheld the 10 Commandments and summarized them as the two great commandments.

Yeshua does speak of "my commandments" (John 14:15, 21; 15:10) and "my words" (John 12:47-48; 14:24; 15:7). But were these commandments or words from Yeshua NEW? Let's look to see if the Messiah's own statements support the theory that he instituted a new law:

JOHN 12:44 Then Jesus cried out and said, "He who believes in me, believes not in me but in Him who sent me. 45 And he who sees me sees Him who sent me. 46 I have come as a light into the world, that whoever believes in me should not abide in darkness. 47 And if anyone hears My words and does not believe, I do not judge him; for I did not come to judge the world but to save the world. 48 He who rejects me, and does not receive my words, has that which judges him – the word that I have spoken will judge him in the last day. 49 For **I have not spoken on my own authority; but the Father who sent me gave me a command, what I should say and what I should speak**. 50 And I know that His command is everlasting life. Therefore, whatever I speak, just as the Father has told me, so I speak." (**NKJV**)

JOHN 14:23 Jesus answered and said to him, "**If anyone loves me, he will keep my word**; and my Father will love him, and we will come to him and make our home with him. 24 He who does not love me does not keep my words; and **the word which you hear is not mine but the Father's who sent me**." (**NKJV**)

When taken at face value, Yeshua's words make it quite clear that he did not come to abolish the Law and replace it with some new legal code. In fact, he explicitly states that was NOT his goal in the Sermon on the Mount:

MATTHEW 5:17 "**Do not think that I came to abolish the Law** or the Prophets; I did not come to abolish but to fulfill. 18 For truly I say to you, until heaven and earth pass away, not the smallest letter or stroke shall pass from the Law until all is accomplished. 19 Whoever then annuls one of the least of these commandments, and teaches others to do the same, shall be called least in the kingdom of heaven; but whoever keeps and teaches them, he shall be called great in the kingdom of heaven. (**NASU**)

The Law of Christ is not a new law instituted to replace the Law given to Israel at Mount Sinai. It is the same Law, expanded from a purely physical perspective to the spiritual level (i.e., Matt. 5:21-30).

GALATIANS 6:3 For if anyone thinks himself to be something, when he is nothing, he deceives himself. 4 But let each one examine his own work, and then he will have rejoicing in himself alone, and not in another. 5 For each one shall bear his own load. (**NKJV**)

Here, Paul suggests that each of the Galatians examine "his own work" to ensure that they remain in the will of God. Paul emphasizes each person's personal responsibility and, consequently, each one's liability.

GALATIANS 6:6 Let him who is taught the word share in all good things with him who teaches. 7 Do not be deceived, God is not mocked; for whatever a man sows, that he will also reap. 8 For he who sows to his flesh will of the flesh reap corruption, but he who sows to the Spirit will of the Spirit reap everlasting life. 9 And let us not grow weary while doing good, for in due season we shall reap if we do not lose heart. 10 Therefore, as we have opportunity, let us do good to all, especially to those who are of the household of faith. (*NKJV*)

In this passage, Paul gives the Galatian congregation an exhortation to do good and to physically provide for those who teach them the truth. But he also gives them a warning to sow according to the Spirit, and not according to the flesh.

GALATIANS 6:11 See with what large letters I have written to you with my own hand! 12 As many as desire to make a good showing in the flesh, these would compel you to be circumcised, only that they may not suffer persecution for the cross of Christ. 13 For **not even those who are circumcised keep the Law**, but they desire to have you circumcised that they may boast in your flesh. (*NKJV*)

Paul, who generally seems to have dictated his letters by the hand of another, personally wrote the end of his letter to the Galatians in his own handwriting. Here Paul claims that the sectarians compelling the Galatians to be circumcised were doing so to avoid persecution and to tout their accomplishment. Apparently, the rest of the Essenes would not have accepted the Galatians as sons of Abraham until they were physically circumcised. In a "no nonsense" fashion, Paul states that even those sectarians who were pushing for legalistic observance of the Law by having them circumcised didn't keep the Law perfectly (Rom. 3:23; Gal. 3:22).

GALATIANS 6:14 But God forbid that I should boast except in the cross of our Lord Jesus Christ, by whom the world has been crucified to me, and I to the world. 15 For in Christ Jesus neither circumcision nor uncircumcision avails anything, but a new creation. 16 And as many as walk according to this rule, peace and mercy be upon them, and upon the Israel of God. 17 From now on let no one trouble me, for I bear in my body the marks of the Lord Jesus. 18 Brethren, the grace of our Lord Jesus Christ be with your spirit. Amen. (*NKJV*)

Paul places his blessing on those who are a new creation through the Messiah. This includes the Jews as well as the Gentiles grafted into "the Israel of God" (Rom. 11:17-24). He concludes his letter with a reminder of what he had suffered to preach the good news of Yeshua the Messiah.

Conclusion

Paul's letter to the Galatians has long been considered to show that the Law of Moses was invalidated and abolished by the Messiah. However, a reevaluation of that premise in light of new information found in the Dead Sea Scrolls indicates that the traditional Christian understanding of Paul's message is incorrect. Instead, we now see that Paul was combating a form of legalistic *Torah* observance in Galatia that focused on keeping the Law by the strength of the flesh rather than by the power of God's Holy Spirit. Paul's letter sought to put the Galatians back on the right path in the face of an extensive 1st-century sectarian heresy.

Bryan T. Huie
July 16, 2004

Revised: July 18, 2010

Heaven:
Our Eternal Home?

Amazingly, the Bible provides very little information regarding heaven. So where do our current beliefs come from? How do they align with the reward promised to believers in the Scriptures?

One of the central doctrines of Christianity is the teaching that believers will spend eternity in heaven. Numerous hymns have been written about those heavenly "streets of gold" that we will walk on in the afterlife. Along with Sunday observance and the Trinitarian concept of the Godhead, the doctrine of going to heaven is one of the foundational beliefs of traditional Christianity.

However, there is no such doctrine taught in the Old Testament. This teaching is based exclusively on New Testament passages. The Synpotic Gospels state that our **treasure** will be **in** heaven:

MATTHEW 6:19 "Do not lay up for yourselves treasures on earth, where moth and rust destroy and where thieves break in and steal; 20 but **lay up for yourselves treasures in heaven**, where neither moth nor rust destroys and where thieves do not break in and steal. 21 For where your treasure is, there your heart will be also." (*NKJV*)

MATTHEW 19:21 Jesus said to him, "If you want to be perfect, go, sell what you have and give to the poor, and **you will have treasure in heaven**; and come, follow Me." (*NKJV*)

MARK 10:21 Then Jesus, looking at him, loved him, and said to him, "One thing you lack: Go your way, sell whatever you have and give to the poor, and **you will have treasure in heaven**; and come, take up the cross, and follow Me." (*NKJV*)

LUKE 18:22 So when Jesus heard these things, He said to him, "You still lack one thing. Sell all that you have and distribute to the poor, and **you will have treasure in heaven**; and come, follow Me." (*NKJV*)

Other passages speak of our **reward** that is **in** heaven:

MATTHEW 5:11 Blessed are you when they revile and persecute you, and say all kinds of evil against you falsely for My sake. 12 Rejoice and be exceedingly glad, for **great is your reward in heaven,** for so they persecuted the prophets who were before you." (*NKJV*)

LUKE 6:20 Looking at his disciples, he said: "Blessed are you who are poor, for **yours is the kingdom of God**. 21 Blessed are you who hunger now, for you will be satisfied. Blessed are you who weep now, for you will laugh. 22 Blessed are you when men hate you, when they exclude you and insult you and reject your name as evil, because of the Son of Man. 23 Rejoice in that day and leap for joy, because **great is your reward in heaven**. For that is how their fathers treated the prophets. (*NIV*)

The disciples were told that their **names were recorded in heaven**:

LUKE 10:19 "Behold, I give you the authority to trample on serpents and scorpions, and over all the power of the enemy, and nothing shall by any means hurt you. 20 Nevertheless do not rejoice in this, that the spirits are subject to you, but rather rejoice because **your names are written in heaven**." (**NKJV**)

HEBREWS 12:22 But you have come to Mount Zion and to the city of the living God, the heavenly Jerusalem, to an innumerable company of angels, 23 to **the general assembly and church of the firstborn who are registered in heaven**, to God the Judge of all, to the spirits of just men made perfect, (**NKJV**)

The apostle Paul stated that believers were **citizens of heaven**:

PHILIPPIANS 3:20 For **our citizenship is in heaven**, from which we also eagerly wait for the Savior, the Lord Jesus Christ, 21 who will transform our lowly body that it may be conformed to His glorious body, according to the working by which He is able even to subdue all things to Himself. (**NKJV**)

Paul also, in agreement with the Synoptic Gospels, wrote that believers have a "**hope laid up in heaven**," an "**enduring possession**" reserved as a **treasure** for them **in** heaven:

COLOSSIANS 1:3 We give thanks to the God and Father of our Lord Jesus Christ, praying always for you, 4 since we heard of your faith in Christ Jesus and of your love for all the saints; 5 because of **the hope which is laid up for you in heaven**, of which you heard before in the word of the truth of the gospel, 6 which has come to you, as it has also in all the world, and is bringing forth fruit, as it is also among you since the day you heard and knew the grace of God in truth; (**NKJV**)

HEBREWS 10:32 But recall the former days in which, after you were illuminated, you endured a great struggle with sufferings: 33 partly while you were made a spectacle both by reproaches and tribulations, and partly while you became companions of those who were so treated; 34 for you had compassion on me in my chains, and joyfully accepted the plundering of your goods, knowing that **you have a better and an enduring possession for yourselves in heaven**. (**NKJV**)

I TIMOTHY 6:17 Instruct those who are rich in this present world not to be conceited or to fix their hope on the uncertainty of riches, but on God, who richly supplies us with all things to enjoy. 18 Instruct them to do good, to be rich in good works, to be generous and ready to share, 19 storing up for themselves **the treasure of a good foundation for**

the future, so that they may take hold of **that which is life indeed**. (**NASU**)

The apostle Peter, in agreement with the author of Hebrews, shows that believers have an "**inheritance incorruptible**" reserved for them **in** heaven:

I PETER 1:3 Blessed be the God and Father of our Lord Jesus Christ, who according to His abundant mercy has begotten us again to a living hope through the resurrection of Jesus Christ from the dead, 4 to **an inheritance incorruptible and undefiled and that does not fade away, reserved in heaven for you,** 5 who are kept by the power of God through faith for salvation ready to be revealed in the last time. (**NKJV**)

A close examination of these Scriptures shows that the focus the New Testament is primarily on the REWARD of believers, which is the TREASURE that they have reserved for them **in** heaven. In II Corinthians, Paul speaks specifically of the nature of this reward:

II CORINTHIANS 5:1 For we know that if our earthly house, this tent, is destroyed, **we have a building from God, a house not made with hands, eternal in the heavens**. 2 For in this we groan, earnestly desiring to be clothed with **our habitation which is from heaven**, 3 if indeed, having been clothed, we shall not be found naked. 4 For we who are in this tent groan, being burdened, not because we want to be unclothed, but further clothed, that mortality may be swallowed up by life. (**NKJV**)

In this passage, Paul speaks figuratively of life in this fleshly body ("our earthly house"). He tells the Corinthians they have a "building from God" in the heavens that awaits them after their fleshly body dies. He speaks longingly of being clothed with his spiritual body, that "habitation which is from heaven." He states that those believers in the flesh groan in travail, waiting to put on their incorruptible spirit body at the resurrection. It is this immortal spirit body that is the **treasure** or **reward** awaiting believers in heaven.

In an earlier letter, Paul told the Corinthians that "**flesh and blood** CANNOT inherit the kingdom of God" (I Cor. 15:50):

I CORINTHIANS 15:50 Now this I say, brethren, that **flesh and blood cannot inherit the kingdom of God**; nor does corruption inherit incorruption. 51 Behold, I tell you a mystery: We shall not all sleep, but **we shall all be changed** – 52 in a moment, in the twinkling of an eye, at the last trumpet. For the trumpet will sound, and **the dead will be raised incorruptible, and we shall be changed.** 53 For **this corruptible must put on incorruption**, and **this mortal must put on**

immortality. 54 So when this corruptible has put on incorruption, and this mortal has put on immortality, then shall be brought to pass the saying that is written: "Death is swallowed up in victory." (*NKJV*)

Paul's teaching is clear to those who can see past the traditions of men. The reward reserved **in** heaven for believers is not a residence **in** heaven itself, but rather an **incorruptible spiritual body** that believers will have after the resurrection.

The Bible **never** explicitly states that believers will be taken to heaven to spend eternity there. In fact, Paul specifically tells us **where** believers will spend eternity in his first letter to the Thessalonians:

I THESSALONIANS 4:13 But I do not want you to be ignorant, brethren, concerning those who have fallen asleep, lest you sorrow as others who have no hope. 14 For if we believe that Jesus died and rose again, even so God will bring with Him those who sleep in Jesus. 15 For this we say to you by the word of the Lord, that we who are alive and remain until the coming of the Lord will by no means precede those who are asleep. 16 For **the Lord Himself will descend from heaven** with a shout, with the voice of an archangel, and with the trumpet of God. And **the dead in Christ will rise** first. 17 Then we who are alive and remain shall be caught up together with them in the clouds to meet the Lord in the air. And **thus we shall always be with the Lord**. (*NKJV*)

Paul clearly states that after the return of Messiah, when the dead are resurrected, those who are "in Christ" will "**always be with the Lord**." Yeshua himself promised to come back and take believers to where he would be:

JOHN 14:1 "Let not your hearts be troubled. Believe in God; believe also in me. 2 **In my Father's house are many rooms**. If it were not so, would I have told you that I go to prepare a place for you? 3 And if I go and prepare a place for you, **I will come again and will take you to myself, that where I am you may be also**. (*ESV*)

Many people think that this Scripture from the Gospel of John is speaking of a heavenly dwelling place. Here Yeshua speaks of his "Father's house." This reference is generally understood to refer to heaven, and many have assumed that Yeshua is promising here to bring his disciples to heaven, that they may dwell there forever.

However, there is another spiritual house of God spoken of in the New Testament: the body of believers. Yeshua knew that God was about to replace the physical temple in Jerusalem with a spiritual temple composed of the assembly of believers. Within this new house of God would be many dwelling places. The physical bodies of believers would become individual rooms or abodes within the Father's spiritual temple. For more information on this concept, refer to my article "Pentecost and the Coming of the Holy Spirit."

One reason that Christians have embraced heaven as their eternal dwelling place is because they do not study the Old Testament enough to know what it teaches about the coming kingdom of God (called the "kingdom of heaven" by Matthew). If believers are to **"always be with the Lord"** after his return, where does the Bible show that the Messiah will be then? We are now going to spend the remainder of this study answering that question.

Let's start with the Messiah's own words, found in the Sermon on the Mount:

MATTHEW 5:2 Then He opened His mouth and taught them, saying: 3 **"Blessed are the poor in spirit, for theirs is the kingdom of heaven**. 4 Blessed are those who mourn, for they shall be comforted. 5 **Blessed are the meek, for they shall inherit the earth**. 6 Blessed are those who hunger and thirst for righteousness, for they shall be filled. 7 Blessed are the merciful, for they shall obtain mercy. 8 Blessed are the pure in heart, for they shall see God. 9 Blessed are the peacemakers, for they shall be called sons of God. 10 **Blessed are those who are persecuted for righteousness' sake, for theirs is the kingdom of heaven."** (*NKJV*)

Many people interpret the phrase "kingdom of heaven" to mean a kingdom that is IN heaven. But that's not what Matthew (the only Gospel author to use "kingdom of heaven") intended to convey by his use of the phrase.

Matthew's Gospel was written to the Jews. Because of their desire not to take the name of God in vain (Exo. 20:7), the Jews often used terms that were understood to be synonymous with God (i.e., "the Power"-Matt. 26:64; Mark 14:62; "heaven"-Luke 15:18) instead of His name. Therefore, in Matthew's writings, the "kingdom of God" is most often referred to as the "kingdom of heaven."

Yeshua stated that the "poor in spirit" (Matt. 5:3) and those "persecuted for righteousness' sake" (Matt. 5:10) are going to receive the "kingdom of heaven." However, the meek are going to "inherit the earth" (Matt. 5:5). Will there be two DIFFERENT rewards for these groups of people? Or are these two actually the same?

A little later in the Sermon on the Mount, Yeshua taught his disciples how to pray. The beginning of this prayer, which is familiar to almost every believer, contains insight into our eternal destiny:

MATTHEW 6:9 "In this manner, therefore, pray: our Father in heaven, hallowed be Your name. 10 **Your kingdom come.** Your will be done **on earth** as it is in heaven. (*NKJV*)

The kingdom of God (or "the kingdom of heaven") will be here on the earth. Yeshua taught his disciples to pray for the coming of this kingdom, so that God's will might be done here on the earth, just as it is now done in heaven.

To conclusively show that the "kingdom of heaven" and the Messiah will be on the earth, we must examine the Old Testament prophecies. These will clearly tell us where believers will enjoy their "heavenly" reward. Let's begin with a prophecy from the book of Zechariah:

ZECHARIAH 8:2 "Thus says the LORD of hosts: 'I am zealous for Zion with great zeal; with great fervor I am zealous for her.' 3 **Thus says the LORD: 'I will return to Zion, and dwell in the midst of Jerusalem**. Jerusalem shall be called the City of Truth, the Mountain of the LORD of hosts, the Holy Mountain.' 4 Thus says the LORD of hosts: 'Old men and old women shall again sit in the streets of Jerusalem, each one with his staff in his hand because of great age. 5 The streets of the city shall be full of boys and girls playing in its streets.' 6 Thus says the LORD of hosts: 'If it is marvelous in the eyes of the remnant of this people in these days, will it also be marvelous in My eyes?' says the LORD of hosts. 7 Thus says the LORD of hosts: 'Behold, I will save My people from the land of the east and from the land of the west; 8 I will bring them back, and they shall dwell in the midst of Jerusalem. They shall be My people and I will be their God, in truth and righteousness.' " (**NKJV**)

Zechariah clearly records that the Messiah (who was given the name of his Father-John 17:11) will return to Jerusalem and will dwell there in the midst of Israel. This is affirmed over and over in the *Tanakh*, as the following prophecies show:

ZECHARIAH 2:4 . . . "Run, speak to this young man, saying: 'Jerusalem shall be inhabited as towns without walls, because of the multitude of men and livestock in it. 5 For I,' says the LORD, 'will be a wall of fire all around her, and I will be the glory in her midst.' " 6 Up, up! Flee from the land of the north," says the LORD; "for I have spread you abroad like the four winds of heaven," says the LORD. 7 "Up, Zion! Escape, you who dwell with the daughter of Babylon." 8 For thus says the LORD of hosts: "He sent Me after glory, to the nations which plunder you; for he who touches you touches the apple of His eye. 9 For surely I will shake My hand against them, and they shall become spoil for their servants. Then you will know that the LORD of hosts has sent Me. 10 Sing and rejoice, O daughter of Zion! For behold, **I am coming and I will dwell in your midst**," says the LORD. 11 "Many nations shall be joined to the LORD in that day, and they shall become My people. And **I will dwell in your midst**. Then you will know that the LORD of hosts has sent Me to you. 12 And the LORD will take possession of Judah as His inheritance in the Holy Land, and will again choose Jerusalem." (**NKJV**)

MICAH 4:1 Now it shall come to pass in the latter days that the mountain of the LORD's house shall be established on the top of the mountains, and shall be exalted above the hills; and peoples shall flow to it. 2 Many nations shall come and say, "Come, and let us go up to the mountain of the LORD, to the house of the God of Jacob; He will teach us His ways, and we shall walk in His paths." For out of Zion the law shall go forth, and the word of the LORD from Jerusalem. 3 He shall judge between many peoples, and rebuke strong nations afar off; they shall beat their swords into plowshares, and their spears into pruning hooks; nation shall not lift up sword against nation, neither shall they learn war any more. 4 But everyone shall sit under his vine and under his fig tree, and no one shall make them afraid; for the mouth of the LORD of hosts has spoken. 5 For all people walk each in the name of his god, but we will walk in the name of the LORD our God forever and ever. 6 "In that day," says the LORD, "I will assemble the lame, I will gather the outcast and those whom I have afflicted; 7 I will make the lame a remnant, and the outcast a strong nation; so **the LORD will reign over them in Mount Zion** from now on, even forever. 8 And you, O tower of the flock, the stronghold of the daughter of Zion, to you shall it come, even the former dominion shall come, the kingdom of the daughter of Jerusalem." (**NKJV**)

JOEL 3:16 The LORD also will roar from Zion, and utter His voice from Jerusalem; the heavens and earth will shake; but the LORD will be a shelter for His people, and the strength of the children of Israel. 17 "So you shall know that **I am the LORD your God, dwelling in Zion My holy mountain. Then Jerusalem shall be holy**, and no aliens shall ever pass through her again." 18 And it will come to pass in that day that the mountains shall drip with new wine, the hills shall flow with milk, and all the brooks of Judah shall be flooded with water; a fountain shall flow from the house of the LORD and water the Valley of Acacias. 19 Egypt shall be a desolation, and Edom a desolate wilderness, because of violence against the people of Judah, for they have shed innocent blood in their land. 20 But Judah shall abide forever, and Jerusalem from generation to generation. 21 For I will acquit them of the guilt of bloodshed, whom I had not acquitted; for **the LORD dwells in Zion.**" (**NKJV**)

ISAIAH 24:17 Fear and the pit and the snare are upon you, O inhabitant of the earth. 18 And it shall be that he who flees from the noise of the fear shall fall into the pit, and he who comes up from the midst of the pit shall be caught in the snare; for the windows from on high are open, and the foundations of the earth are shaken. 19 The earth is violently broken, the earth is split open, the earth is shaken exceedingly. 20 The earth shall reel to and fro like a drunkard, and shall totter like a hut; its transgression shall be heavy upon it, and it will fall, and not rise again. 21 It shall come to pass in that day that the LORD will punish on high the host of exalted ones, and on the earth the kings of the earth. 22 They will be gathered together, as prisoners are gathered in the pit, and will be shut up in the prison; after many days they will be punished. 23 Then the moon will be disgraced and the sun ashamed; for **the LORD of hosts will reign on Mount Zion and in Jerusalem** and before His elders, gloriously. (**NKJV**)

ISAIAH 12:1 And in that day you will say: "O LORD, I will praise You; though You were angry with me, Your anger is turned away, and You comfort me. 2 Behold, God is my salvation, I will trust and not be afraid; 'For YAH, the LORD, is my strength and song; He also has become my salvation.' " 3 Therefore with joy you will draw water from the wells of salvation. 4 And in that day you will say: "Praise the LORD, call upon His name; declare His deeds among the peoples, make mention that His name is exalted. 5 Sing to the LORD, for He has done excellent things; this is known in all the earth. 6 Cry out and shout, O inhabitant of Zion, for great is **the Holy One of Israel in your midst!**" (**NKJV**)

PSALM 2:1 Why do the nations rage, and the people plot a vain thing? 2 The kings of the earth set themselves, and the rulers take counsel together, against **the LORD** and against **His Anointed**, saying, 3 "Let us break Their bonds in pieces and cast away Their cords from us." 4 He who sits in the heavens shall laugh; the LORD shall hold them in derision. 5 Then He shall speak to them in His wrath, and distress them in His deep displeasure: 6 "Yet I have set My King on My holy hill of Zion." 7 "I will declare the decree: The LORD has said to me, 'You are My Son, today I have begotten you. 8 Ask of Me, and I will give you the nations for your inheritance, and the ends of the earth for your possession. 9 You shall break them with a rod of iron; you shall dash them to pieces like a potter's vessel.' " 10 Now therefore, be wise, O kings; be instructed, you judges of the earth. 11 Serve the LORD with fear, and rejoice with trembling. 12 Kiss the Son, lest he be angry, and you perish in the way, when his wrath is kindled but a little. Blessed are all those who put their trust in him. (*NKJV*)

A multitude of Old Testament prophecies speak of the regathering of the Israelites to the Holy Land under the reign of King Messiah. It is clear that Yeshua will be here on earth ruling over the nations from Jerusalem.

According to Paul, we are to forever be with the Lord when he appears. If that is so, then we too will be here on the earth, ruling with him as kings and priests (Rev. 1:6). Isaiah speaks of what we will do at that time:

ISAIAH 1:24 Therefore the Lord says, the LORD of hosts, the Mighty One of Israel, "Ah, I will rid Myself of My adversaries, and take vengeance on My enemies. 25 I will turn My hand against you, and thoroughly purge away your dross, and take away all your alloy. 26 I will restore **your judges** as at the first, and **your counselors** as at the beginning. Afterward you shall be called the city of righteousness, the faithful city." 27 Zion shall be redeemed with justice, and her penitents with righteousness. (*NKJV*)

ISAIAH 30:18 Therefore the LORD will wait, that He may be gracious to you; and therefore He will be exalted, that He may have mercy on you. For the LORD is a God of justice; blessed are all those who wait for Him. 19 For the people shall dwell in Zion at Jerusalem; you shall weep no more. He will be very gracious to you at the sound of your cry; when He hears it, He will answer you. 20 And though the Lord [adonai] gives you the bread of adversity and the water of affliction, yet **your teachers** will not be moved into a corner anymore, but your eyes shall see **your teachers**. 21 Your ears shall hear a word behind you, saying, "This is the way, walk in it," whenever you turn to the right hand or whenever you turn to the left. (*NKJV*)

Resurrected saints with incorruptible spirit bodies will serve as teachers, counselors, and judges for those living in the messianic kingdom of God. As Yeshua's parable of the ten pounds (Luke 19:12-27) shows, Messiah will reward his servants when he returns with positions of rulership within the kingdom of God based on how much spiritual return they generate from the Holy Spirit given to them. They will be given responsibility to lead and teach, as Isaiah's words show us.

We do not go to heaven. At the end of the 1,000-year reign of Messiah, heaven will come to earth:

REVELATION 21:1 Now I saw a new heaven and a new earth, for the first heaven and the first earth had passed away. Also there was no more sea. 2 Then I, John, saw **the holy city, New Jerusalem, coming down out of heaven from God**, prepared as a bride adorned for her husband. 3 And I heard a loud voice from heaven saying, "Behold, **the tabernacle of God is with men, and He will dwell with them**, and they shall be His people. God Himself will be with them and be their God. 4 And God will wipe away every tear from their eyes; there shall be no more death, nor sorrow, nor crying. There shall be no more pain, for the former things have passed away." (*NKJV*)

A time will come, after the reign of the Messiah on the earth, that God Himself will come down from heaven. He will then dwell on the new earth among humanity. The earth, the current version and the new earth that will come after the Millennium, will always be the home of mankind.

Bryan T. Huie
May 25, 2004
Revised: April 17, 2009

How Long Were the Israelites in Egypt?

This comentary examines what the Scriptures show us about the length of time the Israelites were in Egypt. The answer may surprise you.

Determining the correct amount of time that the Israelites were in Egypt takes some biblical detective work. It requires looking at ALL the relevant Scriptures before arriving at a conclusion. Before we get to the specific matter at hand, we need to establish a time line based on the chronology given in the Bible:

EVENT	TIME	SCRIPTURE	DATE
Adam's creation to Seth's birth	130 years	Gen. 5:3	**130 AM**
Seth's birth to Enosh's birth	105 years	Gen. 5:6	**235 AM**
Enosh's birth to Cainan's birth	90 years	Gen. 5:9	**325 AM**
Cainan's birth to Mahalaleel's birth	70 years	Gen. 5:12	**395 AM**
Mahalaleel's birth to Jared's birth	65 years	Gen. 5:15	**460 AM**
Jared's birth to Enoch's birth	162 years	Gen. 5:18	**622 AM**
Enoch's birth to Methuselah's birth	65 years	Gen. 5:21	**687 AM**
Methuselah's birth to Lamech's birth	187 years	Gen. 5:25	**874 AM**
Lamech's birth to Noah's birth	182 years	Gen. 5:28-29	**1056 AM**
Noah's birth to the Flood	600 years	Gen. 7:6	**1656 AM**
Flood to Arphaxad's birth	2 years	Gen. 11:10	**1658 AM**
Arphaxad's birth to Salah's birth	35 years	Gen. 11:12	**1693 AM**
Salah's birth to Eber's birth	30 years	Gen. 11:14	**1723 AM**
Eber's birth to Peleg's birth	34 years	Gen. 11:16	**1757 AM**
Peleg's birth to Reu's birth	30 years	Gen. 11:18	**1787 AM**
Reu's birth to Serug's birth	32 years	Gen. 11:20	**1819 AM**
Serug's birth to Nahor's birth	30 years	Gen. 11:22	**1849 AM**
Nahor's birth to Terah's birth	29 years	Gen. 11:24	**1878 AM**
Terah's birth to Abram's birth	70 years	Gen. 11:26	**1948 AM**
Abram's birth to Isaac's birth	100 years	Gen. 21:5	**2048 AM**

AM = *Anno Mundi* - Year of the Earth (from creation)

As you can see from the chart above, Abram was born in the year 1948 AM (not coincidentally, the modern nation of Israel, composed of Abraham's descendants, was reborn in the year 1948 AD).

GALATIANS 3:16 Now to Abraham and his Seed were the promises made. He does not say, "And to seeds," as of many, but as of one, "And to your Seed," who is Christ. 17 And this I say, that **the law, which was four hundred and thirty years later**, cannot annul the covenant that was confirmed before by God in Christ, that it should make the promise of no effect. (*NKJV*)

In Galatians 3:17, Paul tells us that from the establishment of God's covenant with Abraham until the giving of the Law on Mount Sinai, 430 years elapsed. Genesis 12:1-3 shows us this initial covenant:

GENESIS 12:1 Now the LORD had said to Abram: "Get out of your country, from your family and from your father's house, to a land that I will show you. 2 I will make you a great nation; I will bless you And make your name great; and you shall be a blessing. 3 I will bless those who bless you, and I will curse him who curses you; and in you all the families of the earth shall be blessed." 4 So Abram departed as the LORD had spoken to him, and Lot went with him. And **Abram was seventy-five years old when he departed from Haran**. (*NKJV*)

When was this covenant established? Most would answer that it was established when Abram was 75 years old. This would be an incorrect deduction, however. Elsewhere the Scriptures show that God brought Abram out of Ur of the Chaldees BEFORE he brought him out of Haran (Gen. 11:31; 15:7; Neh. 9:7).

Stephen confirms this fact in his discourse before the Sanhedrin:

ACTS 7:2 And he said, "Brethren and fathers, listen: **The God of glory appeared to our father Abraham when he was in Mesopotamia, BEFORE he dwelt in Haran**, 3 and said to him, 'Get out of your country and from your relatives, and come to a land that I will show you.'" (*NKJV*)

So how do we determine how long Abram was in Haran after God made the covenant with him? Genesis 15 gives us the answer:

GENESIS 15:13 Then He said to Abram: "Know certainly that **your descendants will be strangers in a land that is not theirs, and will serve them, and they will afflict them four hundred years**. 14 And also the nation whom they serve I will judge; afterward they shall come out with great possessions. 15 Now as for you, you shall go to your fathers in peace; you shall be buried at a good old age." (*NKJV*)

According to the cantillation signs placed in the Hebrew text of Genesis 15:13 by the scribes, the phrase "400 years" refers back to the words, "your descendants will be strangers in a land that is not theirs." The years of Abraham's off-spring being strangers in a strange land BEGAN with the birth of Isaac (2048 AM), NOT with the Egyptian enslavement. Therefore the text ought to be understood as follows: "Know certainly that your descendants will be strangers in a land that is not theirs . . . 400 years." Adding 400 years to the date of Isaac's birth brings us to 2448 AM, which is the year of the Exodus and the giving of the Law at Mount Sinai.

The 30-year difference in the number of years mentioned by Paul in Galatians 3:17 and the number of years specified to Abram by God is due to two different starting points for the same ending point. The first covenant (Gen. 12:1-3) was instituted 430 years before the Law was given on Mount Sinai, while Genesis 15:13 refers to 400 years between the birth of Abraham's chosen off-spring, Isaac, and the Exodus from Egypt. This means that God made the first covenant with Abram in 2018 AM, 30 years before Isaac was born. Therefore, we can deduce that Abram left Ur at the age of 70, spent 5 years in Haran, and then left Haran in 2023 AM at the age of 75, as Genesis 12:4 tells us. The covenant of the pieces (Gen. 15) was probably made in the year 2033 AM, just before the birth of Ishmael in 2034 AM.

However, because of a statement made by Stephen, many think that Abram didn't leave Haran until after his father died:

ACTS 7:4 "Then he came out of the land of the Chaldeans and dwelt in Haran. And from there, **when his father was dead**, He moved him to this land in which you now dwell." (**NKJV**)

Based on the biblical chronology shown above, we know that Terah was born in 1878 AM. Genesis 11:32 tells us that Terah lived 205 years. So simple math establishes that Terah didn't physically die until **2083 AM** (35 years AFTER the birth of Isaac). There is no way to reconcile Stephen's statement if we apply it to Terah's physical death. Therefore, unless we assume (incorrectly) that Stephen was mistaken, we have to realize that he was refer-ring to Terah's **spiritual** death, not his physical death.

Many times the Scriptures speak of the living as being dead because of **sin** (Rom. 6:13; Col. 2:13; Eph. 2:1, 5; I Tim. 5:6; I John 3:14; I Pet. 4:6; Rev. 3:1). We know that Terah worshiped other gods (Jos. 24:2). Clearly Stephen was referring to Terah's spiritual state, not his physical state, when he men-tioned his death.

Exodus 12:40-41 tells us the very day that God first made His covenant with Abram:

EXODUS 12:40 Now the **sojourn** of the children of Israel who lived in Egypt was **four hundred and thirty years**. 41 And it came to pass at the end of the **four hundred and thirty years** -- **ON THAT VERY SAME DAY** -- it came to pass that all the armies of the LORD went out from the land of Egypt. (**NKJV**)

The Bible tells us that the Israelites started their trek out of Egypt on the 15th of the month of Abib (Num. 33:3). Therefore, we know that 430 years earlier, on 15 Abib (or Nisan), God first told Abraham to leave Ur of the Chaldees and promised to bless him if he did.

Some argue that Exodus 12:40-41 shows conclusively that the Israelites were slaves in Egypt for 430 years. However, the focus of these verses is the SO-JOURN of the children of Israel. Literally, this sojourn began when Abraham left Ur at the age of 70.

It is easy to prove from the Bible itself that the period of time that the Israelites dwelt in Egypt was not 400 or 430 years:

GENESIS 46:2 Then God spoke to Israel in the visions of the night, and said, "Jacob, Jacob!" And he said, "Here I am." 3 So He said, "I am God, the God of your father; do not fear to go down to Egypt, for I will make of you a great nation there. 4 I will go down with you to Egypt, and I will also surely bring you up again; and Joseph will put his hand on your eyes." 5 Then Jacob arose from Beersheba; and the sons of Israel carried their father Jacob, their little ones, and their wives, in the carts which Pharaoh had sent to carry him. 6 So they took their livestock and their goods, which they had acquired in the land of Canaan, and **went to Egypt**, Jacob and all his descendants with him. 7 His sons and his sons' sons, his daughters and his sons' daughters, and **all his descendants he brought with him to Egypt**. 8 Now **these were the names of the children of Israel, Jacob and his sons, who went to Egypt**: Reuben was Jacob's firstborn. . . . 11 The sons of **Levi** were Gershon, **KOHATH**, and Merari. (*NKJV*)

We see that when Jacob and his descendants left Canaan to move to Egypt, his son Levi and his grandson Kohath were among those who made the journey. After arriving in Egypt, Kohath had a son named Amram (Exo. 6:18). In turn, Amram had a son named Moses (Exo. 6:20). Moses was 80 years old when the Exodus took place (Exo. 7:7).

To find the MAXIMUM possible time between the Israelites move to Egypt and the Exodus, we will make some assumptions. We are told that Kohath lived to be 133 years old (Exo. 6:18), and Amram lived to be 137 years old (Exo. 6:20). Let's assume that Kohath had just been born when Jacob and Levi his father moved to Egypt. We will also assume that Amram had Moses in the last year of his life. To these two life spans, we will add Moses' age at the Exodus (80):

Kohath lived **133** years (Exo. 6:18)
Amram lived **137** years (Exo. 6:20)
Age of Moses at the Exodus was **80** years (Exo. 7:7)
TOTAL – 133 + 137 + 80 = **350**

The **maximum** possible time for the sojourn is only **350 years**. We see that the biblical chronology does not allow for 430 or 400 years in Egypt. So what is the correct number of years in Egypt? To find this out, we need to go back to the year of Isaac's birth and work our way forward.

We've already determined that it was 400 years from the time of Isaac's birth until the Exodus (2048 AM + 400 = 2448 AM). Isaac was 60 when he had Jacob and Esau (Gen. 25:26), which means Jacob was born in 2108 AM. Jacob was 130 years old when he moved his family to Egypt (Gen. 47:28), which indicates that this move occurred in 2238 AM. The time period between 2238 AM and 2448 AM is 210 years. So it was 210 years from the time Jacob moved his family to Egypt until the Exodus took place.

However, it was AFTER the children of Israel had multiplied and filled the land of Egypt, and a new Pharaoh who did not know Joseph had arisen, that the Egyptians enslaved the Israelites. We do not know for sure how long the enslavement lasted. But since Joseph died in 2309 AM (Gen. 50:22), it was probably a generation or two after this that the slavery began. My best guess is that they were enslaved approximately 100 years, give or take a decade or two.

For those of you who haven't studied Jewish sources, the time period of 210 years has long been known and proclaimed by the Jewish sages. But for many reasons, Christian scholars tend to disdain and dismiss Jewish understanding of the Scriptures. By doing so, they (and we) are missing out on some deeper insights into God's word. This is not to say that the Jews are right in all their beliefs and teachings. We are told to prove ALL things, but to only hold fast to that which is GOOD (I The. 5:21).

Conclusion

This question (and the answers most often given) illustrates a weakness of most Christians. I myself have been guilty of this same deficiency many times. We tend not to look deeply enough into the Scriptures to find the **full** answer. "It is the glory of God to conceal a matter, but the glory of kings is to search out a matter" (Pro. 25:2).

This is a case where all the necessary information to arrive at the correct answer is available in the Bible, but most believers don't gather it all and analyze it BEFORE coming to a conclusion. This type of presentation of information is one of the tests God built into the Scriptures to frustrate those who don't truly want to obey Him. God tells us how we must approach our study of the Scriptures: "For precept must be upon precept, precept upon precept, line upon line, line upon line, here a little, there a little" (Isa. 28:10, 13).

Most Christians do not use this method to study. Instead, they proof text and play "trump the verse." Proof texting is finding a Scripture that seems to agree with one's point of view and then using that Scripture to override any apparently contradictory Scriptures. Instead of trying to harmonize ALL the Scriptures on a particular topic, most Christians support those Scriptures that fit their particular beliefs and then ignore or overturn others that don't fit their doctrines. This is one of the main reasons we see so many denominations within Christianity. Is Christ divided (I Cor. 1:13)? Unfortunately, in this age

Lazarus and the Rich Man

This commentary examines the parable of Lazarus and the rich man in depth to uncover its long misunderstood meaning. Sadly, this story is used incorrectly by many in an attempt to understand what happens after death. Yet this parable is really a prophecy of the consequences of the Jewish rejection of their prophesied Messiah.

The parable of Lazarus and the rich man has been the foundation for many of the erroneous beliefs about "hell" within traditional Christianity. Some have viewed it not as a parable, but as a true story Yeshua told to give details about the punishment of sinners in hell. Yet a thorough, unbiased examination of this story will show that the generally accepted interpretations of this passage of Scripture are erroneous and misleading. In this article, we will go through the parable verse by verse to determine what the Messiah was truly teaching.

Those who insist that this is not a parable but a true, literal story Yeshua told to describe the condition of the lost in hell must overlook several facts to arrive at that conclusion. First, Yeshua the Messiah never accuses the rich man of any sin. He is simply portrayed as a wealthy man who lived the good life. Furthermore, Lazarus is never proclaimed to be a righteous man. He is just one who had the misfortune to be poor and unable to care for himself. If this story is literal, then the logical implication is that all the rich are destined to burn in hell, while all the homeless and destitute will be saved. Does anyone believe this to be the case?

If hell is truly as it is pictured in this story, then the saved will be able to view the lost who are burning there. Could anyone enjoy eternal existence if they were able to see lost friends, family, and acquaintances being incinerated in hell, yet never burning up? Additionally, if hell (as it is traditionally taught) is an abyss of fire and brimstone where sinners are tormented forever, does anyone really believe that one drop of water would relieve the pain and anguish of someone suffering in its flames?

These are just some of the difficulties we encounter when we try to make the account of Lazarus and the rich man literal, instead of realizing that it is a PARABLE. If it is a true story, then **all** of the things Yeshua said must be factual. If all the points of the story are not literal, then we must view this tale as an analogy Yeshua used to teach larger spiritual truths.

Many think that the Messiah spoke in parables to make the meaning clearer for the uneducated people he was teaching. Reflecting this belief, an appendix to the *NKJV* says that "Jesus' reputation as a great teacher spread far and wide. And no wonder. He taught in parables, simple stories, that made His lessons clear to all who were ready to learn" (p. 1870, "Man for All Times"). Yet the Messiah said his purpose for speaking to the people in parables was exactly the **opposite** of the explanation cited above:

MATTHEW 13:1 On the same day Jesus went out of the house and sat by the sea. 2 And great multitudes were gathered together to him, so that he got into a boat and sat; and the whole multitude stood on the shore. 3 Then he spoke many things to them in parables . . . 10 And the disciples came and said to him, "**Why do you speak to them in parables?**" 11 He answered and said to them, "Because **it has been given to you** to know the mysteries of the kingdom of heaven, but **to them it has not been given**. 12 For whoever has, to him more will be given, and he will have abundance; but whoever does not have, even what he has will be taken away from him. 13 **Therefore I speak to them in parables, because seeing they do not see, and hearing they do not hear, nor do they understand.** 14 And in them the prophecy of Isaiah is fulfilled, which says: 'Hearing you will hear and shall not understand, and seeing you will see and not perceive; 15 for the hearts of this people have grown dull. Their ears are hard of hearing, and their eyes they have closed, lest they should see with their eyes and hear with their ears, lest they should understand with their hearts and turn, so that I should heal them.' " (***NKJV***)

As this passage and the parallel Scripture in Mark 4 clearly state, Yeshua spoke to the people in parables to **hide** the spiritual meaning of what he was saying. He only intended for his disciples to understand what the parables truly meant. It is no wonder, then, that so many have misunderstood what Yeshua was teaching with the parable of Lazarus and the rich man.

Let's start by getting some background information on the situation in which Yeshua told this parable. Luke tells us that all the tax collectors and sinners were coming to the Messiah to hear what he had to say (Luke 15:1). This made the Pharisees and scribes jealous and they complained, vehemently criticizing Yeshua for receiving sinners and eating with them (Luke 15:2). They were likely envious of his growing fame, afraid that his popularity would diminish their own authority and prestige.

So the Messiah first spoke a trio of related parables (the lost sheep, the lost coin, and the prodigal son) to those gathered around him. They were designed to show the tax collectors and sinners (as well as the Pharisees) that God was concerned for them and that He would seek out the lost and welcome them into His family when they repented and turned back to Him.

The self-righteous Pharisees and scribes, acknowledged by Yeshua as the legitimate religious teachers of the Jews (Matt. 23:1-3), should have been the ones telling these people of God's love for them. They should have been the ones teaching these sinners, exhorting them to return to God and receive His love and forgiveness. However, because of their faith in their own righteousness and their contempt for these tax collectors and sinners who didn't measure up to their standards, the Pharisees and scribes excluded them and considered them accursed (John 7:49).

Afterward, speaking primarily to his disciples but with the Pharisees (and probably the crowd) still listening in, Yeshua related the parable of the unjust steward (Luke 16:1-13). The Pharisees, who were "lovers of money" (Luke 16:14), realized that the Messiah was alluding to them with this parable and took offense. They scoffed at Yeshua. The final part of his response to the derision of the Pharisees and scribes was the parable of Lazarus and the rich man.

We'll now examine this parable in detail to grasp exactly what the Messiah was teaching about the kingdom of God:

LUKE 16:19 "There was a certain rich man who was clothed in purple and fine linen and fared sumptuously every day." (*NKJV*)

We begin by scrutinizing the description Yeshua gives us of the rich man. First, he tells us that this man was clothed in purple and fine linen. This type of clothing would not have been out of the ordinary for one of considerable wealth during this time period. However, this attire also has symbolic meaning. *The Eerdmans Bible Dictionary* says: "The wearing of purple was associated particularly with royalty . . ." (p. 863, "Purple"). In addition, the *New Bible Dictionary* tells us: "The use of linen in OT times was prescribed for priests (Ex. 28:39). The coat, turban and girdle must be of fine linen." (p. 702, "Linen").

So we see that the garments worn by this rich man were symbolic of royalty and the priesthood. With that in mind, let's see what God told Moses just before giving the Israelites the Law on Mount Sinai:

EXODUS 19:6 And ye shall be to me a **royal priesthood** and a **holy nation**: these words shalt thou speak to the children of Israel. (*Brenton's LXX*)

The clothing of the rich man identifies him symbolically with the people of Israel, chosen by God to be His special people. They were called to be a witness to the nations surrounding them, confirming the blessings available to those who would obey God and keep His laws. Unfortunately, they frequently did not live up to the high calling given to them by God. Eventually He sent them into captivity for their refusal to honor their part of the covenant ratified at Mount Sinai. At the time of Yeshua, only the House of Judah continued to have a covenant relationship with God. The rich man in this parable represents the religious Jews of Yeshua's day, exemplified by their teachers, the Pharisees and scribes.

Verse 19 also tells us that the rich man "fared sumptuously every day." Figuratively, this represents the magnificent spiritual feast available only to the Jews, who were the sole remaining part of God's called people, Israel. In the 1st century CE, they were the only people on earth who had the true religion. Indeed, Paul recounts the glorious station of the House of Judah in Romans 9:

ROMANS 9:3 For I could wish that I myself were accursed and cut off from Christ for the sake of my brethren, my kinsmen by race. 4 They are Israelites, and to them belong the sonship, the glory, the covenants, the giving of the law, the worship, and the promises; 5 to them belong the patriarchs, and of their race, according to the flesh, is the Christ. God who is over all be blessed for ever. Amen. (*RSV*)

The Jews were truly rich, feasting on God's spiritual blessings. Yet these very gifts caused them to stumble because they prompted them to self-righteousness. They gloried in the gifts, without glorifying the Eternal God who gave them. Instead of being a "royal priesthood" that was a blessing to all nations, they instead loathed and despised the surrounding peoples. Certainly, as Paul wrote, "their table become a snare and a trap, a stumbling block and a retribution for them" (Rom. 11:9).

LUKE 16:20 "But there was a certain beggar named Lazarus, full of sores, who was laid at his gate, 21 desiring to be fed with the crumbs which fell from the rich man's table. Moreover the dogs came and licked his sores." (*NKJV*)

In contrast to the rich man, we now see Lazarus. The first thing to note is that he is depicted as a beggar. This is an apt description of the Gentiles who "laid at the gate" of Judah. Paul describes the predicament of the Gentiles before they accepted the Messiah in his letter to the Ephesians:

EPHESIANS 2:12 Remember that you were at that time separated from Christ, alienated from the commonwealth of Israel, and strangers to the covenants of promise, having no hope and without God in the world. (*RSV*)

This Scripture is also a fitting representation of the position of the nations before the Messiah's sacrifice for the world's sins. They were certainly "excluded from the commonwealth of Israel," "strangers to the covenants of promise," and "without hope and without God in the world." The Gentiles were beggars, located outside Judah and longing to be fed spiritual crumbs from the table of the divinely blessed Jews.

Additionally, we are told that dogs came and consoled Lazarus in his misery, licking his sores. The Jews considered the surrounding Gentiles to be unclean "dogs." Even Yeshua himself used this unflattering comparison when he conversed with the Greek Syrophoenician woman while in the region of Tyre (Mark 7:24-30).

Also important to the story is the meaning of the name Lazarus. This Greek name is a form of the Hebrew *Eleazer*, and it literally means "he whom God helps." The use of this particular name is very significant to the message of the parable, for the Gentiles would indeed become "those whom God helped" through the sacrifice of His son, Yeshua.

LUKE 16:22 "So it was that the beggar died, and was carried by the angels to Abraham's bosom. The rich man also died and was buried." (*NKJV*)

The next events recorded in this parable are the deaths of Lazarus and then the rich man. Since the parable has been figurative up until this point, there is no reason to assume it becomes literal now.

First, to prove that this language is symbolic and not meant to be taken literally, let's examine exactly what we are told by Yeshua. He says that **first**, Lazarus dies and is taken to the bosom of Abraham. Notice, there is no mention of his burial here. Then **later** the rich man dies, and he is buried (in Hades, according to verse 23). So the time sequence given indicates that upon his death, Lazarus was taken immediately to Abraham's bosom, while afterward the rich man was buried in Hades when he died.

If this story is literal, then we have a contradiction in the Bible. Here, Lazarus is shown to have immediately received the promise of eternal life. Yet the author of Hebrews clearly tells us that Abraham, as well as all the other Old Testament saints, have not yet received the promises given to them by God:

HEBREWS 11:13 All these [Abraham, Noah, Abel, etc.] died in faith, **without receiving the promises**, but having seen them and having welcomed them from a distance, and having confessed that they were strangers and exiles on the earth. . . . 39 And all these [including Abraham], having gained approval through their faith, **did not receive what was promised**, 40 because God had provided something better for us, **so that apart from us they would not be made perfect**. (*NASU*)

The great men and women of faith listed in Hebrews 11 have **not yet** been made perfect and given eternal life. They, along with all the saints of God from every age, are currently sleeping in their graves (Job 3:11-19; Psa. 6:5; 115:17; Ecc. 9:5, 10; I Cor. 15:20; Isa. 57:1-2; Dan. 12:2; Acts 2:29, 34; 13:36). These saints are awaiting the first resurrection, which will take place when Yeshua the Messiah returns at the sounding of the last trumpet (Matt. 24:30-31; I Cor. 15:51-52; I The. 4:16; Rev. 11:15-18).

Clearly, there is no way to reconcile the numerous Scriptures listed above with a literal understanding of the story of Lazarus and the rich man. What, then, does the death of these two men represent?

The deaths of both the rich man (who represented the Jews) and Lazarus (who represented the other nations) are symbolic in this parable. Here, their demise depicts an elemental change in the status and position of the two groups.

To confirm this, let's look at the meaning of Lazarus being "carried to Abraham's bosom." The figurative meaning of being in one's bosom is to be in a position of closeness, to be highly regarded. This symbolism is indicated by the ancient practice of having guests at a feast recline on the chest of their neighbors. The place of highest honor would therefore belong to the one seated next to the host, calling to mind the example of John at the Last Supper (John 13:23).

Paul explains this imagery in his letter to the Galatians by telling us how the Gentiles could be in this place of highest honor:

GALATIANS 3:6 . . . Abraham "believed God, and it was accounted to him for righteousness." 7 Therefore know that **only those who are of faith are sons of Abraham**. 8 And the Scripture, foreseeing that **God would justify the Gentiles by faith**, preached the gospel to Abraham beforehand, saying, "In you all the nations shall be blessed." 9 So then those who are of faith are blessed with believing Abraham. (*NKJV*)

As the passage above (as well as chapters 4 and 9 of Romans) shows, Gentile believers become "sons of Abraham" through faith in the Messiah. This faith allows Gentiles to no longer be "strangers and foreigners, but fellow citizens with the saints and members of the household of God" (Eph. 2:19). For centuries the Jews had received the benefits of being God's chosen people by virtue of being Abraham's physical descendants. But after the sacrifice of Yeshua, this place of honor and blessing would be predominantly given to the people represented by Lazarus. This is the meaning of being "carried to the bosom of Abraham" in this parable.

In contrast to Lazarus, the rich man was **buried** in Hades. An understanding of the original meaning of the Greek word *hades* is necessary to grasp the message of the parable. Regarding the possible etymology of this word, the *The New International Dictionary of New Testament Theology* states that *hades* ". . . comes from *idein* (to see) with the negative prefix, *a-*, and so would mean the invisible . . . In the LXX *hades* occurs more than 100 times, in the majority of instances to translate Heb. *she'ol*, the underworld which receives all the dead. It is the land of darkness . . ." (p. 206, vol. 2).

Most likely, *hades* originally meant "unseen." Later, it came to refer to the hidden state of those buried in the earth. Symbolically, this parable shows that a point would come when the House of Judah would become "unseen" by God, out of favor because of their unbelief. There would come a time when the Jews as a whole would no longer be God's favored nation. God would harden their hearts, leading them to reject their Messiah (John 1:11).

LUKE 16:23 "And being in **torments in Hades**, he lifted up his eyes and saw Abraham afar off, and Lazarus in his bosom." (*NKJV*)

What did Yeshua mean by saying here that the rich man was in "torments in Hades"? The key to discovering the symbolic meaning of this verse is the Greek noun *basanois*, translated "torments" above.

According to Friberg's *Analytical Lexicon of the Greek New Testament*, *basanois*, which is a form of the noun *basanos*, means "strictly, *a touchstone* for testing the genuineness of metals by rubbing against it . . ."

The etymology of *basanos* found in Kittel's *Theological Dictionary of the New Testament* is very helpful in correctly understanding this verse:

In non-biblical Gk. [*basanos*] is a commercial expression, or is used in relation to government. It then acquires the meaning of the checking of calculations, which develops naturally out of the basic sense of [*basanos, basanizein*] . . . **In the spiritual sphere it has the figur[ative] sense, which is closely related to the original concrete meaning, of a means of testing . . .**

The word then undergoes a change in meaning. The original sense fades into the background. [*Basanos*] now comes to denote "torture" or "the rack," espec [ially] used with slaves . . . [*Basanos*] occurs in the sense of "torment" . . .

The change in meaning is best explained if we begin with the object of treatment. If we put men instead of metal or a coin, the stone of testing become[s] torture or the rack. The metal which has survived the testing stone is subjected to harsher treatment. Man is in the same position when severely tested by torture. In the testing of metal an essential role was played by the thought of testing and proving genuineness. The rack is a means of showing the true state of affairs. **In its proper sense it is a means of testing and proving, though also of punishment**. Finally, even this special meaning was weakened and only the general element of torture remained (pp. 561, 562, vol. I).

In this verse, ***basanois*** simply conveys a sense of testing and proving through punishment. When this understanding is combined with a proper discernment of the symbolism of Hades, we can begin to see the point Yeshua is making. As a whole, the House of Judah would to be cut off and replaced during this current age by those from the nations who in faith would accept the sacrifice of the Messiah.

If the Pharisees and scribes understood Yeshua's prophetic parable, it must have astonished and infuriated them. How could the Jews become alienated from God while the elect Gentiles became the "seed of Abraham"? The implication that the House of Judah and those called from the Gentile nations were to change places would have been almost impossible for the Pharisees and scribes to believe.

LUKE 16:24 "Then he cried and said, 'Father Abraham, have mercy on me, and send Lazarus that he may dip the tip of his finger in water and cool my tongue; for I am tormented in this flame.' " (***NKJV***)

First, notice that the rich man identifies Abraham as his father, just as the Pharisees did (John 8:39). The rich man (Judah) is now shown to be undergoing reproof, testing, and punishment in "this flame" (singular, **not** "these flames"). It is quite obvious that the flame is not literal, because a wet fingertip on the tongue would do nothing to quench the pain inflicted by real flames.

The word rendered "torment" here is a form of the Greek verb ***odunao***, which literally means "grief," "pain," or "suffering." Predominantly, it conveys the sense of mental anguish, **not** physical pain. Forms of this word are found only four times in the Scriptures, all in the writings of Luke. It appears twice in this parable, in verses 24 and 25. In Luke 2:48, it is used to describe the anxious distress that Mary and Joseph felt after they discovered the 12-year old Yeshua missing on the trip home from Jerusalem after the Passover feast. In Acts 20:38, it depicts the sorrow the elders of the Ephesian Church felt at Paul's farewell announcement that they would never see him again.

The rich man cries out from the symbolic darkness of Hades for comfort because of the suffering caused by the flame. The explanation of the symbolism of the flame will require a little background information.

In Deuteronomy 11 and 28, Moses delineates God's part in His covenant with Israel. Moses told them that if they obeyed God, they would be the most blessed nation on earth. Conversely, if they disobeyed, God promised to curse and eventually destroy them because of their sins.

As the history of Israel in the *Tanakh* shows, only rarely did they obey God. Although God was patient and forgave them many times when they repented and turned back to Him, eventually He brought about the curses on Israel as He had promised.

First the House of Israel (the 10 tribes that composed the northern kingdom of Samaria) was carried into captivity by Assyria (c. 722 BCE). Hosea, who prophesied during the end of the northern kingdom, said this about God's chosen people who were called to be a royal priesthood and a holy nation:

HOSEA 4:6 My people are destroyed for lack of knowledge. Because you have rejected knowledge, **I also will reject you from being priest for Me**; because you have forgotten the law of your God, I also will forget your children. (*NKJV*)

Then, a little over a century later, the southern kingdom of Judah was subdued and finally carried captive by Babylon (c. 586 BCE). Because of their sins, God had delivered His people to their enemies, as He had promised.

The people of Judah were given another chance, however. After the Persians defeated the Babylonians, the Jews were allowed to return to Judea (c. 538 BCE) and eventually they rebuilt the Temple. Chastened and aware that their sins had brought about the captivity, many sought to obey God's laws upon their return to the land.

But by the time of the Messiah, once again unbelief had become a major problem. Many of the religious teachers of the day had substituted human traditions for the laws God had given Israel (Matt. 15:1-9; Mark 7:1-13). Because of their lack of faith, they didn't really believe the very Scriptures they professed to follow (John 5:39, 45-47). Ultimately, they rejected the anointed one God sent to them and had the Romans crucify him.

Now back to the question at hand. What does the flame in the parable represent?

When one looks at the history of the Jewish people from the time of Yeshua until today, one theme remains constant — PERSECUTION. With the quashing of the Jewish revolts against Rome (66-70 CE and 132-135 CE), the saga of the Jewish people in the Diaspora has been one of persistent and harsh persecution from virtually all quarters. The Inquisition of the 15th century and the Holocaust of the 20th century are two of the more well-known antisemitic episodes, but many more are recorded on the bloody pages of history. Due to their unbelief and rejection of Yeshua, God has brought the "flame" of suffering and grief down upon the Jews through the centuries. Unfortunately, most of that mistreatment has come at the hands of those who called themselves "Christians."

The Jews pictured by the rich man in this parable are in their present state because of their unbelief, which ultimately manifested itself in the rejection of the Messiah, Yeshua. Unfortunately, this parable shows that the punishment and testing they would undergo would not **immediately** lead them to Yeshua. Instead of calling on the Messiah, the rich man calls on his ancestor Abraham to help ease his suffering.

LUKE 16:25 "But Abraham said, 'Son, remember that in your lifetime you received your good things, and likewise Lazarus evil things; but now he is comforted and you are tormented. (*NKJV*)

Abraham clearly identifies the rich man as his descendant by calling him "son." He tells him that things have changed. When the Jews were God's chosen people, they enjoyed the spiritual blessings associated with that status. But now, Abraham says, Lazarus is enjoying those blessings while the rich man is grieving and in sorrow. "Tormented" here is another form of *odunao*, the same Greek verb found above in verse 24.

LUKE 16:26 " 'And besides all this, between us and you there is a great gulf fixed, so that those who want to pass from here to you cannot, nor can those from there pass to us.' " (*NKJV*)

What is the "great gulf" which stands between the rich man and Lazarus? Paul aptly explains it to us in the 11th chapter of Romans. He tells us that God has blinded the Jews and "given them a spirit of stupor, eyes that they should not see and ears that they should not hear, to this very day" (Rom. 11:8). He goes on to say that "a partial hardening would happen to Israel until the fullness of the Gentiles had come in" (Rom. 11:25). In II Corinthians 3:14-15, Paul says that the Jews' "minds were blinded. For until this day the same veil remains unlifted in the reading of the Old Testament, because the veil is taken away in Christ. But even to this day, when Moses is read, a veil lies on their heart."

The "great gulf" mentioned by Abraham is nothing less than God's blinding in this age of the Jews as a whole to the truth about their Messiah! It's not that the Jewish nation won't acknowledge Yeshua as the prophesied Messiah; they **cannot** recognize his true identity because of God's actions! Yet because of the Eternal Father's great mercy, this state of affairs will not last forever (Rom. 11:26).

LUKE 16:27 "Then he said, 'I beg you therefore, father, that you would send him to my father's house, 28 for I have five brothers, that he may testify to them, lest they also come to this place of torment.' " (*NKJV*)

Yielding himself to his destiny, the rich man asks one more thing of his forefather Abraham. He pleads with him to send someone to warn his brothers, so that they may escape "this place of **torment**" (*basanou*), the testing and punishment that he was undergoing.

The fact that the rich man has **five** brothers is a vital clue to his true symbolic identity. Judah, the progenitor of the Jews, was the son of Jacob through Leah (Gen. 29:35). He had five full-blooded brothers: Reuben, Simeon, Levi, Issachar, and Zebulun (Gen. 35:23).

While the significance of this seemingly pointless detail has been neglected by scholars throughout the centuries, you can be certain that it did not escape the notice of the Pharisees and scribes to which Yeshua was speaking. They thoroughly knew their history and were extremely proud of their heritage. Yeshua wanted those self-righteous Pharisees to know exactly who he was referring to with this parable. This detail cements the identity of the rich man as the House of Judah, the Jews!

LUKE 16:29 "Abraham said to him, 'They have Moses and the prophets; let them hear them.' " (*NKJV*)

Once again Abraham refuses the rich man's request, telling him that the brothers already have a witness in the writings of Moses and the prophets that will allow them to escape his fate. Moses, as well as the prophets, are shown several times in the New Testament to support Yeshua's identity as the Messiah (Luke 24:27, 44; John 1:45; 5:46; Acts 3:22-24; 7:37; 26:22-23; 28:23). Abraham tells the rich man that his brothers would have to recognize the prophesied Messiah because of the things written about him in the *Tanakh*. This echoes what Yeshua told the Jews in John's Gospel:

JOHN 5:45 "Do not think that I shall accuse you to the Father; there is one who accuses you — Moses, in whom you trust. 46 For if you believed Moses, you would believe me; for he wrote about me. 47 But if you do not believe his writings, how will you believe my words?" (*NKJV*)

As the Scriptures show, the Jewish leaders of Yeshua's day generally failed to recognize the very one Moses wrote about (Deu. 18:15, 18).

LUKE 16:30 "And he said, 'No, father Abraham; but if one goes to them from the dead, they will repent.' 31 But he said to him, 'If they do not hear Moses and the prophets, neither will they be persuaded though one rise from the dead.' " (*NKJV*)

Yeshua uses the last two verses of this parable as an amazing prophecy of his pending resurrection from the dead. The rich man says that although his brothers may not accept the scriptural evidence for the identity of the Messiah, they will accept the evidence of one who is raised from the dead.

But Abraham answers and plainly tells him that anyone who rejects the Bible's teaching about the Messiah will also refuse to acknowledge the evidence of a miraculous resurrection. This last verse is a sad prophecy about the Jews who, despite God's resurrection of His son from the power of the grave, have failed to recognize Yeshua as the prophesied Messiah.

Yeshua ends this parable abruptly, with no real resolution presented. The picture presented is a bleak one, yet there is hope for the Jews and for all Israel. In Romans 11, Paul laid out that hope in such a manner that scarcely few today have really believed it.

In Romans 11:1 Paul rhetorically asks if God has cast away His people, Israel. He answers his own question emphatically by saying "Certainly not!" He tells us that God has not cast away His people whom He foreknew. Paul writes that there is currently a remnant of Israel that God has elected by His grace. This group is analogous to the 7,000 God reserved for Himself in the time of Elijah (I Kings 19:18). The rest God hardened, Paul says, that the Gentiles might also be saved. He gives the resolution of the situation at the end of chapter 11:

ROMANS 11:25 For I do not desire, brethren, that you should be ignorant of this mystery, lest you should be wise in your own opinion, that blindness in part has happened to Israel until the fullness of the Gentiles has come in. 26 And so **all Israel will be saved**, as it is written: "The Deliverer will come out of Zion, and He will turn away ungodliness from Jacob; 27 for this is My covenant with them, when I take away their sins." 28 Concerning the gospel they are enemies for your sake, but concerning the election they are beloved for the sake of the fathers. 29 For the gifts and the calling of God are irrevocable. 30 For as you were once disobedient to God, yet have now obtained mercy through their disobedience, 31 even so these also have now been disobedient, that through the mercy shown you they also may obtain mercy. 32 For God has committed them all to disobedience, that He might have mercy on all. 33 Oh, the depth of the riches both of the wisdom and knowledge of God! How unsearchable are His judgments and His ways past finding out! (*NKJV*)

The same God that blinded Israel unto disobedience will have mercy on all that have been rebellious due to that blindness. To quote Paul once again, "Oh, the depth of the riches both of the wisdom and knowledge of God! How unsearchable are His judgments and unfathomable His ways!" Praised be the Eternal Creator of all things!

CONCLUSION:

The parable of Lazarus and the rich man, long used by mainstream Christian ministers to teach the "reality of hell," really has nothing to say about punishment or reward in the afterlife. Yeshua used this story, which fit the common misconception about life after death in his day, to show the fate that awaited the Jewish nation because of the unbelief and faithlessness which caused them to reject him as the Messiah. They still suffer from that fate to this very day. Yet the time is soon coming when God will pour on the Jews the Spirit of grace and supplication; then they will look on their Messiah whom they pierced, and they will mourn for him as one mourns for his only son, and grieve for him as one grieves for a firstborn (Zec. 12:10).

Bryan T. Huie
January 9, 1998

Revised: April 8, 2009

Mystery of God:

Predestination or Freewill?

This tackles the question of whether the Bible teaches predestination or free will. It sets the stage by establishing some key traits the heavenly Father reveals about Himself in the Scriptures: His omnipresence, omniscience and omnipotence. Then relevant passages of Scripture are examined to determine what God is truly doing here on the earth. The plan of God is likely much more grandiose than you have been taught.

What is God really trying to accomplish here on earth? This is a question that religious men and women have pondered since the dawn of creation. Paul tells us that the mystery of God was hidden throughout all the ages and generations from the time of creation until the appearance of the Messiah. After his first coming, however, the heavenly Father revealed this mystery to His saints (Col. 1:26). Yet how well do those who profess to have accepted Yeshua the Messiah (Jesus Christ) really understand God's mysterious plan?

Most Christian denominations believe that they have a good grasp of the mystery of God the Father. They think He is saving those who, of their own free will, accept the sacrifice of His son Yeshua. Conversely, they believe that God will condemn and eternally punish those who do not accept that sacrifice (either because of conscious rejection or ignorance).

Under that basic premise, most of Christianity has implicitly decided that God is going to end up saving just a minority of humanity, since even the most optimistic assessment can only conclude that most people throughout history have NOT accepted the saving sacrifice of Yeshua. Yet does this understanding agree with what God says He will do in His Word? In this article we will examine what the Bible truly teaches about this misunderstood mystery of God that even now so few really comprehend.

In order to lay out the mystery of God, we must first understand some things about God that the Father reveals of Himself. God tells us quite a bit about Himself and His abilities in the Bible.

God the Father – Omnipresent, Omniscient and Omnipotent

These three impressive sounding words describe God's presence, knowledge, and power, which are concepts found often in the Scriptures. We will examine each in turn:

OMNIPRESENCE

The term "omnipresent" refers to the ability to be present everywhere at the same time. The Scriptures tell us that God the Father, through His Holy Spirit, maintains a presence in all of His creation:

PSALM 139:7 **Where shall I go from your Spirit? Or where shall I flee from your presence? 8 If I ascend to heaven, you are there! If I make my bed in Sheol, you are there!** 9 If I take the wings of the morning and dwell in the uttermost parts of the sea, 10 even there your hand shall lead me, and your right hand shall hold me. 11 If I say, "Surely the darkness shall cover me, and the light about me be night," 12 even the darkness is not dark to you; the night is bright as the day, for darkness is as light with you. (*ESV*)

JEREMIAH 23:23 "Am I only a God nearby," declares the LORD, "and not a God far away? 24 **Can anyone hide in secret places so that I cannot see him?**" declares the LORD. "**Do not I fill heaven and earth?**" declares the LORD. (*NIV*)

PROVERBS 5:21 For **a man's ways are in full view of the LORD**, and He examines all his paths. (*NIV*)

PROVERBS 15:3 **The eyes of the LORD are in every place**, keeping watch on the evil and the good. (*ESV*)

OMNISCIENCE

To be "omniscient" means that one has total and complete knowledge of all things. What does the Bible tell us about God the Father's knowledge?

ISAIAH 46:9 Remember the former things, those of long ago; I am God, and there is no other; I am God, and there is none like me. 10 **I make known the end from the beginning, from ancient times, what is still to come**. I say: My purpose will stand, and I will do all that I please. (*NIV*)

ISAIAH 48:3 **I foretold the former things long ago, my mouth announced them and I made them known**; then suddenly I acted, and they came to pass. (*NIV*)

ISAIAH 42:9 Behold, the former things have come to pass, and **new things I now declare; before they spring forth I tell you of them**." (*ESV*)

PSALM 139:1 For the director of music. Of David. A psalm. O LORD, You have searched me and You know me. 2 **You know when I sit and when I rise; You perceive my thoughts from afar**. 3 **You discern my going out and my lying down; You are familiar with all my ways**. 4 **Before a word is on my tongue You know it completely, O LORD**. 5 You hem me in — behind and before; You have laid Your hand upon me. 6 Such **knowledge** is too wonderful for me, too lofty for me to attain. (*NIV*)

LUKE 12:6 "Are not five sparrows sold for two small coins? Yet **not one of them has escaped the notice of God**. 7 **Even the hairs of your head have all been counted**. Do not be afraid. You are worth more than many sparrows." (*NAB*)

MATTHEW 24:30 "Then the sign of the Son of Man will appear in heaven, and then all the tribes of the earth will mourn, and they will see the Son of Man coming on the clouds of heaven with power and great glory. 31 And He will send His angels with a great sound of a trumpet, and they will gather together His elect from the four winds, from one end of heaven to the other. . . . 36 **But of that day and hour no one knows**, not even the angels of heaven, **but My Father only**." (*NKJV*)

These Scriptures show that God knows all things, and that He often foretells the future to us through His prophets. But we are told even more here; God does not just make known future events, but He actively works to carry out His plan. It's not simply a case of the heavenly Father being able to see the future. God specifically tells us that He takes action to make prophesied events occur.

OMNIPOTENCE

The term "omnipotence" means having power over all things. Let's see what the Scriptures tell us about God the Father's power:

ISAIAH 44:24 Thus says the LORD, your Redeemer, and the one who formed you from the womb, "**I, the LORD, am the maker of all things**, stretching out the heavens by Myself and spreading out the earth all alone," (*NASU*)

JEREMIAH 10:12 But **God made the earth by His power**; He founded the world by His wisdom and stretched out the heavens by His understanding. (*NIV*)

JEREMIAH 27:5 "**With My great power** and outstretched arm **I made the earth** and its people and the animals that are on it, and I give it to anyone I please." (*NIV*)

JEREMIAH 32:17 Ah Lord GOD! **It is You who made the heavens and the earth by Your great power** and by Your outstretched arm! Nothing is too hard for You. (*NRSV*)

JEREMIAH 51:15 "**He made the earth by His power**; He founded the world by His wisdom and stretched out the heavens by His understanding." (*NIV*)

ISAIAH 40:25 "Who will you compare Me to, or who is My equal?" asks the Holy One. 26 Look up and see: Who created these? He brings out the starry host by number; He calls all of them by name. Because of His **great power and strength**, not one of them is missing. (*CSB*)

JOB 36:22 See, **God is beyond reach in His power**; who governs like Him? (*JPS Tanakh*)

God's power is so great that He created the entire vast universe using it. The power of God is also manifested in His ability to design a plan and ensure that it is carried out to achieve His will and purpose:

ISAIAH 14:24 The LORD of hosts has sworn: **As I have designed, so shall it be**; and as **I have planned, so shall it come to pass**: (*NRSV*)

ISAIAH 14:27 **The LORD of hosts has planned; who can thwart Him?** His hand is stretched out; who can turn it back? (*NAB*)

ISAIAH 43:13 "Even from eternity I am He, and there is none who can deliver out of My hand; **I act and who can reverse it?**" (*NASU*)

ISAIAH 46:10 I foretell the end from the beginning, and from the start, things that had not occurred. I say: **My plan shall be fulfilled; I will do all I have purposed**. (*JPS Tanakh*)

LAMENTATIONS 3:37 Who can speak and have it happen if the Lord has not **decreed** it? (*NIV*)

II CHRONICLES 20:6 [King Jehoshaphat] said: "O LORD, God of our fathers, are You not the God who is in heaven? You rule over all the kingdoms of the nations. **Power and might are in Your hand, and no one can with-**

stand You." (*NIV*)

God's power is such that whatever He has decided to do, that is what will be done. God tells us that He has designed a plan that will be implemented because **no one** (not man nor angel) has the power to thwart or withstand His purpose.

If God truly is all powerful, and if He has a definite plan for mankind, then nothing happens outside the scope of that plan. Logically this means that He is the author of **everything** that happens, both good and bad. Numerous Scriptures confirm this to be the case:

ISAIAH 45:7 I **form the light**, and **create darkness**: I **make peace**, and **create evil**: I the LORD do all these things. (*RWB*)

LAMENTATIONS 3:38 Is it not from the mouth of the Most High that **good and evil** come? (*NIV*)

ECCLESIASTES 7:13 Consider what God has done: Who can straighten what He has made crooked? 14 When times are **good**, be happy; but when times are **bad**, consider: **God has made the one as well as the other**. Therefore, a man cannot discover anything about his future. (*NIV*)

DEUTERONOMY 32:39 "See now that I, I am He, and there is no God besides Me; it is I who **put to death** and **give life**. I have **wounded** and it is I who **heal**, and there is no one who can deliver from My hand." (*NASU*)

I SAMUEL 2:6 The LORD both **kills** and **gives life**; He **brings down to the grave** and **raises up**. (*NET*)

JOB 5:18 For He **wounds**, but He also **binds up**; He **injures**, but His hands also **heal**. (*NIV*)

HOSEA 6:1 "Come, let us return to the LORD. He has **torn us to pieces** but He will **heal us**; He has **injured us** but He will **bind up our wounds**." (*NIV*)

Because He is all powerful, God is the source of everything that happens, both good and bad. The Scriptures show that He is the One who wounds and kills, in addition to being the One who heals and makes alive. As the Almighty Creator and Supreme Power in the entire universe should, God the Father takes complete responsibility for all things in this world, evil as well as good.

Yet very few believe God when He claims to be the source of evil. They refuse to accept the very words of God recorded in the Bible and instead prefer to believe in a different God, one of their own devising. The God of most Christians isn't the source of the evil in the world. Instead, they believe God simply allows His creation to choose evil because He has given them the free will to do so.

Many cite the first half of Habakkuk 1:13 in support of their contention that God, far from being the creator of evil, cannot even so much as look upon it:

HABAKKUK 1:13 **Your eyes are too pure to look on evil**; you cannot tolerate wrong. . . . (*NIV*)

"There! The Bible says it, so I believe it!" proclaim those who hold this view. But if this is really the point the prophet is making here, then he is contradicting the scriptural wisdom of King Solomon (Pro. 15:3). Since the Messiah told us that the Scriptures cannot be broken (John 10:35), let's look at the context of the entire first chapter of Habakkuk to understand what he is really saying about God.

Habakkuk 1:2-4 records the prophet's cries to **YHVH** regarding the sin and violence that were rampant within Judah during the reign of the latter kings. In Habakkuk 1:5-11, God reveals to him that He is going to raise up the Babylonians against Judah to punish them for their sins. This in turn causes Habakkuk to wonder why God would use a people more violent and wicked than Judah to punish His chosen ones:

HABAKKUK 1:12 Are You not from eternity, Yahweh my God? My Holy One, You will not die. **LORD, You appointed them to execute judgment**; my Rock, **You destined them to punish us**. 13 Your eyes are too pure to look on evil, and You cannot tolerate wrongdoing. So why do You tolerate those who are treacherous? Why are You silent while one who is wicked swallows up one who is more righteous than himself? 14 You have made mankind like the fish of the sea, like marine creatures that have no ruler. 15 The Chaldeans pull them all up with a hook, catch them in their dragnet, and gather them in their fishing net; that is why they are glad and rejoice. 16 That is why they sacrifice to their dragnet and burn incense to their fishing net, for by these things their portion is rich and their food plentiful. 17 Will they therefore empty their net and continually slaughter nations without mercy? (*CSB*)

In reality, we see that the words of Habakkuk about God prove the exact opposite point from what most understand from the first half of verse 13. Even though Judah's sins were grievous, Habakkuk was appalled at God's solution after He showed him how He was going to deal with them. Habakkuk wondered how God could choose the treacherous, vicious, arrogant Babylonians (i.e., Chaldeans) to punish His people. Although he realized that the Jews needed to be corrected, Habakkuk could not understand God's choice of people to serve as His instrument of punishment. So Habakkuk's point really was, "God, I know You hate evil, yet You are going to choose a people even more wicked than we are to punish us. WHY?"

God has and continues to make use of various (and often evil) proxies to carry out His will. The heavenly Father uses fallen angels such as Satan (Job 1:6-12; 2:1-7) and the unnamed spirit who enticed King Ahab to his death through deception (I Kings 22:19-23; II Chr. 18:18-22), pagan prophets such as Balaam (Num. 22:5-24:25), and despotic men such as Babylonian king Nebuchadnezzar (Jer. 25:9; 27:6; 43:10) and Persian king Cyrus (Isa. 44:28; 45:1-4; II Chr. 36:22:23; Ezra 1:1-4) to accomplish His will. Despite what men and nations plot in their own minds to do, it is the will of God that is ultimately done:

PSALM 33:10 The LORD foils the plans of the nations; He thwarts the purposes of the peoples. 11 But **the plans of the LORD stand firm forever, the purposes of His heart through all generations**. (*NIV*)

Because God is using His creation to complete His plan, it is often incorrectly assumed that the Father is simply doing His best to rescue a plan gone horribly wrong. For instance, many believe that a powerful angel now called Satan (the Hebrew word for "adversary") rebelled and became the archenemy of God at some point in the distant past. They believe that this Adversary almost succeeded in derailing God's plan to bring many human sons into His family (Luke 3:38) by tempting Adam and Eve into disobeying God.

However (as this line of thought goes), the heavenly Father was able to salvage His plan for humanity by sending His Son Jesus to the earth to provide a means for humanity to be forgiven and saved from the sin and death that entered the world through Adam's choice (Rom. 5:12). It appears that although the devil and his angels will ultimately be defeated, first they will succeed in dragging down most of humanity into the fiery pit of hell with them (Matt. 25:41; Rev. 14:9-11; 20:10).

Yet this imaginary scenario is absolutely contradicted by the Scriptures, which show that the sacrifice of Yeshua for sin was part of God the Father's plan from the very beginning:

1 PETER 1:18 You know that you were ransomed from the futile ways inherited from your ancestors, not with perishable things like silver or gold, 19 but with the precious blood of Christ, like that of a lamb without defect or blemish. 20 **He was destined before the foundation of the world**, but was revealed at the end of the ages for your sake. (*NRSV*)

REVELATION 13:8 All inhabitants of the earth will worship the beast — all whose names have not been written in the Book of Life belonging to **the Lamb that was slain from the creation of the world**. (*NIV*)

II TIMOTHY 1:8 . . . God, 9 who saved us and called us to a holy calling, not because of our works but because of His own purpose and grace, **which He gave us in Christ Jesus before the ages began,** (*ESV*)

ACTS 2:22 "Men of Israel, listen to these words: Jesus the Nazarene, a man clearly attested to you by God with powerful deeds, wonders, and miraculous signs that God performed among you through him, just as you yourselves know — 23 this man, who was handed over **by the predetermined plan and foreknowledge of God**, you executed by nailing him to a cross at the hands of Gentiles." (*NET*)

ISAIAH 53:10 Yet **it was the LORD's will to crush him and cause him to suffer**, and though **the LORD makes his life a guilt offering**, he will see his offspring and prolong his days, and the will of the LORD will prosper in his hand. (*NIV*)

God did not have to improvise because the attack of Satan disrupted His original plan. The Messiah's sacrifice for mankind's salvation was not a revision or addition to the heavenly Father's initial blueprint. It was the focal point of the plan of God even BEFORE the creation.

To believe that **YHVH** had to change or modify His plan in any respect is to believe that it was initially imperfect. How could an omnipresent, omniscient and omnipotent God have designed a flawed plan that required revision to make it work? The simple answer is that a perfect God **would not**, indeed **could not**, have drafted an imperfect plan. Consequently, the design we now see unfolding must be EXACTLY what God intended from the very beginning!

Is "All" Too Lofty A Goal For God?

If taken at face value, the Bible convincingly shows that God the Father is all powerful and that He fully intends to bring His plan to a successful conclusion, despite the best efforts of those in the physical and spiritual realms. Therefore, what we see taking place in the world cannot be God scrambling to make the best of a bad situation, but rather God's original plan unfolding. But, as strange as it seems when viewed logically in the light of Scripture, this obvious conclusion that God the Father is in total control of all things is not acknowledged by most who profess to worship Him.

The reason most have concluded that God is NOT in absolute control is because they have accepted the idea that He has given His creation "free will." Even if the Eternal Father wants to save all of mankind (I Tim. 2:4), many believe that He can't because they have been taught that God will not force anyone to be saved against their will. Effectively, the common belief is that God has ceded His sovereignty to His creation. Therefore, the creation will determine the outcome of the divine plan, not God.

The Father may not want anyone to perish but everyone to come to repentance (II Pet. 3:9), but according to the prevailing view, God will NOT get what He desires. Because it is thought that He has given man the "free will" to choose life or death, some will choose NOT to be saved. In this warped scenario, the choices of mortal men are allowed to override the outcome desired by the immortal God.

Yet does this understanding square with what the Bible says? Let's see what the Scriptures teach about God's plan for ALL mankind:

JOHN 12:32 "And I, when I am lifted up from the earth, will **draw** [helkuso] **ALL people** to myself." (*NRSV*)

In this statement, Messiah Yeshua gives us a glimpse into what God planned to accomplish through the sacrifice of His Son. It's clear from the next verse (John 12:33) that the phrase "lifted up" was a reference to Yeshua's impending crucifixion. The Messiah plainly understood that his sacrificial death was a necessary part of God's plan which would eventually lead to ALL mankind accepting him as their Lord ("Master"). Paul expands on the words of Yeshua to confirm the end result of his atoning death:

PHILIPPIANS 2:8 He humbled himself, by becoming obedient to the point of death — even death on a cross! 9 As a result God exalted him and gave him the name that is above every name, 10 so that at the name of Jesus **EVERY knee** will bow — in heaven and on earth and under the earth — 11 and **EVERY tongue** confess that Jesus Christ is Lord **to the glory of God the Father**. (*NET*)

Yeshua's ability to put aside his own desires and do the will of the Father resulted in God exalting him above all things except Himself (I Cor. 15:27). In the end, the entire creation will bow to Yeshua and confess that he is Lord. This outcome will bring glory to God the Father, because it will signal the successful completion of this phase of His plan.

TITUS 2:11 For the grace of God has appeared **for the salvation of ALL men**, (*RSV*)

Paul tells Titus that God's unmerited favor, which was manifested in the appearance of Messiah Yeshua, will ultimately lead to the salvation of all mankind.

I TIMOTHY 2:3 . . . **God our Saviour**, 4 **who will have ALL men to be saved**, and to come to the knowledge of the truth. (*DRA*)

In his first letter to Timothy, Paul states that God will have all of humanity come to a knowledge of the truth and be saved. He doesn't say how or when this will happen, but it is communicated as a certainty. Because this statement is so definitive, many modern translations try to water it down by rendering it as "God, who **desires** all men to be saved." The implication of translating it this way is that God really does WANT to save everyone, but for some reason He won't be able to accomplish that goal.

Since we have already seen from the Scriptures that God's will and purpose cannot be thwarted, this slight change in rendering does nothing to invalidate the underlying sentiment of Paul's statement. If the omnipotent God truly desires all men to be saved, there is nothing in this universe that can stop that outcome from happening. Therefore, we are left to decide whether we believe God is powerful enough to accomplish His will. Unfortunately, many have believed Satan's deception that He ultimately will not able to achieve this desire.

I CORINTHIANS 15:22 For just as **in Adam ALL die**, so also **in Christ ALL will be made alive**. 23 But each in his own order . . . (*CSB*)

ROMANS 5:18 Therefore just as one man's trespass led to **condemnation for ALL**, so one man's act of righteousness leads to **justification and life for ALL**. (*NRSV*)

We know that everyone since Adam has died because of sin (Rom. 5:12). The only human never to have sinned was Yeshua the Messiah (II Cor. 5:21; Heb. 4:15; I John 3:5), and sin still caused his death because he had to die for the sins of the world (I John 2:2). So when Paul contrasts the death that was brought by Adam with the life that will be brought by Messiah, he has to be talking about the entirety of humanity. "All" humans have been condemned to death because of Adam's decision to disobey; for Paul's comparison to be true, the same "all" must eventually be justified and made alive by Messiah's act of righteousness.

II PETER 3:9 The Lord is not slow in keeping His promise, as some people think of slowness; on the contrary, He is patient with you; for **it is not His purpose that anyone should be destroyed, but that EVERYONE should turn from his sins.** (*CJB*)

If it truly is NOT God's purpose to destroy anyone, but rather to see all mankind repent, how can anyone or anything prevent that from happening? As we are told in the Scriptures, the purpose within *YHVH*'s heart will stand firm forever (Psa. 33:11) and His plan will be fulfilled (Isa. 46:10).

I TIMOTHY 4:10 . . . We have put our hope in **the living God, who is the Savior of ALL men, and especially of those who believe.** (*NIV*)

Paul received his insights into the mystery of God by revelation from the glorified Messiah himself (Gal. 1:11-12; Eph. 3:3). He probably understood what God was accomplishing better than anyone else, before or since. Throughout his letters, Paul casually drops theological bombshells regarding universal salvation. Here in his first letter to Timothy, he plainly states that God will save all mankind, starting specifically with believers in Yeshua the Messiah. Once Paul's universalist view is recognized for what it truly is, it's interesting to note how often he states or alludes to the salvation of all mankind in his letters.

Is Our Destiny Preordained By God?

Another controversial matter that Paul addresses in several places is the topic of predestination. In fact, his letter to the Ephesian congregation contains a considerable exposition on this concept and how it ties in to universalism:

EPHESIANS 1:3 Blessed be the God and Father of our Lord Jesus Christ, who has blessed us in Christ with every spiritual blessing in the heavenly places, 4 even as **He chose us in him before the foundation of the world**, that we should be holy and blameless before Him. In love 5 **He predestined us for adoption as sons through Jesus Christ, according to the purpose of His will**, 6 to the praise of His glorious **grace**, with which He has blessed us in the Beloved. (*ESV*)

Paul gets right to the heart of his message quickly. In verse 4, he tells the believers in Ephesus that God the Father "chose us" (each believer) to be blessed in Messiah Yeshua "before the foundation of the world." Many claim that this choosing refers to the church as a whole, and not to every individual believer. This view, however, is based more on the natural human aversion to the concept of predestination than on the actual teaching of Paul.

In verse 5, Paul tells the Ephesians that in love God **predestined** believers for adoption as His sons through Messiah Yeshua. He did this "according to the pleasure of His will," as the *New English Translation* renders the final part of verse 5. In other words, the heavenly Father did this because it's what He wanted to do. It's the way God decided to achieve His goal of ultimately bringing all mankind into His family.

As Paul explains elsewhere, God does not choose us because of anything we **have done** or **will do** in the future (II Tim. 1:9; Rom. 9:11). Instead, each of us was chosen because God the Father showed us **favor**. The Greek root word translated "grace" in verse 6 is *charis*. Although it is usually rendered "grace" in the New Testament, it literally means to bestow undeserved "favor" on someone. God predestined each one who is called and chosen in this age to the exclusion of all others. When He did this before time as we know it began, He was showing us unmerited favor, as Paul told Timothy:

II TIMOTHY 1:8 . . . God, 9 who has saved us and called us to a holy life — **not because of anything we have done but because of His own purpose and grace**. This grace was given us in Christ Jesus before the beginning of time, (*NIV*)

Paul's comments elevating God's grace above our works must be viewed in the light of his understanding of predestination. Paul never denigrated God's Law (Rom. 7:16; Gal. 3:21) or a believer's observance of it (Rom. 3:31; I Cor. 7:19). Rather, he showed that God's calling does not depend on man's desire or effort, but solely on the Father's mercy (Rom. 9:16). Yeshua himself stated this to the Jews of his day:

JOHN 6:44 "**No one can come to me unless the Father who sent me draws** [helkuse] **him**. And I will raise him up on the last day." (*ESV*)

JOHN 6:63 "It is the Spirit who gives life, the flesh is no help. The words I have spoken to you are Spirit and life, 64 yet some among you do not trust." (For Yeshua knew from the outset which ones would not trust him, also which one would betray him.) 65 "This," he said, "is why I told you that **no one can come to me unless the Father has made it possible for him**." (*CJB*)

Those who truly come to the Messiah do not simply decide for themselves one day to do so. If we believe the words of Yeshua, only those God specifically "draws" come to him. The word translated "draws" in John 6:44 is from the Greek root *helko*. Here is what Bauer, Gingrich, Arndt, and Danker (*BGAD*) have to say about the literal meaning of this word:

To move an object from one area to another in a pulling motion, *draw*, with implication that the object being moved is incapable of propelling itself or in the case of pers[ons] is unwilling to do so voluntarily, in either case with implication of exertion on the part of the mover. (*Greek-English Lexicon of the New Testament and Other Early Christian Literature*, 3rd edition)

Interestingly, *helkuso* (a form of the same Greek root word found in John 6:44) is used in Yeshua's statement that his sacrificial death would eventually "draw" all people to Him (John 12:32). Again, the implication is that these people will not come voluntarily, but will come because of the action of God.

EPHESIANS 1:7 In him we have redemption through his blood, the for-giveness of our trespasses, according to the riches of His **grace**, 8 which He lavished upon us, in all wisdom and insight 9 making known to us **the mystery of His will, according to His purpose**, which He set forth in Christ 10 as **a plan for the fullness of time, to unite ALL things in him, things in heaven and things on earth.** *(ESV)*

Paul plainly tells us here that the mystery of God's will is that He is uniting all things in heaven and earth to Himself through His Son, Yeshua. Every facet of the Father's plan is aimed at achieving the goal of reconciling all things back to Himself, as Paul also stated in his second letter to the Corinthians:

II CORINTHIANS 5:18 All this is from **God, who reconciled us to Himself through Christ** and gave us the **ministry of reconciliation:** 19 that **God was reconciling the world to Himself in Christ**, not counting men's sins against them. And He has committed to us the message of reconciliation. *(NIV)*

God's goal is for us to develop His godly character and become spiritually complete; He wants His children to "grow up" to become just like Him (Matt. 5:48). The way we become like Him is through the work of His Holy Spirit in us during the process of reconciliation. God is NOT working with everyone at this time; instead, He is only calling a few in this age (John 6:44) who were predestined before the beginning of time to fulfill God's purpose:

EPHESIANS 1:11 In him we have obtained an inheritance, **having been pre-destined according to the purpose of Him who works all things according to the counsel of His will,** 12 so that we who were the first to hope in Christ might be to the praise of his glory. 13 In him you also, when you heard the word of truth, the gospel of your salvation, and believed in him, were sealed with the promised Holy Spirit, 14 who is the guarantee of our inheritance until we acquire possession of it, to the praise of his glory. *(ESV)*

In the 2nd chapter of Ephesians, Paul specifically states that our predestined salvation is not based on our works. Rather, the favor God shows us is a gift:

EPHESIANS 2:4 But God, being rich in mercy, because of the great love with which He loved us, 5 even when we were dead in our trespasses, made us alive together with Christ — by **grace** you have been saved — 6 and raised us up with him and seated us with Him in the heavenly places in Christ Jesus, 7 so that in the coming ages He might show the immeasurable riches of His **grace** in kindness toward us in Christ Jesus. 8 For by **grace** you have been saved through faith. And **this is not your own doing; it is the gift of God,** 9 **not a result of works,** so that no one may boast. 10 For **we are His workmanship, created in Christ Jesus for good works, which God prepared beforehand, that we should walk in them**. *(ESV)*

Our salvation does not give us cause to boast. We are God's handiwork, His creation. He has made us what we are; the good works we do were preor-dained before the beginning of time. Therefore, we can take no credit for doing them. We earn NONE of the good things God does for us; they are a divine gift:

JAMES 1:17 **Every good gift and every perfect gift is from above**, coming down from the Father of lights with whom there is no variation or shadow due to change. (*ESV*)

In his letter to Titus, Paul reiterates that our good works (which he urges believers to maintain) do not save us:

TITUS 3:4 But when the kindness and the love of God our Savior toward man appeared, 5 **not by works of righteousness which we have done, but according to His mercy He saved us**, through the washing of regeneration and renewing of the Holy Spirit, 6 whom He poured out on us abundantly through Jesus Christ our Savior, 7 that having been justified by His **grace** we should become heirs according to the hope of eternal life. 8 This is a faithful saying, and these things I want you to affirm constantly, that those who have believed in God should be careful to maintain **good works**. These things are good and profitable to men. (*NKJV*)

Continuing in his letter to the Ephesians, Paul spells out how the mystery of God applied to those Gentiles in Ephesus:

EPHESIANS 3:1 This is the reason that I Paul am a prisoner for Christ Jesus for the sake of you Gentiles — 2 for surely you have already heard of the commission of God's **grace** that was given me for you, 3 and how **the mystery was made known to me by revelation**, as I wrote above in a few words, 4 a reading of which will enable you to perceive my understanding of **the mystery of Christ**. 5 **In former generations this mystery was not made known to humankind**, as it has now been revealed to his holy apostles and prophets by the Spirit: 6 that is, **the Gentiles have become fellow heirs, members of the same body, and sharers in the promise in Christ Jesus through the gospel**. (*ESV*)

Paul was a very learned man, having studied extensively at the feet of Gamaliel the Elder (Acts 22:3; cf. 5:34), one of the brightest Jewish sages of his day. However, he takes no credit for having figured out for himself the mystery of God. Instead, Paul clearly states that this mystery (which had been hidden from all former generations) was made known to him by revelation from the Messiah Yeshua (Acts 26:15-18; Gal. 1:11-12). This mystery was that just as the remnant of God's chosen people (the Jews) were destined for salvation, so were the rest of the people from all the nations ("the Gentiles").

Paul addresses this universal salvation of all mankind in his letter to the Roman assembly:

ROMANS 11:25 Lest you be wise in your own sight, I want you to understand this **mystery**, brothers: A partial hardening has come upon Israel, until the fullness of the Gentiles has come in. 26 And **in this way all Israel will be saved**, as it is written, "The Deliverer will come from Zion, he will banish ungodliness from Jacob"; 27 "and this will be my covenant with them when I take away their sins." 28 As regards the gospel, they are enemies of God for your sake. But as regards election, they are beloved for the sake of their forefathers. 29 For the gifts and the calling of God are irrevocable. 30 For just as you were at one time disobedient to God but now have received mercy because of their disobedience, 31 so they too have now been disobedient in order that by the mercy shown to you they also may now receive mercy. 32 For **God has consigned** [sunekleisen] **ALL to disobedience, that he may have mercy on ALL.** 33 Oh, the depth of the riches and wisdom and knowledge of God! How unsearchable are his judgments and how inscrutable his ways! 34 "For who has known the mind of the Lord, or who has been His counselor?" 35 "Or who has given a gift to Him that he might be repaid?" 36 For from Him and through Him and to Him are all things. To Him be glory forever. Amen. (*ESV*)

In this chapter, Paul addresses how the salvation of all Israel will be achieved. He clearly states that the unbelieving Jews, those who don't accept Yeshua because God Himself blinded them (Rom. 11:7-10), are still loved by Him. But he goes on to show that the salvation of all Israel is not the final goal of God's plan. In verse 32 he uses a form of the Greek root word *sugkleio* (which literally means to "hem in," "enclose" or "imprison") to describe what God has done to **all** men. Specifically, Paul tells us that God has **imprisoned** ALL mankind (both Jew and Gentile) in disobedience.

Why would God do this? Paul tells us the reason is so that in the end He might have mercy on all. This aspect of God's plan is so awesome to Paul that he launches into a praise of God's unsearchable and unknowable ways, which are beyond man's ability to understand. To paraphrase Paul, everything is FROM God, THROUGH God, and TO God. As humans, we can take credit for nothing.

EPHESIANS 3:7 Of this gospel I have become a servant according to the gift of God's **grace** that was given me by the working of His power. 8 Although I am the very least of all the saints, this **grace** was given to me to bring to the Gentiles the news of the boundless riches of Christ, 9 and to make everyone see what is the plan of **the mystery hidden for ages in God** who created all things; 10 so that through the church the wisdom of God in its rich variety might now be made known to the rulers and authorities in the heavenly places. 11 **This was in accordance with the eternal purpose that He has carried out in Christ Jesus our Lord**, 12 in whom we have access to God in boldness and confidence through faith in him. (*ESV*)

Here Paul says that even though he is the least of those whom God has called (cf. I Tim. 1:13; I Cor. 15:9), through the gift of God's favor he was chosen to bring this good news about the mystery of God to the people of the nations. This is according to God's age-lasting purpose, which is being accomplished through the Lord Yeshua the Messiah.

EPHESIANS 3:18 I pray that you may have the power to comprehend, with all the saints, what is the breadth and length and height and depth, 19 and to know the love of Christ that surpasses knowledge, so that you may be filled with all the fullness of God. 20 Now to **Him who by the power at work within us is able to accomplish abundantly far more than all we can ask or imagine**, 21 to Him be glory in the church and in Christ Jesus to all generations, forever and ever. Amen. (*NRSV*)

Paul realized that God's mysterious plan was very hard for man to grasp. Here he prays that God would help the saints understand the fullness ("breadth, length, height and depth") of His plan. He finishes this section of his letter by stating that the **power of God** (i.e., the Holy Spirit) working within us is able to accomplish much more than we can request or even understand.

Paul also speaks of predestination in his letter to the Romans:

ROMANS 8:28 And we know that for those who love God all things work together for good, for those who are called according to His purpose. 29 For **those whom He foreknew He also predestined to be conformed to the image of His Son**, in order that he might be the firstborn among many brothers. 30 And **those whom He predestined He also called**, and **those whom He called He also justified**, and **those whom He justified He also glorified**. (*ESV*)

Messiah Yeshua is the focal point of the Father's plan, the firstborn of many sons of God to come. Paul here states that for those who love God, everything that happens eventually works out for their benefit. God predestined those who are being called by Him to be justified in Messiah. Those He justified by the Messiah's sacrifice will also be glorified and used to further His plan.

When the topic of predestination is understood properly, we have to realize that nothing happens apart from God's plan. Even though we occasionally go through painful trials, these are ultimately for our good and will help us to reach spiritual maturity, as James explains:

JAMES 1:2 Consider it a great joy, my brothers, whenever you experience various trials, 3 knowing that **the testing of your faith produces endurance**. 4 But endurance must do its complete work, so that you may be **mature and complete**, lacking nothing. (*CSB*)

In the 9th chapter of Romans, Paul used the example of Jacob and Esau to illustrate how God has predestined those He calls:

ROMANS 9:10 And even more to the point is the case of Rivkah; for both her children were conceived in a single act with Yitz'chak, our father; 11 and before they were born, before they had done anything at all, either good or bad (**so that God's plan might remain a matter of His sovereign choice, not dependent on what they did, but on God, who does the calling**), 12 it was said to her, "The older will serve the younger." 13 This accords with where it is written, "Ya'akov I loved, but Esav I hated." (*CJB*)

As a good illustration of God's predestination, Paul cites the example of Jacob and Esau. He tells us that before their birth, before they had done anything (good or bad), God decided to use Jacob in His plan, but to reject Esau. Paul clearly states that the choice God made was based on Him being the supreme ruler of the universe, not on anything Jacob or Esau did. Some try and make this Scripture mean that God foresaw what each of the twins WOULD do later in their lives and then chose Jacob over Esau based on that fore-knowledge. But that interpretation specifically denies the point Paul is making here about God's absolute authority, not foreknowledge, being the basis for the selection.

Human nature causes most people confronted with this scenario to assert that God was unfair to Esau. Paul anticipated this objection and addressed it next:

ROMANS 9:14 What then shall we say? Is God unjust? Not at all! 15 For He says to Moses, "I will have mercy on whom I have mercy, and I will have compassion on whom I have compassion." 16 **It does not, therefore, depend on man's desire or effort, but on God's mercy**. 17 For the Scripture says to Pharaoh: "I raised you up for this very purpose, that I might display My power in you and that My name might be proclaimed in all the earth." 18 Therefore God has mercy on whom He wants to have mercy, and He hardens whom He wants to harden. (*NIV*)

No, God is not unjust, according to Paul. The reason is because God's plan is not based on what a man wants or what a man does, but rather on God's mercy. God used Pharaoh for a specific purpose, so that the whole world might understand His awesome power. God had mercy on the children of Israel, but He hardened Pharaoh's heart, bringing destruction upon the land of Egypt. All of these events were orchestrated by God the Father to further His plan and purpose for mankind.

Again, Paul expects that what he has just said will elicit hostile questions from his readers. "If God hardens my heart and makes me stand in opposition to His will (just as He did with Pharaoh), why does He still punish me? How am I truly to blame? Who can withstand God's purpose?"

ROMANS 9:19 One of you will say to me: "Then why does God still blame us? For who resists His will?" 20 But **who are you, O man, to talk back to God?** "Shall what is formed say to Him who formed it, 'Why did You make me like this?'" 21 Does not the potter have the right to make out of the same lump of clay some pottery for noble purposes and some for common use? 22 What if God, choosing to show His wrath and make His power known, bore with great patience the objects of His wrath — prepared for destruction? 23 What if He did this to make the riches of His glory known to **the objects of His mercy, whom He prepared in advance for glory** — 24 **even us, whom He also called**, not only from the Jews but also from the Gentiles? (*NIV*)

Paul answers these questions simply. Since **YHVH** the Father is the Creator and Ruler of the universe, He can do as He pleases. Those created have no right to ask the Creator why they are made a certain way. He shows that God, the Master Potter, has created some vessels for holy use and some for common use (cf. II Tim. 2:20-21). Paul goes on to state that the common vessels will be broken during the process of God's plan being carried out to show the holy vessels the riches of God's glory.

Paul's response regarding God's process for accomplishing His plan closely mirrors the Father's words to Job, when he questioned God following the occurrence of a series of tragedies in his life. God allowed Satan to test Job by destroying his children, his material goods (Job 1:13-19), and his health (Job 2:7). Being a righteous man, Job did not understand why God was putting him through such pain and suffering.

After repeatedly professing his innocence and asking God to **prove** that He was justified in causing his suffering, God finally answered Job with a series of questions designed to illustrate His magnificance and power (Job 38:1-41:34). Delineating His awesome acts of creation, God caused Job to see that His power and authority gave the heavenly Father the right to do as He pleased in his life:

JOB 42:1 1 Then Job answered the Lord: 2 "**I know that You can do all things and that no plan of Yours can be ruined**. 3 You asked, 'Who is this that made My purpose unclear by saying things that are not true?' **Surely I spoke of things I did not understand; I talked of things too wonderful for me to know**. 4 You said, 'Listen now, and I will speak. I will ask you questions, and you must answer Me.' 5 My ears had heard of You before, but now my eyes have seen You. 6 So now I hate myself; I will change my heart and life. I will sit in the dust and ashes." (**NCV**)

If we accept the biblical position that God **does** have the right to make some human vessels for honor and some for destruction, the question then becomes: "Will those broken vessels of wrath be cast away forever by God after their use, or will the Master Potter reshape them into holy vessels at some future point?" By recognizing the scriptural doctrine of universal salvation, we can see that God has committed to eventually remake those common vessels into holy vessels.

PHILIPPIANS 2:12 Therefore, my dear friends, as you have always obeyed — not only in my presence, but now much more in my absence — continue to work out your salvation with fear and trembling, 13 for **it is God who works in you to will and to act according to His good purpose**. (**NIV**)

Paul tells us that we are to "work out our salvation with fear and trembling." However, he goes on to show that it really isn't us who does the work, but God. It is the heavenly Father who causes us to "will" (want to do something) and to "act" on those desires. This is according to His purpose, which ultimately is for our good.

Paul clearly teaches predestination. What Calvin, Luther, and others who recognized this teaching missed was that Paul also taught universal salvation. They did not understand the timing aspect of Paul's teaching. Yes, some were predestined to be saved in this age. However, this did not mean that the rest who are not saved in this age are forever lost. God will save all mankind, but He will do so in the way and at the time He decides. Each person will be saved when it is his or her time (I Cor. 15:22).

Predestination – Does the Rest of the Bible Support Paul's Teaching?

There are very few today who accept the doctrine of predestination. Most steadfastly assert that humanity has free will, and that God does not limit the will of man, but allows him to exercise that will even to the point that it overrides His own. But what do the rest of the Scriptures have to say about God's will and the fulfillment of His purpose? Let's examine some passages from the Old Testament to see if this teaching was a new innovation by Paul, or if it had its roots in the Hebrew Scriptures:

JEREMIAH 10:23 You know, O LORD, that **man is not master of his way; man's course is not within his choice, nor is it for him to direct his step.** (*NAB*)

This is a very straightforward and direct statement from Jeremiah. He clearly states that man does not control his destiny, does not choose his own path or direct his own steps. The clear implication is that it is God who does these things.

PROVERBS 16:9 In his mind a man plans his course, but **the LORD directs his steps**. (*NAB*)

The *Artscroll Tanach Series* is a set of Jewish commentaries on the Hebrew Scriptures from talmudic, midrashic, and rabbinic sources. Here is what the commentary on Proverbs says about this proverb and its companion statement from Jeremiah:

Like many other verses in Scripture, this verse teaches that man is not in control of his own destiny. He can only make plans; the ultimate outcome, however, is in the hands of Hashem. The prophet Jeremiah also proclaims that (*Jeremiah* 10:23) . . . *a man's path is not his own.* Accordingly, we must learn to place our trust in Hashem and fervently pray that He set us on the path of success so that we may see our plans reach fruition (*Meiri*). (p. 301, vol. 2, *Mishlei / Proverbs*)

Similar comments are found elsewhere in the psalms of David, as well as in the proverbs of Solomon:

PSALM 139:16 Your eyes saw my unformed body. **All the days ordained for me were written in Your book before one of them came to be.** (*NIV*)

PSALM 37:23 **The steps of a man are established by the LORD**, and He delights in his way. (*NASU*)

PROVERBS 20:24 **Man's steps are ordained by the LORD**, how then can man understand his way? (*NASU*)

The *Artscroll Tanach Series* commentary on Proverbs ties together the theme of these final two verses:

This oft-quoted verse (similar to *Psalms* 37:23 . . . *By Hashem are a man's footsteps established*) expresses the limited extent of our ability to understand Divine Providence. Man is a puppet in the hands of Hashem and as such often has no comprehension of the circumstances of his mortal existence. But this itself can be a source of encouragement, for we trust that whatever our condition, Hashem has our best interests at heart. (p. 408, vol. 2, *Mishlei / Proverbs*)

Notice how similar this rabbinic view is to that of the apostle Paul, who stated that God causes everything that happens to work together for the good of those who love Him and are called in accordance with His purpose (Rom. 8:28).

PROVERBS 19:21 The human mind may devise many plans, but **it is the purpose of the LORD that will be established**. (*NRSV*)

PROVERBS 16:1 A man may arrange his thoughts, but **what he says depends on the LORD**. (*JPS Tanakh*)

These two related statements from Solomon indicate that the mind of a man does have some ability to formulate independent thoughts and schemes. However, when it comes to actions and spoken words to express those thoughts, man is dependent upon God. There is no such thing as "chance" or "luck"; God is in control of all things:

PROVERBS 16:33 The lot is cast into the lap, but **its every decision is from the LORD**. (*CSB*)

Numerous stories from the Old Testament show the hand of God in planning and carrying out His will through the actions of men. Let's look at some of them to see how God guided events to fulfill His purpose.

JOSEPH

First, let's look at the story of Joseph, the favorite son of Jacob by his beloved wife Rachel. Because of the special treatment that Joseph received from Jacob, the rest of his brothers hated him (Gen. 37:3-4). Eventually, this hatred caused them to plot to kill Joseph. Reuben, the oldest son of Jacob, was able to keep the other brothers from slaying him. However, they did sell Joseph into slavery and deceive his father into believing that he had been killed by a wild animal.

Joseph ended up as a slave in Egypt, but God was with him in everything that he did. Thirteen years after being betrayed by his brothers, while Joseph was being held unjustly in prison, God gave Pharaoh a prophetic dream that he did not understand. But God also gave Joseph the ability to accurately interpret that dream for the ruler of Egypt of the famine that He was about to send upon the land (Gen. 41:25, 28). Because of the wisdom and discernment that Joseph displayed in regard to the dream, Pharaoh elevated him to the second highest position in all the land. He also placed him in charge of the effort to prepare the land for the famine that was coming after seven years.

When the prophesied famine struck, Jacob heard that there was food in Egypt. He sent his 10 oldest sons down from Canaan to Egypt to purchase grain. Joseph immediately knew them when they arrived, but they did not recognize him. After testing his brothers to see if their hearts had changed since their earlier actions against him, Joseph revealed himself to them. In doing so, he stated that **everything** that had happened to him was predestined by God:

GENESIS 45:4 And Joseph said to his brothers, "Please come near to me." So they came near. Then he said: "I am Joseph your brother, whom you sold into Egypt. 5 But now, do not therefore be grieved or angry with yourselves because you sold me here; for **God sent me before you to preserve life**. 6 For these two years the famine has been in the land, and there are still five years in which there will be neither plowing nor harvesting. 7 And **God sent me before you to preserve a posterity for you in the earth, and to save your lives by a great deliverance**. 8 So now **it was not you who sent me here, but God**; and He has made me a father to Pharaoh, and lord of all his house, and a ruler throughout all the land of Egypt." (*NKJV*)

Joseph realized that everything he had suffered was part of the plan of God. Therefore, he didn't hold his brothers liable for what happened to him, but rather understood that God the Father was responsible. This realization was what allowed Joseph to forgive his brothers for their plot against him:

GENESIS 50:18 His brothers then came and threw themselves down before him. "We are your slaves," they said. 19 But Joseph said to them, "Don't be afraid. Am I in the place of God? 20 **You intended to harm me, but God intended it for good to accomplish what is now being done, the saving of many lives**." (*NIV*)

Although his brothers acted against him out of hatred (motivated in large part by divinely-inspired events such as his dreams), Joseph did not hold them accountable for their actions. He forgave them because he realized that God accomplished His will through them. In this, we see that Joseph was a type of the Messiah, who also forgave his brothers the Jews for their persecution and crucifixion of him (Luke 23:34).

The Jews of Yeshua's day did what they did because God blinded them to His plan (John 12:37-40; Rom. 11:7-10), in order for His atoning sacrifice for mankind to be successfully offered:

ACTS 3:13 "The God of Abraham, Isaac and Jacob, the God of our fathers, has glorified His servant Jesus. You handed him over to be killed, and you disowned him before Pilate, though he had decided to let him go. 14 You disowned the holy and righteous one and asked that a murderer be released to you. 15 You killed the author of life, but God raised him from the dead. We are witnesses of this. 16 By faith in the name of Jesus, this man whom you see and know was made strong. It is Jesus' name and the faith that comes through him that has given this complete healing to him, as you can all see. 17 Now, **brothers, I know that you acted in ignorance, as did your leaders.** 18 But **this is how God fulfilled what He had foretold through all the prophets, saying that His Christ would suffer.**" (*NIV*)

I CORINTHIANS 2:7 But we speak God's wisdom in a **mystery,** the **hidden wisdom which God predestined before the ages** to our glory; 8 the wisdom which none of the rulers of this age has understood; for **if they had understood it they would not have crucified the Lord of glory**; (*NASU*)

By understanding that God is ultimately responsible for all things, it is possible to see why God commanded us to forgive those who oppose, oppress and attack us:

MATTHEW 5:44 "But I say to you, **love your enemies, bless those who curse you, do good to those who hate you, and pray for those who spitefully use you and persecute you,** 45 that you may be sons of your Father in heaven; for He makes His sun rise on the evil and on the good, and sends rain on the just and on the unjust." (*NKJV*)

To really forgive our enemies, it helps for us to recognize that God's blinding has caused them to be against us. They are "vessels of wrath" which God is using to make known to us "the riches of His glory" (Rom. 9:22-23). This realization of God's sovereignty and His control of events was why Joseph could truly forgive his brothers of their transgression against him.

PHARAOH

The story of the Pharaoh of the Exodus is of great benefit in understanding how God brings events to pass in order to fulfill His will. As quoted earlier from the 9th chapter of Romans, Paul clearly stated that God hardened Pharaoh's heart in order for Him to prove something to the world (Rom. 9:17-18). Let's start the story with God's words to Abram 430 years prior to the Exodus:

GENESIS 15:13 Then the LORD said to Abram, "Know for certain that your offspring will be sojourners in a land that is not theirs and will be servants there, and they will be afflicted for four hundred years. 14 But I will bring judgment on the nation that they serve, and afterward they shall come out with great possessions." (*ESV*)

This prophecy from God to Abram specifies an exact time period – 400 years. According to the cantillation signs in the Hebrew text of Genesis 15:13, the phrase "400 years" refers back to the words, "your descendants will be strangers in a land that is not theirs." The years of Abraham's offspring being strangers in a strange land began with the birth of Isaac, NOT with the Egyptian enslavement. Therefore the text ought to be understood as follows: "Know certainly that your descendants will be strangers in a land that is not theirs . . . 400 years." It was 400 years from the date of Isaac's birth until the Exodus, and 430 years (Exo. 12:40-41; Gal. 3:17) from the time of God's covenant with Abram.

Notice that God pronounced a very specific time period for these very specific events. God didn't just allow them to happen or foresee them happening. He directly acted to cause them to happen at a precise point in time. In his commentary on the Exodus, the Jewish sage Rashi wrote that the covenant of the pieces (Gen. 15:13), the angelic announcement of Isaac's birth (Gen. 18:10), his actual birth (Gen. 21:2), and the Exodus from Egypt (Exo. 12:41) all took place on exactly "the selfsame day" on the Hebrew calendar:

On the fifteenth of Nisan the ministering angels came to Abraham to announce (it) to him, and on the fifteenth of Nisan Isaac was born, and on the fifteenth of Nisan there was decreed the decree "between the pieces." (p. 121, vol. II, *The Pentateuch and Rashi's Commentary*)

Clearly, the fact that all these events occurred on the same date was not coincidence, but part of the design of God's plan. For that plan to be fulfilled precisely as God desired, Pharaoh had to do exactly as God intended. When Moses first received instructions from the Angel of *YHVH* from the burning bush, a brief outline of the events that would occur during the Exodus was given to him:

EXODUS 3:16 "Go and gather the elders of Israel together and say to them, 'The LORD, the God of your fathers, the God of Abraham, of Isaac, and of Jacob, has appeared to me, saying, "I have observed you and what has been done to you in Egypt, 17 and I promise that I will bring you up out of the affliction of Egypt to the land of the Canaanites, the Hittites, the Amorites, the Perizzites, the Hivites, and the Jebusites, a land flowing with milk and honey." ' 18 And they will listen to your voice, and you and the elders of Israel shall go to the king of Egypt and say to him, 'The LORD, the God of the Hebrews, has met with us; and now, please let us go a three days' journey into the wilderness, that we may sacrifice to the LORD our God.' 19 But **I know that the king of Egypt will not let you go unless compelled by a mighty hand**. 20 So I will stretch out My hand and strike Egypt with all the wonders that I will do in it; after that he will let you go. 21 And I will give this people favor in the sight of the Egyptians; and when you go, you shall not go empty, 22 but each woman shall ask of her neighbor, and any woman who lives in her house, for silver and gold jewelry, and for clothing. You shall put them on your sons and on your daughters. So you shall plunder the Egyptians." (*ESV*)

God later added some additional details about the reaction of Pharaoh to the miracles God would grant Moses to perform:

EXODUS 4:21 And the LORD said to Moses, "When you go back to Egypt, see that you do before Pharaoh all the miracles that I have put in your power. But **I will harden his heart**, so that he will not let the people go. 22 Then you shall say to Pharaoh, 'Thus says the LORD, Israel is My firstborn son, 23 and I say to you, "Let My son go that he may serve Me." If you refuse to let him go, behold, I will kill your firstborn son.' " (*CJB*)

Here we see the first mention of God hardening the heart of Pharaoh. For the will of God to be carried out according to His plan in this matter, all 10 plagues (culminating with the death of the firstborn) had to occur. By hardening his heart, God ensured that Pharaoh didn't abandon his rebellion before God accomplished His objectives. He specifically tells Moses His plan shortly thereafter:

EXODUS 7:1 And the LORD said to Moses, "See, I have made you like God to Pharaoh, and your brother Aaron shall be your prophet. 2 You shall speak all that I command you, and your brother Aaron shall tell Pharaoh to let the people of Israel go out of his land. 3 But **I will harden Pharaoh's heart**, and though I multiply My signs and wonders in the land of Egypt, 4 Pharaoh will not listen to you. Then I will lay My hand on Egypt and bring My hosts, My people the children of Israel, out of the land of Egypt by great acts of judgment. 5 The Egyptians shall know that I am the LORD, when I stretch out my hand against Egypt and bring out the people of Israel from among them." (*ESV*)

The first time we specifically see it stated that God hardened Pharaoh's heart is after the 6th plague of boils:

EXODUS 9:11 The magicians could not stand before Moses because of the boils, for the boils were on the magicians as well as on all the Egyptians. 12 And **the LORD hardened Pharaoh's heart**, and he did not listen to them, just as the LORD had spoken to Moses. (*NASU*)

After hardening his heart to ensure that the punishment would continue, God then threatened Pharaoh and Egypt with another horrible plague:

EXODUS 9:13 Then the LORD said to Moses, "Get up early in the morning, confront Pharaoh and say to him, 'This is what the LORD, the God of the Hebrews, says: Let My people go, so that they may worship Me, 14 or this time I will send the full force of My plagues against you and against your officials and your people, so you may know that there is no one like Me in all the earth. 15 For by now I could have stretched out My hand and struck you and your people with a plague that would have wiped you off the earth. 16 But I **have raised you up for this very purpose, that I might show you My power and that My name might be proclaimed in all the earth**. 17 You still set yourself against My people and will not let them go. 18 Therefore, at this time tomorrow I will send the worst hailstorm that has ever fallen on Egypt, from the day it was founded till now.' " (*NIV*)

God clearly stated through Moses that He had raised up Pharaoh for the very purpose of revealing His power and glorifying His name through him. Could Pharaoh have stopped the plagues by giving in to God's demand to let His people go? No, we see from the very words of God that this was not an option. God's plan required that all 10 plagues be poured out on Egypt, and nothing (not even Pharaoh himself) could have been allowed to stop that from happening. **YHVH** the Father clearly and unambiguously states this fact over and over in the Exodus narrative:

EXODUS 10:1 Then the LORD said to Moses, "Go to Pharaoh, for **I have hardened his heart and the hearts of his officials** so that I may perform these miraculous signs of Mine among them 2 that you may tell your children and grandchildren how I dealt harshly with the Egyptians and how I performed My signs among them, and that you may know that I am the LORD." (*NIV*)

Again, after the 8th plague of locusts, Pharaoh seemed ready to give in (Exo. 10:16-17). However, we see that God once more intervened and hardened the heart of Pharaoh to stop him from accepting Moses' demands:

EXODUS 10:20 But **the LORD hardened Pharaoh's heart**, and he did not let the Israelites go. (*CSB*)

Likewise, after the 9th plague of darkness, Pharaoh was ready to acquiesce to Moses' request (Exo. 10:24). But once again, God did not allow him to do so:

EXODUS 10:27 But **the LORD hardened Pharaoh's heart**, and he would not let them go. (*JPS*)

In Exodus chapter 11, Moses told Pharaoh of the 10th and final plague that would fall upon Egypt: the death of the firstborn. Hot with anger at Pharaoh's refusal to let the Israelites go, Moses left Pharaoh's presence:

EXODUS 11:9 Then the LORD said to Moses, "**Pharaoh will not listen to you, that My wonders may be multiplied in the land of Egypt.**" 10 Moses and Aaron did all these wonders before Pharaoh, and **the LORD hardened Pharaoh's heart**, and he did not let the people of Israel go out of his land. (*ESV*)

Did Pharaoh have free will in this incident? A literal reading and acceptance of the biblical account at face value shows that the intervention of God was what caused Pharaoh to reject the requested release of the Israelites numerous times. God's hardening of Pharaoh's heart was the reason that the Egyptian firstborn died, and the reason that the Passover sacrifice was ultimately required.

Clearly this episode was NOT primarily about getting His people freed from slavery. Rather it was about establishing a literal salvation from Egypt for the Israelite firstborn that would symbolize the later salvation the spiritual firstborn would have through the sacrifice of Yeshua the Messiah, our Passover (I Cor. 5:7). The original was necessary to foreshadow the future. Consequently, God made sure that Pharaoh reacted in such a way that allowed that first Passover to occur as He had planned.

Now, back to the question Paul raised in Romans chapter 9: Was God unjust to punish Pharaoh after causing him to rebel against Him? Paul initially deflected this question by saying that the created have no right to question what the Creator does (Rom. 9:19-21). However, the apostle to the Gentiles then went on to explain that God is using most in this age simply as "vessels of wrath" (Rom. 9:22) in the process of showing mercy to His "assembly of the firstborn" (Heb. 12:23). Through these spiritual firstborn, God will eventually have mercy on all (Rom. 11:30-31).

SENNACHERIB

For another example of predestination in the *Tanakh*, let's look at the story of Sennacherib, the king of Assyria. Sennacherib came against Jersalem during the reign of Jewish king Hezekiah. His envoy proclaimed to the Jews that they should not look to King Hezekiah or to *YHVH* their God to save them. After putting on sackcloth, King Hezekiah sent Eliakim, Shebna, and the senior priests to the prophet Isaiah for God's input on the matter. Here is the message from *YHVH* that Isaiah sent back to the king:

ISAIAH 37:21 Then Isaiah son of Amoz sent a message to Hezekiah: "This is what the LORD, the God of Israel, says: Because you have prayed to Me concerning Sennacherib king of Assyria, 22 this is the word the LORD has spoken against him: "The Virgin Daughter of Zion despises and mocks you. The Daughter of Jerusalem tosses her head as you flee. 23 Who is it you have insulted and blasphemed? Against whom have you raised your voice and lifted your eyes in pride? Against the Holy One of Israel! 24 By your messengers you have heaped insults on the Lord. And you have said, 'With my many chariots I have ascended the heights of the mountains, the utmost heights of Lebanon. I have cut down its tallest cedars, the choicest of its pines. I have reached its remotest heights, the finest of its forests. 25 I have dug wells in foreign lands and drunk the water there. With the soles of my feet I have dried up all the streams of Egypt.' 26 Have you not heard? **Long ago I ordained it. In days of old I planned it; now I have brought it to pass, that you have turned fortified cities into piles of stone**. 27 Their people, drained of power, are dismayed and put to shame. They are like plants in the field, like tender green shoots, like grass sprouting on the roof, scorched before it grows up. 28 But I know where you stay and when you come and go and how you rage against Me. 29 Because you rage against Me and because your insolence has reached My ears, **I will put My hook in your nose and My bit in your mouth, and I will make you return by the way you came**." (*NIV*)

Through Isaiah, God told Hezekiah that He had long ago planned that which was then happening. God clearly stated that He had predestined and raised up Sennacherib and He had given him his victories over the nations he had conquered. To punish his impudence, pride, and lack of recognition of God's hand in his successes, God told King Hezekiah that He would drag Sennacherib back to Assyria in shame.

That very night, God fufilled His word regarding King Sennacherib:

II KINGS 19:35 And that night the angel of the LORD went out and struck down 185,000 in the camp of the Assyrians. And when people arose early in the morning, behold, these were all dead bodies. 36 Then Sennacherib king of Assyria departed and went home and lived at Nineveh. 37 And as he was worshiping in the house of Nisroch his god, Adrammelech and Sharezer, his sons, struck him down with the sword and escaped into the land of Ararat. And Esarhaddon his son reigned in his place. (*ESV*)

Clearly portrayed in this story is the fact that God alone is sovereign and that He organizes the rise and fall of world leaders (cf. Jer. 27:5 below).

NEBUCHADNEZZAR

In the prophecies of Jeremiah and Ezekiel, God shows that Babylonian king Nebuchadnezzar was His servant, used to accomplish His divine will. In addition, God stated that the Babylonian kingdom would continue under Nebuchadnezzar, his son (Nabonidus), and his grandson (Belshazzar). It was under the rule of Belshazzar that God would raise up Cyrus the Persian to conquer Babylon:

JEREMIAH 25:9 "I will summon all the peoples of the north and **My servant Nebuchadnezzar king of Babylon**," declares the LORD, "and I will bring them against this land and its inhabitants and against all the surrounding nations. I will completely destroy them and make them an object of horror and scorn, and an everlasting ruin." (*NIV*)

JEREMIAH 27:5 "It is I who by My great power and My outstretched arm have made the earth, with the men and animals that are on the earth, and **I give it to whomever it seems right to Me. 6 Now I have given all these lands into the hand of Nebuchadnezzar, the king of Babylon, My servant, and I have given him also the beasts of the field to serve him. 7 All the nations shall serve him and his son and his grandson**, until the time of his own land comes. Then many nations and great kings shall make him their slave. 8 But if any nation or kingdom will not serve this Nebuchadnezzar king of Babylon, and put its neck under the yoke of the king of Babylon, I will punish that nation with the sword, with famine, and with pestilence, declares the LORD, until I have consumed it by his hand. 9 So do not listen to your prophets, your diviners, your dreamers, your fortune-tellers, or your sorcerers, who are saying to you, 'You shall not serve the king of Babylon.' 10 For it is a lie that they are prophesying to you, with the result that you will be removed far from your land, and I will drive you out, and you will perish. 11 But any nation that will bring its neck under the yoke of the king of Babylon and serve him, I will leave on its own land, to work it and dwell there, declares the LORD." (*ESV*)

EZEKIEL 29:18 "Son of man, Nebuchadnezzar king of Babylon made his army labor hard against Tyre. Every head was made bald, and every shoulder was rubbed bare, yet neither he nor his army got anything from Tyre to pay for the labor that he had performed against her. 19 Therefore thus says the Lord GOD: Behold, I will give the land of Egypt to Nebuchadnezzar king of Babylon; and he shall carry off its wealth and despoil it and plunder it; and it shall be the wages for his army. 20 I have given him the land of Egypt as his payment for which he labored, because **they worked for Me**, declares the Lord GOD. (*ESV*)

JEREMIAH 43:10 "Then say to them, 'This is what the LORD Almighty, the God of Israel, says: I will send for **My servant Nebuchadnezzar king of Babylon**, and I will set his throne over these stones I have buried here; he will spread his royal canopy above them. 11 He will come and attack Egypt, **bringing death to those destined for death, captivity to those destined for captivity, and the sword to those destined for the sword.** 12 He will set fire to the temples of the gods of Egypt; he will burn their temples and take their gods captive. As a shepherd wraps his garment around him, so will he wrap Egypt around himself and depart from there unscathed. 13 There in the temple of the sun in Egypt he will demolish the sacred pillars and will burn down the temples of the gods of Egypt.' " (*NIV*)

God gave Nebuchadnezzar victory and used him to afflict those nations He purposed to punish. This Babylonian king was predestined by God to accomplish His purpose during a critical period of Judah's history.

CYRUS

Pharaoh, Sennacherib, and Nebuchadnezzar were not the only ancient rulers used by God to further His divine plan. The Persian king Cyrus was specifically named by God through the prophet Isaiah as one who would be given victory by God and then be used to fulfill His will:

ISAIAH 44:28 "**It is I who says of Cyrus, 'He is My shepherd! And he will perform all My desire.'** And he declares of Jerusalem, 'She will be built,' and of the temple, 'Your foundation will be laid.' " (*NASU*)

ISAIAH 45:1 "**Thus says the LORD to His anointed, to Cyrus, whose right hand I have held — to subdue nations before him** and loose the armor of kings, to open before him the double doors, so that the gates will not be shut: 2 'I will go before you and make the crooked places straight; I will break in pieces the gates of bronze and cut the bars of iron. 3 I will give you the treasures of darkness and hidden riches of secret places, **that you may know that I, the LORD, who call you by your name**, am the God of Israel. 4 For Jacob My servant's sake, and Israel My elect, **I have even called you by your name; I have named you, though you have not known Me.** 5 I am the LORD, and there is no other; there is no God besides Me. **I will gird you, though you have not known Me,** 6 **that they may know from the rising of the sun to its setting that there is none besides Me.** I am the LORD, and there is no other;' " (*NKJV*)

EZRA 1:1 Now in the first year of Cyrus king of Persia, that the word of the LORD by the mouth of Jeremiah might be fulfilled, **the LORD stirred up the spirit of Cyrus king of Persia**, so that he made a proclamation throughout all his kingdom, and also put it in writing, saying, 2 **Thus says Cyrus king of**

Persia: All the kingdoms of the earth the LORD God of heaven has given me. And He has commanded me to build Him a house at Jerusalem which is in Judah. *(NKJV)*

God raised up Cyrus for the express purpose of bringing about the downfall of Babylon and allowing His people, the Jews, to return to Jerusalem and rebuild the Temple there. Cyrus was predestined to accomplish a specific task for Almighty God, and the Eternal Father ensured that he successfully completed His purpose.

JEREMIAH

The prophet Jeremiah is one of several people mentioned in the Scriptures who was known by God before they were born:

JEREMIAH 1:4 The word of the LORD came to me, saying, 5 **"Before I formed you in the womb I knew you, before you were born I set you apart**; I appointed you as a prophet to the nations." 6 "Ah, Sovereign LORD," I said, "I do not know how to speak; I am only a child." 7 But the LORD said to me, "Do not say, 'I am only a child.' **You must go to everyone I send you to and say whatever I command you.**" *(NIV)*

According to the very words of God, Jeremiah did not have the free will to do anything other than what He told him to do.

Now let's move on to the New Testament to see others, both good and bad, who were predestined to fulfill God's purpose:

JOHN THE BAPTIST

The story of John the Baptist is generally well known to most Christians. The words of the angel Gabriel to his priestly father, Zechariah, plainly show that John was predestined from before his birth to be the prophesied messenger announcing the first appearance of the Messiah:

LUKE 1:13 But the angel said to him: "Do not be afraid, Zechariah; your prayer has been heard. Your wife Elizabeth will bear you a son, and you are to give him the name John. 14 He will be a joy and delight to you, and many will rejoice because of his birth, 15 for he will be great in the sight of the Lord. He is never to take wine or other fermented drink, and he will be filled with the Holy Spirit even from birth. 16 Many of the people of Israel will he bring back to the Lord their God. 17 And he will go on before the Lord, in the spirit and power of Elijah, to turn the hearts of the fathers to their children and the disobedient to the wisdom of the righteous — to make ready a people prepared for the Lord." *(NIV)*

John was a relative of Yeshua due to his mother Elizabeth being kin to Mary (Luke 1:36). He had no say in how his life would turn out. John was selected by God before his birth and tasked with a particular mission (the preaching of repentance in preparation for the kingdom of God) that ended with his death at the hands of Herod Antipas. From before his conception until his death, John's path was charted by God.

THE BLIND MAN AT THE TEMPLE

JOHN 9:1 As he passed by, he saw a man blind from birth. 2 And his disciples asked him, "Rabbi, who sinned, this man or his parents, that he was born blind?" 3 Jesus answered, "**It was not that this man sinned, or his parents, but that the works of God might be displayed in him.**" (*ESV*)

According to the words of the Messiah himself, this man had been born blind in order for Yeshua to bring praise to God's name by giving him sight. This man's entire life, including the years of suffering he experienced due to his blindness, was a prelude to Yeshua's miraculous healing. He was predestined for just that moment and just that miracle, so Yeshua could glorify God through him.

JUDAS ISCARIOT

The eternal fate of Judas Iscariot, the betrayer of the Messiah, has long been debated in the Christian world. However, what does not appear to be debatable is whether or not Judas acted of his own free will when he betrayed Yeshua. The Scriptures clearly indicate that Judas was preordained to be a traitor to Yeshua's cause, leading to his crucifixion:

JOHN 6:64 "But there are some of you who do not believe." For Jesus knew from the beginning who they were who did not believe, and **who would betray Him**. (*NKJV*)

JOHN 17:12 While I was with them, I kept them in your name, which you have given me. I have guarded them, and **not one of them has been lost except the son of destruction, that the Scripture might be fulfilled.**" (*ESV*)

ACTS 1:16 "Friends, **the Scripture had to be fulfilled, which the Holy Spirit through David foretold concerning Judas, who became a guide for those who arrested Jesus** — 17 for he was numbered among us and was allotted his share in this ministry." (*NRSV*)

GENTILES IN ANTIOCH IN PISIDIA

Are there some who are destined by the Eternal Father to be in the millennial kingdom of God?

ACTS 13:44 On the next Sabbath almost the whole city gathered to hear the word of the Lord. 45 When the Jews saw the crowds, they were filled with jealousy and talked abusively against what Paul was saying. 46 Then Paul and Barnabas answered them boldly: "We had to speak the word of God to you first. Since you reject it and do not consider yourselves worthy of eternal life, we now turn to the Gentiles. 47 For this is what the Lord has commanded us: 'I have made you a light for the Gentiles, that you may bring salvation to the ends of the earth.' " 48 When the Gentiles heard this, they were glad and honored the word of the Lord; and **all who were appointed for eternal life believed.** (*NIV*)

Clearly, the Scriptures teach that those Gentiles in Antioch in Pisidia who believed the preaching of Paul and Barnabas were preordained by God to enjoy age-lasting life during the millennial reign of Messiah Yeshua.

PAUL THE APOSTLE

After his conversion, Paul understood God had predestined him from the time that he was born for the work of taking the gospel to the Gentiles:

GALATIANS 1:15 But when **God, who set me apart from birth and called me by His grace**, was pleased 16 to reveal His Son in me so that I might preach him among the Gentiles, I did not consult any man, (*NIV*)

Paul knew that this preordained responsibility was not due to anything he had personally done. Rather, it was that God showed him unmerited favor ("grace") in calling him. Paul's letters indicate that he fully realized just how personally unworthy he was for the task that God assigned him:

I CORINTHIANS 15:9 For **I am the least of the apostles, and not fit to be called an apostle**, because I persecuted the church of God. (*NASU*)

EPHESIANS 3:8 To me, **though I am the very least of all the saints**, this grace was given, to preach to the Gentiles the unsearchable riches of Christ, (*ESV*)

Paul was the most prolific writer in the New Testament regarding the doctrine of predestination. Having been personally instructed by the glorified Messiah, he understood God's plan. Paul knew God had charted out the path of his life, and that he was destined to run the race on the course God had laid out for him:

ACTS 20:22 "And now, compelled by the Spirit, I am going to Jerusalem, not knowing what will happen to me there. 23 I only know that in every city the Holy Spirit warns me that prison and hardships are facing me. 24 However, I consider my life worth nothing to me, **if only I may finish the race** and complete the task the Lord Jesus has given me — the task of testifying to the gospel of God's grace." (*NIV*)

HEBREWS 12:1 Therefore, since we are surrounded by such a great cloud of witnesses, let us throw off everything that hinders and the sin that so easily entangles, and **let us run with perseverance the race marked out for us**. (*NIV*)

At the end of his life, Paul recognized that he had successfully completed the race God had set before him to run:

II TIMOTHY 4:6 For I am already being poured out like a drink offering, and the time has come for my departure. 7 I have fought the good fight, **I have finished the race**, I have kept the faith. 8 Now there is in store for me the crown of righteousness, which the Lord, the righteous Judge, will award to me on that Day — and not only to me, but also to all who have longed for his appearing. (*NIV*)

At the end of his life, after he had successfully completed that which God had assigned him to do, Paul realized that he would be one of the few chosen from among the many that God calls (Matt. 20:16; 22:14). He understood that because he had faithfully carried out God's will, he would be rewarded with a place in the coming kingdom of God.

The "many are called but few are chosen" principle is God's counterbalance to an understanding of predestination. Even Paul, who was aware that God had predestined him to take the gospel to the Gentiles, did not know for sure if he would finish his race successfully (I Cor. 9:24-27). God only chooses a few from among the many that He calls in order to conceal from those who are now called their immediate fate. If He didn't do this, being called by God during this age could be absolutely equated with qualifying for a position as a priest/king in the coming Messianic kingdom. Since God doesn't want His saints to be complacent, the "many called/few chosen" formula is a way to introduce uncertainty into the equation.

Is God Responsible for Man's Suffering?

"OK," some will say, "there appears to be biblical evidence that some people are predestined by God for certain things. But surely that can't mean that He involves Himself in the lives of every single human being on the planet, can it?"

Well, let's see what the Messiah has to say about the extent of God's control over the physical world in the fulfillment of His divine will:

MATTHEW 10:29 "Are not two sparrows sold for a penny? Yet **not one of them will fall to the ground apart from the will of your Father**. 30 And **even the very hairs of your head are all numbered**. 31 So don't be afraid; **you are worth more than many sparrows**." (*NIV*)

If not one single **sparrow** falls to the ground apart from the will of God the Father, how much control do you think He exercises over **mankind**? We don't have to wonder, because the Messiah clearly tells us that WE are much more important to God than many sparrows. If He has numbered the very hairs of our heads, does God care enough about us to be intricately involved in our everyday lives? The scriptural and logical answer is "Yes."

Most cannot fathom the idea that God has preordained the destinies of billions of people. Despite numerous Scriptures to the contrary, the concept of free will is so deeply ingrained in the religious beliefs of most that they cannot accept that God has predestined the lives (and ultimately, the salvation) of all mankind.

Many will object that God cannot be in charge of every detail of each person's life, because if He was, then He would be **directly** responsible for all human suffering and pain on the earth. Most cannot accept that God would cause the horrific misery that is evident in this world. Therefore, they rationalize that God doesn't specifically cause what happens, but rather He simply **allows** it to occur because He has given His sentient creatures free will, and many of them have chosen to do evil.

Unfortunately, this rationalization doesn't let God off the hook. If He truly is omnipresent, omniscient and omnipotent, He has the presence, knowledge, and power to stop the suffering that happens. To have that power and not make use of it to end human misery means God is complicit in the suffering. Either way it is viewed, God bears responsibility for the suffering that humanity endures.

If God is powerful enough to stop all suffering (and the Scriptures assert that He is), then why does God not end it? Could it be because this suffering ultimately serves God's purpose of bringing many sons into His family?

ROMANS 8:18 I consider that **our present sufferings are not worth comparing with the glory that will be revealed in us**. 19 The creation waits in eager expectation for the sons of God to be revealed. 20 **For the creation was subjected to frustration, not by its own choice, but by the will of the One who subjected it**, in hope 21 that **the creation itself will be liberated from its bondage to decay and brought into the glorious freedom of the children of God**. 22 We know that the whole creation has been groaning as in the pains of childbirth right up to the present time. 23 Not only so, but we ourselves, who have the firstfruits of the Spirit, groan inwardly as we wait eagerly for our adoption as sons, the redemption of our bodies. 24 For in this hope we were saved. But hope that is seen is no hope at all. Who hopes for what he already has? 25 But if we hope for what we do not yet have, we wait for it patiently. (*NIV*)

Paul states that God subjected His creation to frustration and decay, but that He will liberate it from these impediments when His children are revealed. While Paul doesn't go into the details, he clearly conveys a certainty that the present sufferings of humanity will pale in comparison to the glory that will be manifested in mankind when this portion of God's plan is completed.

The prophet Isaiah quotes a promise from God that all the pain and suffering of this present world will one day be forgotten when He creates a new heavens and a new earth:

ISAIAH 65:17 "Behold, I will create new heavens and a new earth. **The former things will not be remembered, nor will they come to mind**." (*NIV*)

Even the Messiah was required to suffer while he was on this earth. This wasn't suffering simply for the sake of suffering, but rather suffering with a purpose and goal. This suffering contributed to Yeshua becoming complete, as the author of Hebrews tells us twice:

HEBREWS 2:9 But we see Jesus, who was made a little lower than the angels, now crowned with glory and honor because he suffered death, so that **by the grace of God he might taste death for everyone**. 10 In bringing many sons to glory, **it was fitting that God**, for whom and through whom everything exists, **should make the author of their salvation perfect through suffering**. (*NIV*)

HEBREWS 5:7 In the days of his flesh, Jesus offered up prayers and supplications, with loud cries and tears, to Him who was able to save him from death,
and he was heard because of his reverence. 8 Although he was a son, **he
learned obedience through what he suffered.** 9 And **being made perfect**, he
became the source of eternal salvation to all who obey him, (*ESV*)

If the Messiah had to suffer in order to learn obedience and be made "perfect"
or "complete," why should we expect anything different? Is a slave greater
than his master? No, the best we should expect is to be like our Master (Matt.
10:24-25). Since the Father decreed that our Master Yeshua had to suffer in
order to be perfected, we too should expect God the Father to put us through
trials and tribulations in order for us to reach spiritual maturity and attain godly
character (Jam. 1:2-4).

The primary difference between Yeshua and us is that he had a preexistent relationship with *YHVH* the heavenly Father and fully understood God's will and
what was expected of him. We, unfortunately, do not always know God's will
for us. We can only determine it by studying the Scriptures, developing a relationship with God through regular prayer, and asking Him to reveal His will to
us through His Holy Spirit.

Conclusion:

The Scriptures portray God the Father as being omnipotent. Because of His
incomparable power, there is nothing that God cannot achieve. Since He created and sustains all things through His Holy Spirit, no being within God's creation is able to thwart His plan or purpose. Several times, God states in the
Scriptures that His will is to eventually save all mankind. His chosen vessel
for accomplishing this salvation is His son Yeshua the Messiah.

Per His plan, God has called many people now to worship Him. However,
from those many called, only a few will be chosen to be saved (Matt. 20:16;
22:14) **in this age**. God's purpose in saving those few now is so that they can
in turn help save others later. Most are destined to be used by God at this time
to extend His mercy to those few. God's plan calls for using most people in
this age to show His wrath and to make His power and glory known to those
on whom He is having mercy (Rom. 9:22-23). Seeing and recognizing God's
wrath and power causes those He has called and chosen to **fear** Him. According to the Scriptures, the fear of *YHVH* leads to obedience, which brings us
wisdom (Job 28:28; Psa. 111:10; Pro. 9:10; 15:33), knowledge (Pro. 1:17; 2:5),
and life (Pro. 10:27; 14:27; 19:23; 22:4).

God planned in exquisite detail how to bring many sons into His family before
He created the universe. Unfortunately, as the apostle Paul stated, God's decrees are unfathomable and His ways incomprehensible to most of mankind
(Rom. 11:33). He has blinded the majority so that they cannot understand His
plan or how it is being accomplished. Even among believers, what God is doing is not well understood. However, when all is said and done, it will be rec-

ognized by everyone that God alone is responsible for the salvation of humanity. No one will be able to boast that they played any part in their own salvation. It is by God's grace alone, not our works, that our Father will bring us into His divine family. In this way, God the Father will receive all the praise and glory from His children for His merciful act of salvation.

Bryan T. Huie

May 7, 2008

Revised: June 10, 2010

Pharisees and Sadducees

This study details the origin and beliefs of the two principal sects in 1st-century Judaism, the Pharisees and Sadducees. Which group was most closely aligned with the teachings of Yeshua? What impact did the Pharisees and Sadducees have on the early church? These and more questions are answered in this article from Scripture and history.

The Pharisees and the Sadducees are the two most well-known Jewish sects from the time of Yeshua the Messiah. Both, to some extent, opposed Yeshua during his ministry and received condemnation from him. In this article, I am going to examine the origins, beliefs, and impact of these two rival groups.

Historically, all of our knowledge of the Pharisees and Sadducees has been derived from three main sources: the works of the Jewish historian Flavius Josephus; the early rabbinical writings (200 CE and later); and the New Testament. Recently, however, references to these parties have also been found in some of the Dead Sea Scrolls unearthed at Qumran. Each of these sources has its limitations, but I will seek to achieve a historically accurate depiction of the Pharisees and Sadducees which is supported by all the available information.

First, let's look at the derivation of each party's name. It is commonly believed that "Pharisee" is derived from the Hebrew *perusim*, which means "separated ones." However, recently it has been suggested that "Pharisee" may instead come from the Hebrew *parosim*, meaning "specifier," since they sought to specify the correct meaning of God's law to the people.

The Sadducees are widely assumed to have been named after Zadok, a priest in the time of King David and King Solomon, although a less accepted theory alleges that they took their name from a later Zadok who lived in the 2nd century BCE. Alternately, some scholars have theorized that the name "Sadducee" comes from the Hebrew *tsadiq*, which means "righteous."

The origin of these two sects cannot be definitively traced. The first specific mention we see of them is during the reign of John Hyrcanus (134-104 BCE). The scant evidence available suggests that they coalesced as distinctive groups soon after the Maccabean revolt. To fully grasp the basis for the emergence of the Pharisees and Sadducees, it's helpful to understand the political climate in which they developed. I would encourage you to study the history of Judea in the two centuries before the ministry of Messiah.

Regarding the factors which led to the establishment of the Pharisees as a distinct party, British historian Paul Johnson writes:

In their battle against Greek education, pious Jews began, from the end of the second century BC, to develop a national system of education. To the old scribal schools were gradually added a network of local schools where, in theory at least, all Jewish boys were taught the Torah. This development was of great importance in the spread and consolidation of the synagogue, in the birth of Pharisaism as a movement rooted in popular education, and eventually in the rise of the rabbinate. (p. 106, *A History Of The Jews*)

Addressing this same topic in his history of the Hasmonean dynasty, Elias Bickerman states:

The Pharisees . . . wished to embrace the whole people, and in particular through education. It was their desire and intention that everyone in Israel achieve holiness through the study of the Torah . . . (p. 93, *The Maccabees*)

While the Pharisees primarily came from middle-class families and were zealous for the Mosaic law, the Sadducees were generally wealthy members of the Jewish aristocracy who had embraced hellenism. Because of their support for the program of economic and military expansion instituted by the Hasmonean rulers, the Sadducees came to exercise considerable influence in the court of John Hyrcanus. During this same period, the Pharisees became distinct from the *Hasidim* who had fought against the hellenizing forces in the Maccabean revolt. The Pharisees emerged as a significant force in Jewish affairs because of their influence with the common people.

According to Josephus' classic history, *The Antiquities of the Jews*, John Hyrcanus was originally a disciple and supporter of the Pharisees. However, a Pharisee named Eleazer opposed Hyrcanus serving as high priest because of doubts about his genealogy. Eleazer alleged that his mother had been raped during the persecution of Antiochus Epiphanes, calling Hyrcanus' lineage into question. When Hyrcanus proved that this story was a lie, a Pharisaic court recommended a lenient punishment of lashes for the slanderer. This angered Hyrcanus, who, with the encouragement of a Sadducean friend, quit the popular Pharisees and became a Sadducee. He even went so far as to abolish the Pharisaic practices that had been enacted into law and punish those who observed them. The hellenistic Sadducees consequently amassed considerable power during his reign.

Things got much worse for the Pharisees during the reign of Hyrcanus' son, Alexander Jannaeus (103-76 BCE). One year during the Feast of Tabernacles, Alexander, performing as high priest, corrupted the libation ceremony by pouring the water over his feet instead of on the altar as the Pharisees decreed. For this, he was pelted by the religious Jews with lemons. Outraged at this affront, he had his soldiers slay 6,000 of the offenders. This brought on a civil war which lasted six years and cost 50,000 Jewish lives. When the war eventually ended, Josephus records that Alexander transported some of his Jewish prisoners of war, most of them probably Pharisees, "to Jerusalem, and did one of the most barbarous acts in the world to them; for as he was feasting with his concubines, in the sight of all the city, he ordered about eight hundred of them to be crucified; and while they were living, he ordered the throats of their children and wives to be cut before their eyes " (bk. 13, ch. 14, sec. 2, *The Antiquities of the Jews*).

Alexander became increasingly unpopular among the Jews because of the civil war and his pro-Sadducee, hellenizing tendencies. The influence of the Sadducees was prevalent until his death in 76 BCE. On his deathbed, Alexander encouraged his wife, Salome Alexandra, to make peace with the Pharisees, since they had influence with the majority of the population. In a statement which calls to mind a major criticism Yeshua had of some of the Pharisees of his day, the *Babylonian Talmud* records Alexander telling Salome, "Fear not the Pharisees and the non-Pharisees, but the hypocrites who ape the Pharisees " (*Sotah* 22b). Once in power, Salome took her husband's advice and began favoring the Pharisees. This was not difficult for her, because her brother, Simon ben She-tech, was the leader of the Pharisees at this time.

During Salome's reign (76-67 BCE), the Sadducees lost much of their authori-ty. Although Salome was the recognized leader of the nation, it soon became obvious that the Pharisees had gained significant influence. They were brought into the Sanhedrin and became the major force in national politics. In reality, they became the actual power behind the throne. Now in a position to avenge earlier persecution from the pro-Saducean faction, they had some of those who had advised Alexander put to death. After an outcry from the Sadducees, including her son Aristobulus II, Salome allowed them to leave Jerusalem for several surrounding fortresses.

Herod the Great's rule (37-4 BCE) brought changing fortunes for both sects. One of Herod's initial political goals was to reduce the power of the Pharisees, who held enormous sway with the people. As the *Dictionary of Jesus and the Gospels* states, Herod's "first adversaries, the people and the Pharisees, object-ed both to his being Idumean, a half-Jew, as well as his friendship with the Romans. Those who opposed him were punished, and those who took his side were rewarded with favors and honors" (p. 319, "Herodian Dynasty").

Josephus records that two of those rewarded were a Pharisee named Pollio and his disciple Sameas, who had encouraged the Jews to accept Herod because they felt the rule by a foreigner resulted from divine judgement and the people should willingly bear it. Perhaps because of this intervention, Herod was on fairly good terms with the Pharisees throughout most of his reign and generally avoided conflict with them until just before his death. By that time, it appears that the Pharisees as a party had essentially withdrawn from politics, although individual Pharisees may have remained politically active.

Herod also sought to diminish the position of the Sadducees, who had regained their power after the death of Salome and held the high priesthood and the ma-jority of the seats on the Sanhedrin. One of the first things Herod did upon be-coming king in 37 BCE was to order the execution of 45 Saducean members of the Sanhedrin for their support of his rival for the kingship, Antigonus; in addition, he confiscated their property to pay Marc Antony, the Roman who had appointed him king. He also turned the Sanhedrin into a religious court only, taking away its power in secular matters.

Since he was only half Jewish, Herod knew the people would not tolerate him serving as high priest in addition to being king, as some of the Hasmoneans had. So he separated the two positions and began appointing high priests at his pleasure.

Eusebius, in his 4th-century *Ecclesiastical History*, wrote:

When Herod was appointed king by the Romans, he no longer nominated the chief priests from the ancient lineage, but conferred the honour upon certain obscure individuals. . . . Herod was the first that locked up the sacred vesture of the high priest, and having secured it under his own private seal, no longer permitted the high priests to have it at their disposal. (p. 31, ch. VI, pop. ed.) This broke the custom of the high priesthood being attached to a particular family. Herod also abolished the practice of the high priest holding the position for life. According to Josephus, in the 107 years from the beginning of Herod's reign to the fall of Jerusalem, there were 28 high priests. The Talmud records that by the time of Messiah, the high priest bought the office from the government and the position was changed every year. But even after he was out of office, the ex-high priest kept his rights to the dignity of the office. These policies resulted in a group of wealthy Sadducean priestly families (primarily the Boethus, Anan, and Phiabi families) being appointed to the office on a regular basis.

Herod's decision to appoint the high priest had a major impact on the operation of the Temple. British historian Paul Johnson writes:

By downgrading the importance of the high-priest, a hated Sadducee, Herod automatically raised in importance his deputy, the *segan*, a Pharisee, who got control over all the regular Temple functions and ensured that even the Sadducee high-priests performed the liturgy in a Pharisaical manner. (pp. 117-118, *A History Of The Jews*)

While most of the priests in the service of the Temple belonged to the party of the Sadducees, there were some who were Pharisees. *The International Standard Bible Encyclopedia* states:

The difference between the Sadducees and the Pharisees was not a simple one of priests versus laymen (many Pharisees were also priests - mostly of the lower ranks, but probably some even in the upper levels) . . . (p. 279 vol. 4, "Sadducees")

There is some dispute among scholars about who actually controlled the Temple sacrifices and rituals before and during the time of Messiah. While many accept the witness of Josephus and the rabbinical writings, some scholars have taken the position that these Jewish historical sources cannot be trusted because they were written after 70 CE. They have rejected the claims made in post-destruction rabbinic literature that the Pharisees were the dominant religious group in the affairs of the Temple as early as the Maccabean period. However, new evidence found among the Dead Sea Scrolls tends to discredit this skeptical view.

In reference to this dispute, Lawrence H. Schiffman, professor of Hebrew and Judaic studies at New York University, writes:

. . . Any light that might be cast on the history of the Pharisees and their teachings in the pre-destruction period would be critically important. With new evidence from the Dead Sea Scrolls it is now possible to demonstrate that for much of the Hasmonean period Pharisaic views were indeed dominant in the Jerusalem Temple . . . (pp. 30-31, *Bible Review*, June 1992, "New Light on the Pharisees: Insight from the Dead Sea Scrolls")

One of the Dead Sea Scrolls, known as MMT, sheds light on the prestige the Pharisees enjoyed prior to the ministry of Yeshua. According to Schiffman:

MMT is a foundation text of the Qumran sect. It was written in the early Hasmonean period when the Temple was managed and its rituals conducted in accord with Pharisaic views. The Hasmoneans made common cause with the Pharisees in order to cleanse the Temple of the excessive hellenization that they blamed to a great extent on the Sadducean priests who had become, in their view, too hellenized. Various elements in MMT and in the Temple Scroll [another Dead Sea document] represent the polemic of those who continued piously to hold fast to Sadducean views against the Hasmoneans and their Pharisaic allies. . . . It can no longer be claimed that there is no evidence for the Pharisees earlier than the tannaitic materials and the first-century Jewish historian Josephus, who wrote after the Roman destruction of Jerusalem. In fact, the scrolls provide extensive and wide-ranging testimony about the pre-destruction history of the Pharisees and their ideology. MMT and the Temple Scroll provide evidence of Pharisaic dominance over the Temple ritual in the early days of the Hasmonean period. (*Ibid.*, p. 54)

Regarding later Pharisaic control of the Temple, *The Eerdmans Bible Dictionary* says:

By the time of Jesus they [the Sadducees] included the families who supplied the high priests, as well as other wealthy aristocrats of Jerusalem. Most members of the Sanhedrin, the central judicial authority of Jewish people, were Sadducees. Thus, the Sadducees were the party of those with political power, those allied with the Herodian and Roman rulers, but they were not a group with influence among the people themselves. The views of the Pharisees prevailed among the common people, so that even though the two groups differed with regard to items in the laws of purity and details of temple procedure during the feasts, the Sadducean priests were compelled to operate according to the Pharisees' views. (p. 902, "Sadducees")

Emil Schürer, in his extensive history of the Jews during this period, wrote:

The Pharisees maintained their leadership in spiritual matters, especially in urban circles. It is true that the Sadducean high priests stood at the head of Sanhedrin. But in fact it was the Pharisees, and not the Sadducees, who made the greatest impact on the ordinary people . . . The Pharisees had the masses for their allies, the women being especially devoted to them. They held the greatest authority over the congregations, so that everything to do with worship, prayers, and sacrifice took place according to their instructions. Their popularity is said to have been so high that they were listened to even when they criticized the king or the high priest. They were in consequence able to restrain the king. For the same reason, also, the Sadducees in their official functions complied with the pharisaic requirements because otherwise the people would not have tolerated them (p. 402, vol. II, rev. ed., *The History of the Jewish People in the Age of Christ (175 B.C. - A.D. 135)*)

Addressing the differences between the Pharisees and Sadducees regarding religious observances, Alfred Edersheim, a noted 19th-century Jewish scholar, wrote:

Even greater importance attached to differences on *ritual* questions, although the controversy here was purely theoretical. For, the Sadducees, when in office, always conformed to the prevailing Pharisaic practices (p. 320, ch. II, bk. III, *The Life and Times of Jesus the Messiah*)

Because of their fear of the people, this Sadducean adaptation to Pharisaic views extended to all official duties the Sadducees performed. Josephus verifies this fact; of the Sadducees, he states:

They are able to do almost nothing of themselves; for when they become magistrates, as they are unwillingly and by force sometimes obliged to be, they addict themselves to the notions of the Pharisees, because the multitudes would not otherwise bear them." (bk. 18, ch. 1, sec. 4, *The Antiquities of the Jews*)

The New Unger's Bible Dictionary confirms this severe restriction on the power of the Sadducees during the time of Yeshua:

Although the spiritual power of the Pharisees had increased greatly, the Sadducean aristocracy was able to keep at the helm in politics. The price at which the Sadducees had to secure themselves power at this later period was indeed a high one, for they were in their official actions to accommodate themselves to Pharisaic views.(p. 1112, "Sadducee")

Even though the high priest was a Sadducee, history shows that the Sadducees were compelled to follow Pharisaic customs in the Temple rituals because of their fear of the people. This gave the Pharisees effective control of Temple observances, which was probably most noticeable during the annual feasts.

Alfred Edersheim recorded the practical effects of the Pharisees' control of Temple:

When a Sadducean high-priest, on the Feast of Tabernacles, poured out the water on the ground instead of into the silver funnel of the altar, Maccabean king though he was, he scarce escaped with his life, and ever afterwards the shout resounded from all parts of the Temple, "Hold up thy hand," as the priest yearly performed this part of the service. The Sadducees held, that on the Day of Atonement the high-priest should light the incense before he actually entered the Most Holy Place. As this was contrary to the views of the Pharisees, they took care to bind him by an oath to observe their ritual customs before allowing him to officiate at all. It was in vain that the Sadducees argued, that the daily sacrifices should not be defrayed from the public treasury, but from special contributions. They had to submit, and besides to join in the kind of half-holiday which the jubilant majority inscribed on their calendar to perpetuate the memory of the decision. The Pharisees held, that the time between Easter [Passover] and Pentecost should be counted from the second day of the feast; the Sadducees insisted that it should commence with the literal "Sabbath" after the festive day. But despite argument, the Sadducees had to join when the solemn procession went on the afternoon of the feast to cut down the "first sheaf," and to reckon Pentecost as did their opponents. (p. 220, *Sketches of Jewish Social Life*)

Pharisaic control of the local synagogues was more direct. Synagogues first came into being after the Jews returned from the Babylonian exile. They were not intended to replace the Temple, but were meant to be places of prayer and instruction in the Torah. At first, the teachers of the law in the synagogues were priests and Levites. But some in the priesthood became hellenized and lost the respect of the people because of their accommodation of Greek ideas at the expense of the law. The apocryphal book of *II Maccabees* shows that, by the reign of Antiochus Epiphanes, even the priests at the Temple in Jerusalem had become enamored with the Greek way of life; so much so "that the priests had no courage to serve any more at the altar, but despising the Temple, and neglecting the sacrifices, hastened to be partakers of the unlawful allowance in the place of exercise, after the game of Discus called them forth" (*II Macc.* 4:14).

Because of this, the scribes, who were lay teachers of the law, eventually supplanted the priests in the synagogues. The model for the scribes was Ezra, who was designated by the Hebrew title *soper*. After the Jewish return from exile in Babylon, this term came to mean one who was learned in the Hebrew Scriptures, especially the Torah. In the New Testament, these men are primarily called "scribes," but they are also referred to as "lawyers" and "teachers of the law."

Although not all Pharisees were scribes, the vast majority of the scribes were Pharisees, and they regulated the synagogues, teaching and interpreting the law. The Pharisees were solidly devoted to the daily application and observance of the Mosaic law and the "oral law," known as the Oral Torah.

Paul Johnson describes this "oral law" of the Pharisees as follows:

They followed ancient traditions inspired by an obscure text in Deuteronomy, "put it in their mouths", that God had given Moses, in addition to the written Law, an Oral Law, by which learned elders could interpret and supplement the sacred commands. The practice of the Oral Law made it possible for the Mosaic code to be adapted to changing conditions and administered in a realistic manner. (p. 106, *A History Of The Jews*)

Dr. Brad Young, a professor at Hebrew University in Jerusalem, writes of the oral law:

The Oral Torah clarified obscure points in the written Torah, thus enabling the people to satisfy its requirements. If the Scriptures prohibit work on the Sabbath, one must interpret and define the meaning of work in order to fulfill the divine will. Why is there a need for an oral law? The answer is quite simple: Because we have a written one. The written record of the Bible should be interpreted properly by the Oral Torah in order to give it fresh life and meaning in daily practice. . . . Moreover, it should be remembered that the Oral Torah was not a rigid legalistic code dominated by one single interpretation. The oral tradition allowed a certain amount of latitude and flexibility. In fact, the open forum of the Oral Torah invited vigorous debate and even encouraged diversity of thought and imaginative creativity. Clearly, some legal authorities were more strict than others, but all recognized that the Sabbath had to be observed. (p. 105, *Jesus the Jewish Theologian*)

The Sadducees however, rejected everything except the written Scriptures (primarily the Pentateuch) and their own **Book of Decrees**, which specified a system of capital punishment: who was to be stoned, who strangled, who burned, and who beheaded. To the Law of Moses they adhered strictly to the letter, without making allowances for the spiritual intent.

This was one of the major points of contention between the Pharisees and Sadducees; however, it wasn't the only difference of belief. Both the New Testament and Josephus show that the Pharisees believed in the resurrection from the dead and the existence of spirit beings such as angels and demons. They believed humans had freedom to make their own choices, but that God could and did interpose His will in mens' lives. Josephus also wrote that the Pharisees believed "souls have an immortal vigor in them," and that men would be punished or rewarded in the next age based on how they conducted themselves in this life. Josephus further states that "on account of which doctrines, they are able greatly to persuade the body of the people; and whatsoever they do about divine worship, prayers, and sacrifices, they perform them according to their direction" (bk. 18, ch. 1, sec. 4, *The Antiquities of the Jews*).

Regarding the beliefs of the Pharisees, *The International Standard Bible Encyclopedia* states:

The presentation of the Pharisees in the Gospels is generally negative. Jesus is seen to be disputing with them continually, which suggests that his teaching was the antithesis of pharisaism. Closer investigation, however, does not support this suggestion. The NT evidence shows Jesus in agreement with beliefs and practices vitally important to the Pharisees. (p. 828, vol. 3, "Pharisees")

The Sadducees had very different beliefs from the Pharisees. They denied the resurrection of the dead, as well as the existence of spirit beings. The Sadducees believed, according to the teachings of the Greek philosopher Epicurus, that the soul dies with the body. Therefore, they taught that there were no rewards or punishments after death. The Sadducees had a deistic view of God; they saw Him as uninterested in human affairs and therefore unwilling to intervene. Regarding their views on the resurrection, Messiah issued a strong denunciation, telling them that they were wrong because they did not know the Scriptures or the power of God (Matt. 22:29; Mark 12:24).

The average Jew rejected the teachings of the Sadducees, and they had very little support among the common people. While some scholars have interpreted these beliefs as a conservative effort by the Sadducees to resist religious innovations by the Pharisees, Messiah's teachings were clearly much closer to those of the Pharisees than the Sadducees. It's more likely that the doctrines of the Sadducees simply represented a corrupt elite's attempt to minimize the impact of religion on their secular lives.

The International Standard Bible Encyclopedia states the following about the motivation of the Sadducees:

As a result of their high social status the Sadducees were dominated by political interests, and in these areas they were rigidly conservative, it naturally being in their best interest to maintain the status quo. Maintaining the status quo necessarily entailed collaboration with the Roman occupiers, by whom their power was delegated, and for this self-serving policy the masses despised the Sadducees. (p. 279, vol. 4, "Sadducees")

During the time of Messiah's ministry the two parties are thought to have been relatively small; the number of Pharisees is estimated to have been about 6,000, while the Sadducees were only half as many. Both groups came into conflict with Yeshua during his ministry; however, it was the scribes and Pharisees who first opposed him.

Concerning the primary cause of this conflict, Dr. Brad Young writes:

Many scholars and Bible students fail to understand the essence of Jesus' controversial ministry. Jesus' conflict with his contemporaries was not so much over the doctrines of the Pharisees, with which he was for the most part in agreement, but primarily over the understanding of his mission. He did sharply criticize hypocrites . . . (p. 100, ***Jesus the Jewish Theologian***)

Yeshua strongly and frequently condemned the Pharisees for being self-righteous and hypocritical. Does this mean that **all** Pharisees at the time of Yeshua were self-righteous hypocrites? Regarding this question, Dr. Brad Young writes:

A Pharisee in the mind of the people of the period was far different from popular conceptions of a Pharisee in modern times . . . The image of the Pharisee in early Jewish thought was not primarily one of self-righteous hypocrisy . . . The Pharisee represents piety and holiness. . . . The very mention of a Pharisee evoked an image of righteousness . . . (***Ibid.***, pp.

184, 188)

Dr. Young continues:

While Jesus disdained the hypocrisy of some Pharisees, he never attacked the religious and spiritual teachings of Pharisaism. In fact, the sharpest criticisms of the Pharisees in Matthew are introduced by an unmistakable affirmation, "The scribes and Pharisees sit on Moses' seat; so practice and observe whatever they tell you, but not what they do; for they preach, but do not practice" (Matt. 23:2-3). The issue at hand is one of practice. The content of the teachings of the scribes and Pharisees was not a problem . . . The rabbis offered nearly identical criticisms against those who teach but do not practice . . . Unfortunately, the image of the Pharisee in modern usage is seldom if ever positive. Such a negative characterization of Pharisaism distorts our view of Judaism and the beginnings of Christianity . . . The theology of Jesus is Jewish and is built firmly upon the foundations of Pharisaic thought . . . (*Ibid.*, pp. 184, 187, 188)

Jamieson, Fausset, and Brown's commentary on Matthew 23:2-3 concurs with Dr. Young's interpretation above. Of this passage they write:

Saying, The scribes and the Pharisees sit. The Jewish teachers *stood* to read, but *sat* to expound the Scriptures . . . **in Moses' seat** - that is, as interpreters of the law given by Moses. **3. All therefore** - that is, all which, as *sitting in that seat*, and teaching *out of that law*, **they bid you observe, that observe and do**. The word "therefore" is thus, it will be seen, of great importance, as limiting those injunctions which He would have them obey to what they fetched from the law itself . . . (p. 108, vol. III, *A Commentary: Critical, Experimental, and Practical*)

Addressing the character of the Pharisees, researcher John D. Keyser writes the following: " As a result of the harsh portrayal in the New Testament of these teachers of Jewish law, the very name Pharisee has become synonymous with hypocrisy and self-righteousness." He goes on to say that many modern scholars "have failed to realize that the Pharisaic religion was divided into TWO SEPARATE SCHOOLS - the School of Shammai and the School of Hillel. The group that Christ continually took to task in the New Testament was apparently the School of Shammai - a faction that was very rigid and unforgiving in their outlook" (p. 1, "Dead Sea Scrolls Prove Pharisees Controlled Temple Ritual!").

Although Pharisees were frequently the adversaries of Yeshua, it should also be noted that not all their interactions were hostile. Pharisees asked him to dine with them on occasion (Luke 7:36; 11:37; 14:1), and he was warned of danger by some Pharisees (Luke 13:31). Additionally, it appears that some of the Pharisees (including Nicodemus) believed in him, although they did so secretly because of the animosity of their leaders toward Yeshua.

The New Testament shows that Yeshua did not clash with the Sadducees until near the end of his ministry. This was because they were a political party, not the religious teachers of the people. The Sadducees were not primarily concerned with religion, but with the power they could acquire through the high priesthood and the political system. They used their position in society to increase their wealth and affluence.

In his Bible dictionary, James Hastings describes why the Sadducees became antagonistic toward Yeshua:

It was only toward the close of His life that our Saviour came into open conflict with them. They had little influence with the people, especially in religious matters; His criticism was therefore mainly directed against the Pharisees and scribes, the supreme religious authorities, although, according to Matt. 16:6, 11, He also warned His disciples against the leaven of the Sadducees, meaning, probably, their utterly secular spirit. They, on their part, seem to have ignored Him, until, by driving the moneychangers out of the Temple (Matt. 21:12, Mark 11:15, Luke 19:45), He interfered with the prerogatives of the Sanhedrin. His acceptance of the Messianic title "son of David" also filled them with indignation against Him (Matt. 21:15). They accordingly joined the scribes and Pharisees in opposition to Him, and sought to destroy Him (Mark 11:18, Luke 19:47), first, however, attempting to discredit Him in the eyes of the people, and to bring down upon Him the vengeance of the Romans, by their questions as to His authority, as to the resurrection, and as to the lawfulness of paying tribute to Caesar (Matt. 21:23, 22:23, Mark 11:27, 12:18, Luke 20:1, 19, 27). In the Sanhedrin that tried Him they probably formed the majority, and the "chief priests," who presided, belonged to their party. (p. 351, vol. IV, *Hastings Dictionary of the Bible*, "Sadducees")

For a number of reasons, a group of leading Pharisees and Sadducees conspired to put Yeshua to death. But because of his popularity, they knew they had to do so secretly or risk the wrath of the people, because many of them considered him at the very least a prophet, and quite possibly the long-awaited Messiah. Due to the treachery of Judas Iscariot, the Pharisees and Sadducees managed to capture Yeshua by force in the dead of night. He was illegally tried and crucified before the Passover feast.

This isn't the last we hear of these two groups in the New Testament, however. The book of Acts shows that they both impacted the Church of God, each in a different way.

The Sadducees were the continual opponents of the early Church and the apostles. No Sadducees are ever mentioned as having become part of the community of believers in the Bible. *The Zondervan Pictorial Bible Dictionary* says:

After the day of Pentecost the Sadducees were very active against the infant Church. Along with the priests and the captain of the temple they arrested Peter and John and put them in prison. A little later, they arrested all the apostles and took counsel to slay them (Acts 5:17, 33). Their hostile attitude persisted throughout the rest of the Acts of the Apostles. There is no record of a Sadducee being admitted into the Christian Church. According to Josephus (Antiq. xx, 9, 1), they were responsible for the death of James, the brother of the Lord. (p. 742, "Sadducees")

Conversely, the New Testament records that there were Pharisaic Christians in the early Church. Acts 15:5 shows some of the Pharisees who had accepted Yeshua as the Messiah voicing their opinion on the circumcision question. Some commentators believe that the zealous Jews mentioned in Acts 21:20 were actually Christian Pharisees. And Pharisaic scribes on the Sanhedrin council stood up for the apostle Paul when he was brought before them in 58 CE (Acts 23:9).

In fact, the man responsible for writing more of the New Testament than anyone else was unquestionably a member of the sect of the Pharisees. Paul affirms his affiliation in several places. In Acts 22:3, Paul states that he was a Jew brought up in Jerusalem at the feet of Gamaliel, a leading Pharisee who had intervened for Peter and the apostles soon after the beginning of the Church (Acts 5:33-39).

In Acts 23:6, Paul publicly declared, "**I am** a Pharisee, the son of a Pharisee" (Acts 23:6). It is very telling that more than twenty years after his miraculous conversion on the road to Damascus, Paul still claims to be a Pharisee. This alone should be proof that, on a basic level, Pharisaism and Christianity did not conflict.

Regarding Paul's speech before the Sanhedrin, Luke depicts "Christianity and Pharisaism as natural allies, hence the direct continuity between the Pharisaic branch of Judaism and Christianity. The link is expressed directly in Paul's own testimony: he is (now) a Pharisee, with a Pharisaic heritage (23:6). His Pharisaic loyalty is a present commitment, not a recently jettisoned stage of his religious past (cf. Phil 3:5-9). His Christian proclamation of a risen Lord, and by implication, of a risen humanity (Acts 23:6), represents a particular, but defensible, form of Pharisaic theology " (p. 1111, *Harper's Bible Commentary*).

In Philippians 3:5, Paul states that he was "concerning the law, a Pharisee." In verse 6, he goes on to say that he was "concerning the righteousness which is in the law, blameless."

Regarding Paul's exultation in this Scripture, the *Dictionary of Paul and His Letters* says:

As a further cause for boasting in Philippians, Paul claims to be a Pharisee. Here the term was defined with precision. The expression 'as to the Law a Pharisee' refers to the oral Law. . . . Paul thereby understood himself as a member of the scholarly class who taught the twofold Law. By saying that the Pharisees sit on Moses' seat (Mt 23:2), Jesus was indicating they were authoritative teachers of the Law. . . . In summary, Paul was saying that he was a Hebrew-speaking interpreter and teacher of the oral and written Law. (p. 504, "Jew, Paul the")

The formal end of both the Pharisees and the Sadducees came after the Romans quelled the Jewish revolt of 66-70 CE. After the destruction of Jerusalem in 70 CE, Pharisaism gradually died out. But the basic Pharisaic tenets lived on in an altered form, that of rabbinic Judaism. However, with the Temple destroyed and the support of the Romans withdrawn, the Sadducees ceased to exist as a party. It wasn't until the 8th century CE that Sadducean principles were revived by the Karaite movement.

Nearly 2,000 years after the life and death of Yeshua the Messiah, we have a tendency to view biblical events through the filter of our own modern western culture. But Yeshua is intricately linked to the Jewish religion and society of his day. To truly grasp his message, it's vital that we have a historical understanding of the time in which Yeshua lived. This requires a basic knowledge of 1st-century Jewish culture and society. Hopefully this article has been helpful in arriving at a better appreciation of our Messiah through a more complete understanding of the Pharisees and Sadducees.

Bryan T. Huie
March 16, 1997
Revised: April 8, 2009

Resurrection of Jesus Christ

When was Jesus (Yeshua) resurrected? A seemingly simple and foundational question is actually quite difficult to pinpoint from the Scriptures. Simple math quickly eliminates a Good Friday death - Easter Sunday resurrection as is commonly believed. Digging into the ancient Greek text, combined with a foundational Hebraic mindset towards the festivals of the Lord, reveals the amazing answer to this question.

Yeshua gave only ONE sign to prove that he was the Messiah prophesied in the *Tanakh*:

MATTHEW 12:39 But he answered and said to them, "An evil and adulterous generation seeks after a sign, and no sign will be given to it except the sign of the prophet Jonah. 40 For as Jonah was **THREE DAYS and THREE NIGHTS** in the belly of the great fish, so will the Son of Man be **THREE DAYS and THREE NIGHTS** in the heart of the earth. (*NKJV*)

For numerous centuries, most Christians have held a belief that directly contradicts this unique sign that Messiah said would identify him. Untold generations of Christians have been taught that Jesus died on Good Friday and was resurrected on Easter Sunday. So prevalent is this satanic deception that most never even stop to consider that such a scenario denies that Yeshua is the prophesied Messiah. In this article, we're going to see what God's Word **really** has to say about the death and resurrection of the Messiah, Jesus Christ. First, let's examine the position of those who claim Yeshua was crucified on Good Friday and raised very early on Easter Sunday morning. Below is a graphic representation of these claims:

"THREE DAYS & THREE NIGHTS" According to Good Friday – Easter Sunday scenario

Friday	Saturday	Sunday
Nisan 14	**Nisan 15**	**Nisan 16**

Chronology - Friday Crucifixion / Sunday Morning Resurrection

Yeshua dies and is buried in late afternoon - **1st day & 1st night**		Yeshua in the grave for the **2nd day & 2nd night**		Yeshua raised from the dead early in the morning before sunrise (X) - John 20:1 (**no 3rd day or 3rd night**)	
1–	----1----	----2----	----2---X		
Friday (day)	Friday (night)	Saturday (day)	Saturday (night)	Sunday (day)	Sunday (night)
Nisan 14	Nisan 15		Nisan 16		Nisan 17
Roman Friday		Roman Saturday		Roman Sunday	

As you can see, this scenario only allows for parts of **two** days and **two** nights. So how do those who advocate this perspective get around the obvious lack of a third day and night? Quite ingeniously, the advocates of the Good Friday/Easter Sunday position use the debate over an *onah* (period of time) in the Jewish *Talmud* to substantiate their view.

They use quotes from Rabbi Ismael and Rabbi Eliezar ben Azariah regarding the counting of THREE DAYS to supposedly shore up their position. Here is the talmudic discussion of an *onah*, as presented by John B. Lightfoot in defense of the Good Friday/Easter Sunday timeline:

Weigh well that which is disputed in the tract *Schabbath*, concerning the uncleanness of a woman for three days; where many things are discussed by the Gemarists concerning the computation of this space of three days. Among other things, these words occur; "R. Ismael saith, *Sometimes it contains four Onoth*, sometimes five, sometimes six. But how much is the space of *an Onah*? R. Jochanon saith either a day or a night." And so also the Jerusalem Talmud; "R. Akiba fixed a day for an *Onah*, and a night for *an Onah*: but the tradition is, that R. Eliezar Ben Azariah said, *A day and a night make an Onah, and a part of an Onah is as a whole*." And a little after, *R. Ismael computeth a part of the Onah for the whole*. (p. 210, vol. 2, ***Commentary on the New Testament from the Talmud and Hebraica***)

By merging the conflicting opinions of Rabbi Ismael and Rabbi Eliezar, Good Friday/Easter Sunday proponents claim that Friday evening before sunset to Sunday morning before sunrise can be viewed as three days and three nights. If nothing else, the Good Friday/Easter Sunday advocates should certainly get credit for creativity.

However, the talmudic argument they cite as proof deals with the Jewish computation of an idiomatic THREE DAYS as it relates to the rabbinic period of time called an *onah*. The point of contention between the Jewish rabbis was whether an *onah* (a unit of time not mentioned in the Bible) was 12 hours or 24 hours in length. Rabbi Ismael, Rabbi Jochanan, and Rabbi Akiba all agreed that an *onah* was 12 hours long, either a day or a night. Rabbi Eliezar ben Azariah, on the other hand, considered an *onah* to be a 24-hour day. Yet it appears each side of this argument agreed that the count should be inclusive (that is, any portion of an *onah* should be counted as a full *onah*). This talmudic discussion does **not** address how to determine a literal THREE DAYS and THREE NIGHTS (a computation that is fairly self-evident to those without a theological axe to grind).

For example, according to Rabbi Ismael's opinion, an idiomatic THREE DAYS in Jewish thought can contain from **FOUR** *onahs* . . .

	1st ONAH	2nd ONAH	3rd ONAH	4th ONAH	
Thursday night	Friday day	Friday night	Saturday day	Saturday night	Sunday day
Nisan 14		Nisan 15		Nisan 16	

. . . up to **SIX** *onahs*:

1st ONAH	2nd ONAH	3rd ONAH	4th ONAH	5th ONAH	6th ONAH
Thursday night	Friday day	Friday night	Saturday day	Saturday night	Sunday day
Nisan 14		Nisan 15		Nisan 16	

As the graphic plainly shows, a period of six *onah*s would also be a literal three days and three nights.

HOWEVER, a period of only **four** *onah*s, while it may be idiomatically considered "three days" in rabbinical Jewish thought, clearly has only TWO days and TWO nights within it. Since the Messiah **explicitly** stated that he was going to be in the grave for **THREE** days and **THREE** nights, he could not have been speaking idiomatically of a period of only four *onah*s. Therefore, the Jewish debate over the length of an *onah* does **not** confirm the Good Friday/Easter Sunday position, as many claim.

Even using the inclusive reckoning employed by Jews when counting days, the Good Friday/Easter Sunday doctrine falls short. In the final analysis, this scenario suffers from several fatal flaws, not the least of which is the fact that **two** days and **two** nights do NOT equal **three** days and **three** nights.

Because of the contradictions in the Good Friday/Easter Sunday theory, a belief arose among some groups that Yeshua was in the grave exactly 72 hours:

"THREE DAYS & THREE NIGHTS"
Maximum literal interpretation — Seventy-two hours

Nisan 14	Nisan 15	Nisan 16	Nisan 17	Nisan 18

This chronology has Messiah being buried on Wednesday afternoon, just before sunset, and resurrected late on the afternoon of the weekly Sabbath, as depicted on the graphic below:

Chronology - Wednesday Crucifixion / Sabbath Evening Resurrection

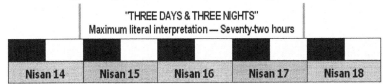

Yeshua crucified from 9-3, and buried in late afternoon of the 1st day (inclusive count)		Yeshua spends 1st night and 2nd day in the grave		Yeshua spends 2nd night and 3rd day in the grave		Yeshua spends 3rd night and 4th day in grave; resurrected at sunset (X) on Saturday evening		Yeshua appears to Mary early on Sunday morning, to disciples on road to Emmaus, to assembled disciples	
Tue. night	Wed. day 1-	Wed. night —1—	Thu. day —2—	Thu. night —2—	Fri. day —3—	Fri. night —3—	Sat. day —4-X	Sat. night	Sun. day
Nisan 14		Nisan 15		Nisan 16		Nisan 17		Nisan 18	
	Roman Wednesday	Roman Thursday		Roman Friday		Roman Saturday		Roman Sunday	

While this scenario is more honest and credible than the Good Friday/Easter Sunday doctrine, it also suffers from some flaws. As shown above, the 72-hour Wednesday evening/Sabbath evening theory has Yeshua in the grave one day too long using the Jewish inclusive method of counting days.

It was not necessary for Yeshua to have been in the grave for a full 72 hours in order for him to fulfill his prophecy (Matt. 12:40). The Jews counted days and nights inclusively. That means that at the beginning or end of the count, a part of a day or night was counted as a whole day or night. The Scriptures clearly show this principle in the book of Esther:

ESTHER 4:15 Then Esther told them to reply to Mordecai: 16 "Go, gather all the Jews who are present in Shushan, and fast for me; neither eat nor drink for **THREE DAYS, NIGHT or DAY**. My maids and I will fast likewise. And so I will go to the king, which is against the law; and if I perish, I perish!" 17 So Mordecai went his way and did according to all that Esther commanded him. 5:1 Now it happened **on the third day** that Esther put on her royal robes and stood in the inner court of the king's palace, across from the king's house, while the king sat on his royal throne in the royal house, facing the entrance of the house. (*NKJV*)

A graphic representation of the nights and days of this fast is most instructive:

	1st night	1st day	2nd night	2nd day	3rd night	3rd day
Mordecai tells the Jews in Shushan to fast with Queen Esther for three days, **night** and **day**; the fast begins on the night which starts the next day	The **1st night** and **day** of fasting by Esther and the Jews in Shushan		The **2nd night** and **day** of fasting by Esther and the Jews in Shushan		After the **3rd night** and during the **3rd day** of fasting, Esther goes in to King Ahasuerus	

Esther told Mordecai that the Jews of Shushan should fast with her for three nights and days, beginning at night. She then went in to the king **during** the third day of the "three nights and three days" of fasting. Clearly, the sequence shown from the Scriptures indicates that when the Bible says "three days and three nights," the beginning and ending day and/or night need not be totally complete.

According to the Jewish practice of counting parts of a day or night as a whole, "three days and three nights" at a minimum has to include two full days, two full nights, and at least portions of another day and another night. Below is a graph of the minimum amount of time Jews would have considered to be "three days and three nights":

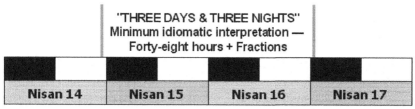

"THREE DAYS & THREE NIGHTS"
Minimum idiomatic interpretation —
Forty-eight hours + Fractions

Nisan 14   Nisan 15   Nisan 16   Nisan 17

There is a theory that places Yeshua in the grave for three days and three nights per the Jewish method of inclusive counting **and** agrees with the Scriptures which speak of a morning resurrection (a weakness that the Sabbath evening resurrection doctrine cannot overcome). This hypothesis is detailed on the following graphic:

Chronology - Wednesday Crucifixion / Sabbath Morning Resurrection

Yeshua crucified from 9-3, and buried in late afternoon; 1st day in grave		Yeshua spends 1st night and 2nd day in the grave		Yeshua spends 2nd night and 3rd day in the grave		Yeshua's 3rd night in grave; resurrected before sunrise (X) on Saturday morning			
Tue. night	Wed. day 1-	Wed night ---1---	Thu. day ---2---	Thu. night ---2---	Fri. day ---3---	Fri. night ---3-X	Sat. day	Sat. night	Sun. day
Nisan 14		**Nisan 15**		**Nisan 16**		**Nisan 17**		**Nisan 18**	
Roman Wednesday		Roman Thursday		Roman Friday		Roman Saturday		Roman Sunday	

As shown above, this doctrine has Yeshua in the grave for three days and three nights in the proper order (day first, and then night). It also concurs with the Scriptures which speak of a morning resurrection, as we will see in the next portion of this article.

Which one of the chronologies presented above has the best scriptural support? The available evidence, when viewed objectively, shows that Yeshua was buried late on Wednesday afternoon (Nisan 14) and resurrected early on the morning of the weekly Sabbath (Nisan 17), before sunrise.

In the remainder of the article, we'll look at the burial and resurrection passages in the Gospels and consult the original Greek language of the New Testament to determine what the Scriptures actually say about this pivotal event in human history. All Greek language citations are from the Byzantine Majority Text published by Robinson-Pierpont in 1995; this compilation represents the standard text of the majority of Greek manuscripts currently in our possession. Let's start in the Gospel of Luke to see what events took place from the time of Yeshua's burial to his resurrection:

LUKE 23:50 Now behold, *there was* a man named Joseph, a council member, a good and just man. 51 He had not consented to their decision and deed. *He was* from Arimathea, a city of the Jews, who himself was also waiting for the kingdom of God. 52 This man went to Pilate and asked for the body of Jesus. 53 Then he took it down, wrapped it in linen, and laid it in a tomb that was hewn out of the rock, where no one had ever lain before. 54 **That day was the Preparation, and the Sabbath drew near**. 55 And the women who had come with him from Galilee followed after, and they observed the tomb and how his body was laid. 56 Then they returned and prepared spices and fragrant oils. And they rested on the Sabbath according to the commandment. 24:1 Now on the first *day* of the week, very early in the morning, they, and certain *other women* with them, came to the tomb bringing the spices which they had prepared. (*NKJV*) even ask a question in a formal worship service, but she must ask her own husband at home because it would be shameful for her to speak in church.

Why would God forbid a woman to ask a question in the church meeting? What would be the harm of a simple question?

Questions are seldom neutral. While some questions are sincerely asked to gain information or insight, many are posed for other reasons. Satan, for example, commenced his conversation with Eve with a question ("Has God indeed said, 'You shall not eat of every tree of the garden'?" - Gen. 3:1). He was not trying to learn from Eve, but instead, he was laying the groundwork to deceive her and tempt her into sin.

The opposition which Yeshua faced from the Jewish religious leaders of his day frequently came in the form of apparently innocent questions (e.g., "Is it lawful to pay taxes to Caesar, or not?" - Matt. 22:17). Many who ask questions are really trying to make a point or to challenge the position of the one being questioned. The power to question is the authority to lead and to correct, and thus it should be exercised by the men of the congregation, whom God has appointed to authority (I Cor. 11:3).

Paul used the principle of BUILDING UP the assembly in verse 26 to form the basis for his commands. Therefore, there should also be positive reasons why women are prohibited from asking questions in a formal worship setting.

There are at least two ways that this prohibition teaches men:

First, the men will be stimulated to more serious study when their wives look to THEM for the answers to their biblical questions. As long as the wife looks to someone other than her husband for spiritual guidance, he will not feel the weight of his responsibility as the leader of the home. That is why Paul says, "let them ask their own husbands at home."

Additionally, the husband's authority will not be threatened and he will not be put on the spot publicly if he is asked at home. If he does not know the answer, he will not be embarrassed in front of the congregation, but will be able to investigate the matter more fully before taking a stand.

I CORINTHIANS 14:36 Or was it from you that the word of God came? Or are you the only ones it has reached? (*ESV*)

The almost bitter words that Paul adds in verse 36 show that he was very displeased with what had happened in Corinth. In this verse, he reproaches the Corinthians for the innovation of permitting women to speak in the formal worship assembly. Paul sarcastically reminds them that they were not the source of the Scriptures, nor were they the only ones who possessed them. He encouraged them to observe the order in the *Torah* that God had established at the beginning and not to seek some new way of their own devising. This order was the common practice among all the other messianic congregations of God.

I CORINTHIANS 14:37 If anyone thinks that he is a prophet, or spiritual,

he should acknowledge that **the things I am writing to you are a command of the Lord**. 38 If anyone does not recognize this, he is not recognized. 39 So, my brothers, earnestly desire to prophesy, and do not forbid speaking in tongues. 40 But all things should be done decently and in order. (*ESV*)

Paul clearly states that these teachings were not **his** opinion, but rather the commands of the Lord (v. 37). Those who rejected them would themselves be rejected (v. 38). His overriding concern was that things be done according to the proper order.

What must be noted in conclusion to our review of this passage in I Cor. 14 is:

1.   The prohibition of speaking in the church to women is specific, absolute, and all-inclusive. They are to keep silent in all formal public worship services. They are not to ask questions;

2.   This prohibition is given precisely for the related matters of teaching and ruling (specifically to avoid challenging the elders' functions of teaching and overseeing the congregation, and the right of each husband to rule his own household); and

3.   The grounds on which the prohibition is founded are universal and based on the different fundamental roles each sex has been given by God in this age of mankind.

In addition to the instructions given to the Corinthian church, Paul spoke specifically of the role of women in his first instructional letter to Timothy also:

I TIMOTHY 2:8 I desire therefore that the men [andras] pray everywhere, lifting up holy hands, without wrath and doubting; 9 in like manner also, that the **women** [gunaikas] adorn themselves in modest apparel, with propriety and moderation, not with braided hair or gold or pearls or costly clothing, 10 but, which is proper for **women** [gunaixin] professing godliness, with good works. 11 Let a **woman** [gune] learn in **silence** [hesuchia] with all **submission** [hupotage]. 12 **And I do not permit a woman** [gunaiki] to **teach** or to have **authority** over a **man** [andros], but to be in **silence** [hesuchia]. (*NKJV*)

The words of Paul regarding women here are difficult for 21st-century western Christians to accept. But they are plain and unequivocal, and support his earlier comments to the Corinthian church regarding the role of women in church services.

Paul follows up these clear instructions with his rationale for giving them:

I TIMOTHY 2:13 For Adam was formed first, then Eve. 14 And Adam was not deceived, but the **woman** [gune] being deceived, fell into transgression. 15 Nevertheless she will be saved in childbearing if they continue in

Luke clearly states that the day on which Yeshua was buried was the Preparation, and the Sabbath was fast approaching. The Greek word translated

παρασκευή

"preparation" here is   . The Good Friday/Easter Sunday proponents fervently insist that this word is a Jewish technical term which can ONLY mean the Friday before a weekly Sabbath. However, this position is refuted by many reputable sources, including those cited below:

παρα-σκευή   . . . 3. in the N.T. in a Jewish sense, *the day of preparation*, i.e. the day on which the Jews made the necessary preparation to celebrate a sabbath **or a feast**: (p. 486, ***Thayer's Greek-English Lexicon of the New Testament***, emphasis added)

PREPARATION (Gk. *paraskeue*, a "making ready"). In the Jewish sense, the day of preparation . . . was the day on which the Jews made the necessary preparation to celebrate a *Sabbath* . . . **or festival** . . . (p. 1028, ***The New Unger's Bible Dictionary***, emphasis added)

All the Gospel passages where *paraskeue* occurs identify the Jewish day of Preparation as the day of the crucifixion of Our Lord. But inasmuch as the sabbath mentioned in the narratives of the crucifixion is evidently the Passover sabbath of that year (Mk. 15:42; Lk. 23:54, 56; Jn. 19:31), and the Fourth Gospel expressly calls the preparation day in question "the Preparation of the Passover" (Jn. 19:14), the determination of the exact day for "the Preparation" during which Christ was crucified depends on the time when the Passover was celebrated that year. Passover takes place on the 14th of the Jewish lunar month Nisan (*Ant.* iii.10.5[248]), and is the greatest of the "special sabbaths" in the Jewish year. . . . But as a fixed date in a lunar month, its relation to the days of the week varied. . . . Thus, while Friday is the usual day of preparation for the normal weekly sabbath, the precise dating of the preparation for the Passover sabbath mentioned in the Gospels depends on the dating of the Passover for that year. (p. 953, vol. 3, "Preparation, Day of," ***The International Standard Bible Dictionary***)

The Good Friday/Easter Sunday proponents' contention that "the Preparation Day" ONLY refers to Friday is clearly unsupportable. As the Wednesday burial/Sabbath morning resurrection chronology above shows, this "Preparation Day of the Passover" (John 19:14) would have been Wednesday, Nisan 14 (see the Jewish calendar for 30 CE to verify this date).

Getting back to the sequence of events of the burial/resurrection recorded by Luke, let's look at ***Young's Literal Translation*** for another rendering of this passage:

LUKE 23:54 And the day was a preparation, and Sabbath was approaching, 55 and the women also who have come with him out of Galilee having followed after, beheld the tomb, and how his body was
placed, 56 and having turned back, they made ready spices and ointments . . . (*YLT*)

Luke tells us that the women followed Joseph to the tomb and watched the
burial of Yeshua. Then we are informed that "having returned, they made
ready spices and ointments." Since the Passover Sabbath was rapidly approaching while Yeshua was being buried, the women could **not** have obtained and prepared the spices for Yeshua's body that night (Wednesday
night) or the next day (Thursday day). Luke tells us here WHAT the women
did, but he doesn't tell us WHEN they did it. To answer the question of **when**
the women acquired and made ready the spices, we must go to the Gospel of
Mark:

MARK 15:47 And Mary Magdalene and Mary *the mother* of Joses observed where he was laid. 16:1 **Now when the Sabbath was past**,
Mary Magdalene, Mary *the mother* of James, and Salome **bought
spices**, that they might come and anoint him. (*NKJV*)

We see from Mark's parallel account that Mary Magdelene, Mary the mother
of James, and Salome bought the spices **after** "the Sabbath." The Sabbath
being referred to here is the same Sabbath mentioned in Leviticus 23:11, 15
— the annual Passover Sabbath of Nisan 15 (which occurred this particular
year on Wednesday night/Thursday day). Therefore, the women would have
purchased the spices during the day on Friday, Nisan 16.

The next verse in Luke's account confirms Mark's timeline. Let's look at a
literal translation of the Greek text of Luke 24:1 for verification of this (the
last part of Luke 23:56 should actually be the first part of Luke 24:1):

LUKE 24:1 Καὶ [And] τὸ [*on* the] μὲν [on the one hand] σάββατον [Sabbath] ἡσύχασαν [they
rested] κατὰ [according to] τὴν [the] ἐντολήν [commandment], τῇ [on] δὲ [but on the other
hand], μ.ᾷ [*on* one] τῶν [of the] σαββάτων [Sabbaths] ὄρθρου [*at* dawn] βαθέος [deep]
ἦλθον [they came] ἐπ. [to] τὸ [the] μνῆμα [tomb], φέρουσαι [bearing] ἃ [that which]
ἡτοίμασαν [they prepared] ἀρώματα [*the* spices], καὶ [and] τινες [certain *others*] σὺν [with]
αὐταῖς [them].

Robert Young translates this passage as follows:

LUKE 23:56b . . . And on the Sabbath, indeed, they rested, according
to the command. 24:1 And **on the first of the Sabbaths**, at early
dawn, they came to the tomb, bearing the spices they made ready, and
certain {others} with them, (*YLT*)

The Greek $\mu\grave{\epsilon}\nu \ldots \delta\grave{\epsilon}$ construction Luke uses here is meant to emphasize **contrast** (μὲν "indeed, on the one hand" . . . δέ "but, on the other hand"). Let's look at a literal translation of this passage which clearly shows the contrast Luke was portraying.

LUKE 23:56b And on the one hand, they rested on the Sabbath according to the commandment; but on the other hand, on one of the Sabbaths, at deep dawn, they came to the tomb, bearing the spices which they prepared, and certain others with them, (*literal translation*)

The contrast Luke wanted to point out to his readers with the use of the

μὲν . . . δέ pairing is between the Passover Sabbath (on which the women rested according to the commandment recorded in Lev. 23:6-7) and "one of the Sabbaths" (on which the women came to the tomb before sunrise to anoint Yeshua's body with spices).

LEVITICUS 23:6 "On the fifteenth day of that month the LORD's Feast of Unleavened Bread begins; for seven days you must eat bread made without yeast. 7 **On the first day hold a sacred assembly and do no regular work.**" (*NIV*)

Understood properly, Luke 23:56b-24:1 tells us that there were two Sabbaths that week: the annual Passover Sabbath on Nisan 15 and "one of the [weekly] Sabbaths" (the first one) in the count from Passover to Pentecost:

LEVITICUS 23:15 "And you shall count for yourselves from the day after the Sabbath, from the day that you brought the sheaf of the wave offering: **seven Sabbaths shall be completed.** 16 Count fifty days to the day after the seventh Sabbath; then you shall offer a new grain offering to the LORD." (*NKJV*)

The *Concordant Literal New Testament* renders Luke 24:1 this way:

LUKE 24:1 Now in the early depths of **one of the Sabbaths**, they, and certain others together with them, came to the tomb, bringing the spices which they make ready. (*CLNT*)

The Greek phrase μιᾷ τῶν σαββάτων literally means "one of the Sabbaths." The Greek word μιᾷ is "one," NOT "first." Additionally, the Greek word σαββάτων is plural. Grammatically, it doesn't make sense to translate this phrase as the "first *day* of the week," an alleged reference to Sunday. However, most English translators render the cardinal "one" as the ordinal "first," the plural "sabbaths" as the singular "week" and insert the missing word "day" into the phrase in order to try and make it fit the traditionally accepted Sunday resurrection scenario.

In his translation, Young renders the phrase as "first of the sabbaths." What would "First of the Sabbaths" have meant to a 1st-century Jew? Is there such a thing that would have been understood by those living at that time in Judea? Absolutely! In fact, Luke 6:1 gives us a clue regarding this phrase:

LUKE 6:1 Now it happened **on the SECOND Sabbath after the FIRST** that he went through the grainfields. And his disciples plucked the heads of grain and ate *them*, rubbing *them* in *their* hands. (**NKJV**)

What is "the Second Sabbath after the First," and how does it tie in to "one of the sabbaths" mentioned in the Gospels in relation to Yeshua's resurrection? We can find the answer to both questions in Johnston Cheney's discussion of this verse:

Seven sabbaths were to be counted from the Γeast of Γirst-fruits or Passover. Consequently, these came to be known as "First Sabbath," "Second Sabbath" etc., down to the seventh. And according to Julian Morgenstern, former President of Hebrew University, this practice continued in Galilee till the time of Christ or the Common Era. It is still observed by some groups in Palestine today. Thus, there was an annual date known as "First Sabbath," just after Passover. (p. 230, **The Life of Christ in Stereo**)

According to Leviticus 23:15, there were seven weekly Sabbaths between Passover and Pentecost that were to be counted. When referring to any of these seven Sabbaths, the Jews would simply call them "one of the Sabbaths." There was an annual date just after Passover at the time of Yeshua known as the "First Sabbath"; this was the first weekly Sabbath after the Passover high Sabbath. "One of the Sabbaths," mentioned by all of the Gospel writers (Matt. 28:1; Mark 16:2; Luke 24:1; John 20:1, 19), refers to this very "First Sabbath"! When English translators render the Greek text

μιᾷ τῶν σαββάτων   as "first *day* of the week," they do so because of tradition. The most logical translation would be the most literal: "One of the Sabbaths."

Some raise the objection that the women could not have gone to anoint Yeshua's body on the weekly Sabbath because it would have been against the Law (Exo. 20:8-11; Deu. 5:12-15). The Jewish **Mishnah** (which records the oral law as it most likely would have been observed in Yeshua's day) addresses the legality of anointing a dead body on a weekly Sabbath. Let's see what the **Mishnah** says would have been allowed:

A. They prepare all that is needed for a corpse.

B. **They anoint** and rinse **it**,

C. on condition that they not move any limb of the corpse.

D. They remove the mattress from under it.

E. And they put on [cool] sand so that it will keep.

F. They tie the chin,

G. not so that it will go up, but so that it will not droop [further].

H. And so in the case of a beam which broke —

I. they support it with a bench or the seams of a bed,

J. not so that it will go up, but so that it will not droop [further].

K. They do not close the eyes of a corpse on the Sabbath,

L. nor on an ordinary day at the moment the soul goes forth.

M. And he who closes the eyes of a corpse at the moment the soul goes forth, lo, this one sheds blood. (p. 207, **The Mishnah, A New Translation**, Shabbat 23:5)

The women rested according to the Law on the Passover Sabbath (Lev. 23:6-7), but they had legal justification to go to the tomb on the weekly Sabbath. It was the Jewish custom (in fact, an obligation) for grieving friends and relatives to go to a grave on the third day to pay last respects. It was at this point in time that death was considered permanent. So a Sabbath morning visit to Yeshua's tomb by the women for the purpose of anointing his body would have been in accord with the Jewish oral law and would **not** have broken the Sabbath commandment (Exo. 20:8-11).

Now let's move on to Matthew's chronicle of these same events:

MATTHEW 27:57 Now when evening had come, there came a rich man from Arimathea, named Joseph, who himself had also become a disciple of Jesus. 58 This man went to Pilate and asked for the body of Jesus. Then Pilate commanded the body to be given to him. 59 When Joseph had taken the body, he wrapped it in a clean linen cloth, 60 and laid it in his new tomb which he had hewn out of the rock; and he rolled a large stone against the door of the tomb, and departed. 61 And Mary Magdalene was there, and the other Mary, sitting opposite the tomb. 62 **On the next day, which followed the Day of Preparation**, the chief priests and Pharisees gathered together to Pilate, 63 saying, "Sir, we remember, while he was still alive, how that deceiver said, '**After three days I will rise**.' 64 Therefore command that the tomb be made secure until the third day, lest his disciples come by night and steal him *away*, and say to the people, 'He has risen from the dead.' So the last deception will be worse than the first." 65 Pilate said to them, "You have a guard; go your way, make it as secure as you know how." 66 So they went and made the tomb secure, sealing the stone and setting the guard. 28:1 Now after the Sabbath, as the first *day* of the week began to dawn, Mary Magdalene and the other Mary came to see the tomb. (**NKJV**)

Matthew gives us some additional pieces of the story in his account. He tells us of the "evening" (just before sunset) burial by Joseph with the women watching. But he adds details about the visit of the Sadducees and Pharisees to Pilate to request a guard be established at the tomb of Yeshua. These rulers appeared before Pilate on the day following the Preparation Day, which would have been the Passover Sabbath (Nisan 15). Since they would have eaten the Passover meal the night before, they no longer had to be concerned with making themselves unclean by entering the Praetorium (John 18:28). They were afraid that Yeshua's disciples would steal his body from the tomb "after three days" and make it appear that he had risen from the dead. Their plea to make the tomb "secure until the third day" should be understood to mean "until the third day had ended," or until the time frame for Yeshua's prophesied resurrection had passed. Pilate agreed and assigned some soldiers to guard the tomb.

The pivotal verse of this passage is the first verse of chapter 28:

MATTHEW 28:1 And on the eve of the Sabbaths, at the dawn, toward the **first of the Sabbaths**, came Mary the Magdalene, and the other Mary, to see the sepulchre, (*YLT*)

MATTHEW 28:1 Now it is the evening of the Sabbaths. At the lighting up into **one of the Sabbaths** came Mary Magdalene and the other Mary to behold the sepulcher. (*CLNT*)

MATTHEW 28:1 Ὀυέ [*the* later of] δέ [And *on*] σαββάτων [*the* Sabbaths], τῇ [at the] ἐπιφωσκούσῃ [dawn] εἰς [to] μίαν [one of] σαββάτων [*the* Sabbaths], ἠλθε [came] Μαρία [Mary] ἡ [the] Μαγδαληνή [Magdalene] καί [and] ἡ [the] ἄλλη [other] Μαοία [Mary] θεωρῆσαι [to see] τὸν [the] τάφον [tomb].

The Greek word 'ουέ is generally translated "after" in this particular verse. However, it primarily means "late," in reference to time. Depending on context, it can also be translated "eve," "even," or "evening." *A Greek-English Lexicon of the New Testament and Other Early Christian Literature* (*BAGD*) shows that the use of this word in "Polyaenus 5, 2, 5

'ουέ τῆς ὥρας = later than the hour [decided upon]" (p. 601). Regarding translating 'ουέ as "after" in Matthew 28:1 and elsewhere, Thayer states: ". . . an examination of the instances just cited (and others) will show that they fail to sustain the rendering *after* . . ." (p. 471).

As Thayer asserts, translating 'ουέ as "after" is not valid in Matthew 28:1. While Young translates it as "eve of," the best rendering of 'ουέ in this verse is "later of." Using that translation, Matthew 28:1 confirms that there were indeed TWO Sabbaths during the week of the crucifixion, as the following literal translation shows:

MATTHEW 28:1 And **on the later of the Sabbaths**, at the dawn to **one of the Sabbaths**, came Mary the Magdalene, and the other Mary, to see the tomb, (*literal translation*)

Matthew very specifically tells us WHEN the women went to the tomb. It was on the later of the two Sabbaths that occurred that week, on "one of the [weekly] Sabbaths" of the seven counted to Pentecost. Just before dawn on this weekly Sabbath, Mary Magdalene and the other Mary brought spices to anoint Yeshua's body.

Now let's look at the record of Yeshua's burial and resurrection in Mark's Gospel:

MARK 15:45b . . . He granted the body to Joseph. 46 Then he bought fine linen, took him down, and wrapped him in the linen. And he laid him in a tomb which had been hewn out of the rock, and rolled a stone against the door of the tomb. 47 And Mary Magdalene and Mary *the mother* of Joses observed where he was laid. 16:1 Now **when the Sabbath was past**, Mary Magdalene, Mary *the mother* of James, and Salome bought spices, that they might come and anoint him. 2 Very early in the morning, on the first *day* of the week, they came to the tomb when the sun had risen. (*NKJV*)

This passage establishes the same series of events we have previously seen in the other Gospel accounts. Mark 16:1 shows that the women went and bought spices after the Passover Sabbath. As pointed out earlier, this would have taken place during the day on Friday, Nisan 16. Mark 16:2 tells us exactly when the women went to the tomb to anoint Yeshua's body with these spices:

MARK 16:2 And **early in the morning of the first of the Sabbaths**, they come unto the sepulchre, **at the rising of the sun**, (*YLT*)

MARK 16:2 And, **very early in the morning on one of the Sabbaths**, they are coming to the tomb **at the rising of the sun**. (*CLNT*)

Mark tells us that the women came to the tomb "at the rising of the sun." This would have been just before the sun rose, while it was still somewhat dark (John 20:1). Mark begins his summation of these events in verse 9, where he tells us specifically when Yeshua was resurrected:

MARK 16:9 And **he, having risen in the morning of the first of the sabbaths**, did appear first to Mary the Magdalene, out of whom he had cast seven demons; (*YLT*)

Young's use of the plural "sabbaths" in verse 9 is grammatically inaccurate;

the Greek noun σαββάτου is singular. A better translation of σαββάτου would be "Sabbath." Additionally, unlike the other passages where forms of the Greek word μιᾳ (the cardinal "one") are used, here the Greek word is πρώτη (the ordinal "first"). Again, the *Concordant Literal New Testament* renders this verse more accurately:

MARK 16:9 Now, **rising in the morning in the first Sabbath**, he appeared first to Mary Magdalene, from whom He had cast out seven demons. (*CLNT*)

MARK 16:9 Ἀναστὰς [having arisen] δὲ [Now] πρω. [early] πρώτη [on *the* first] σαββάτου [Sabbath], ἐφάνη [he appeared] πρῶτον [first] Μαρίᾳ [to Mary] τῇ [the] Μαγδαληνῇ [Magdalene], ἀφ' [from] ἧς [whom] ἐκβεβλήκει [He had cast out] ἑπτὰ [seven] δαιμόνια [demons].

MARK 16:9 Now **having arisen in the morning on the First Sabbath**, he appeared first to Mary the Magdalene, from whom he had cast out seven demons; (*literal translation*)

Mark tells us clearly that Yeshua rose from the dead **in the morning** on the First Sabbath. "In the morning" comes from the Greek adverb πρωΐ, which literally means "early." According to Friberg's *Analytical Lexicon to the Greek New Testament* (*ALGNT*), πρωΐ is, "in Jewish time reckoning, the fourth watch of the night, from three to six a.m." So we have recorded here by Mark a clear time frame for the resurrection: 3-6 AM on the first weekly Sabbath of the seven enumerated between Passover and Pentecost. Now let's examine the final Gospel account of the burial/resurrection from the apostle John:

JOHN 19:38 After this, Joseph of Arimathea, being a disciple of Jesus, but secretly, for fear of the Jews, asked Pilate that he might take away the body of Jesus; and Pilate gave *him* permission. So he came and took the body of Jesus. 39 And Nicodemus, who at first came to Jesus by night, also came, bringing a mixture of myrrh and aloes, about a hundred pounds. 40 Then they took the body of Jesus, and bound it in strips of linen with the spices, as the custom of the Jews is to bury. 41 Now in the place where he was crucified there was a garden, and in the garden a new tomb in which no one had yet been laid. 42 So there they laid Jesus, because of the Jews' Preparation *Day*, for the tomb

was nearby. 20:1 Now on the first *day* of the week Mary Magdalene
went to the tomb early, while it was still dark, and saw *that* the stone
had been taken away from the tomb. (*NKJV*)

John adds to our knowledge of the burial by including the fact that Nicodemus
the Pharisee (John 3:1) brought a hundred pounds of spices to the sepulcher to
prepare Yeshua's body for entombment. We get the sense from John's comment about the garden tomb being nearby that the Preparation Day for the
Passover Sabbath was about to end soon, requiring Joseph and Nicodemus to
hurry their burial of Messiah.

Let's look at John 20:1 a little closer:

JOHN 20:1 Τῇ [on the] δὲ [And] μιᾷ [one] τῶν [of the] σαββάτων [Sabbaths] Μαρία [Mary]
ἡ [the] Μαγδαληνή [Magdalene] ἔρχεται [came] πρωὶ [early] σκοτίας [dark] ἔτι [yet] οὔσης
[being], εἰς [to] τὸ [the] μνημεῖον [tomb], καὶ [and] βλέπει [seeing] τὸν [the] λίθον [stone]
ἠρμένον [having been taken away] ἐκ [from] τοῦ [the] μνημείου [tomb].

Here are two literal translations of this verse:

JOHN 20:1 And **on the first of the Sabbaths**, Mary the Magdalene
doth come early (there being yet darkness) to the tomb, and she seeth
the stone having been taken away out of the tomb, (*YLT*)

JOHN 20:1 Now, **on one of the Sabbaths**, Miriam Magdalene is coming to the tomb in the morning, there being still darkness, and is observing the stone taken away from the door of the tomb. (*CLNT*)

Once again, we see that John's resurrection account matches that of the Syn-
optists. He adds the fact that the sun had not yet risen on the morning of the
First Sabbath when Mary Magdalene arrived at the tomb.

Having now covered all the Gospel accounts of the burial and resurrection, it
is clear that the Greek text does not support a SUNDAY morning resurrection
at all. In fact, the overwhelming evidence is that Messiah Yeshua rose from
the dead early on the morning of the weekly Sabbath, "one of the Sabbaths" in
the seven week count toward *Shavuot* (Pentecost).

There are some additional pieces to this story that the Scriptures give us. Let's
go back to Luke's Gospel for a moment and look at an event that occurred a
little later that same Sabbath day:

LUKE 24:12 But Peter arose and ran to the tomb; and stooping down,
he saw the linen cloths lying by themselves; and he departed, mar-
veling to himself at what had happened. 13 Now behold, two of them
were traveling **that same day** to a village called Emmaus, which was
seven miles from Jerusalem. 14 And they talked together of all these
things which had happened. 15 So it was, while they conversed and
reasoned, that Jesus himself drew near and went with them. 16 But
their eyes were restrained, so that they did not know him. 17 And he
said to them, "What kind of conversation *is* this that you have with one

another as you walk and are sad?" 18 Then the one whose name was Cleopas answered and said to him, "Are you the only stranger in Jerusalem, and have you not known the things which happened there in these days?" 19 And he said to them, "What things?" So they said to him, "The things concerning Jesus of Nazareth, who was a prophet mighty in deed and word before God and all the people, 20 and how the chief priests and our rulers delivered him to be condemned to death, and crucified him. 21 But we were hoping that it was he who was going to redeem Israel. Indeed, besides all this, TODAY is the THIRD DAY SINCE these things happened. 22 Yes, and certain women of our company, who arrived at the tomb early, astonished us. 23 When they did not find his body, they came saying that they had also seen a vision of angels who said he was alive. 24 And certain of those *who were* with us went to the tomb and found *it* just as the women had said; but him they did not see." 25 Then he said to them, "O foolish ones, and slow of heart to believe in all that the prophets have spoken! 26 Ought not the Christ to have suffered these things and to enter into his glory?" 27 And beginning at Moses and all the Prophets, he expounded to them in all the Scriptures the things concerning himself. 28 Then they drew near to the village where they were going, and he indicated that he would have gone farther. 29 But they constrained him, saying, "Abide with us, for it is toward evening, and the day is far spent." And he went in to stay with them. 30 Now it came to pass, as he sat at the table with them, that he took bread, blessed and broke *it*, and gave it to them. 31 Then their eyes were opened and they knew him; and he vanished from their sight. 32 And they said to one another, "Did not our heart burn within us while he talked with us on the road, and while he opened the Scriptures to us?" 33 So they rose up that very hour and returned to Jerusalem, and found the eleven and those *who were* with them gathered together, 34 saying, "The Lord is risen indeed, and has appeared to Simon!" 35 And they told about the things *that had happened* on the road, and how he was known to them in the breaking of bread. 36 Now as they said these things, Jesus himself stood in the midst of them, and said to them, "Peace to you." (**NKJV**)

Luke records the Sabbath flight of two of Yeshua's disciples out of Jerusalem to Emmaus. This account is sometimes used by Good Friday/Easter Sunday proponents to "prove" that this day, the "same day" (Luke 24:13) as the resurrection, was a Sunday. They use Luke 24:21b ("**today is the third day**

SINCE these things happened") to try and support their position. However, the Greek text of this verse confirms that this day was the weekly Sabbath, NOT Easter Sunday! Here is the literal translation of that phrase in the Greek:

LUKE 24:21b τρίτην [third] ταύτην [this] ἡμέραν [day] ἄγει [brings] σήμερον [today], ἀφ
[from] οὗ [which] ταῦτα [these *things*] ἐγένετο [happened].

The Greek words translated "since" in the *NKJV* are   ἀφ οὗ   . A literal translation of Luke 24:21b is ". . . Today brings this third day **from which** these things happened." The use of the Greek preposition/pronoun pair

ἀφ οὗ   indicates that these men were NOT using the customary inclusive counting here, but rather were counting FROM Yeshua's crucifixion and burial on Wednesday, as the following graphic shows:

	X		1st day since		2nd day since		3rd day since		
Tue. night	Wed. day	Wed night	Thu. day	Thu. night	Fri. day	Fri. night	Sat. day	Sat. night	Sun. day
Nisan 14		**Nisan 15**		**Nisan 16**		**Nisan 17**		**Nisan 18**	

The daylight portion of the weekly Sabbath (the "First Sabbath" of the seven counted to Pentecost) was the "third day FROM WHICH" the crucifixion and burial had happened. The two men were referencing Yeshua's prophecy that he would rise again AFTER three days (Mark 8:31).

As Cleopas and Simon (not Peter) traveled toward Emmaus, they were sad (Luke 24:17). They had expected **something** to happen, but that Sabbath morning when news reached them that the tomb was found empty and Yeshua was not seen, they apparently did **not** believe that he had risen from the dead. Instead, they likely assumed that someone had stolen the body and they (Yeshua's disciples) were going to receive the blame for it. In fear they left Jerusalem so they wouldn't be arrested by the Jewish leaders for this supposed crime.

Some claim that Cleopas and Simon could not have been traveling to Emmaus if this day were indeed the Sabbath due to the restriction on traveling more than a "Sabbath day's journey" (slightly less than a mile). However, two points negate this objection. First, these disciples were probably uneducated Galileans who did not observe all points of the oral law of the Pharisees (cf. Matt. 15:1-2; Mark 7:1-5). And even if they did normally observe this oral statute regarding walking, it was permissible to break the law if a life were at stake. These two disciples may very well have thought that their lives would be at risk if they stayed in Jerusalem. After all, their leader had just been executed at the behest of the Jewish authorities, and now his body was missing.

Yeshua appeared to Cleopas and Simon sometime during their trip, but they did not recognize him. He spoke to them about the Scriptures that told of him, amazing them with the things he said. They reached Emmaus probably sometime in mid-afternoon, within a few hours of sunset, as the day was winding down. A literal translation of Luke 24:29 shows the time-frame of their arrival:

LUKE 24:29 And they constrained him, saying, "Stay with us, because toward evening it is, and the day has declined. And he went in to stay with them. (*literal translation*)

It was sometime "toward evening," when the sun had started to set in the mid-afternoon sky. Having traveled out of Jerusalem and walked about seven miles during the middle of the day, the two disciples were tired and hungry. Since they had enjoyed hearing the Scriptures expounded to them during their trip, they implored the unknown traveler to stay with them. However, as they were eating, their eyes were opened and they recognized Yeshua. When they did, he vanished from before them.

Cleopas and Simon were so excited that they immediately headed back late that Sabbath afternoon to Jerusalem to tell the rest of the disciples that Yeshua was indeed alive. One would certainly imagine that they were motivated to get back to Jerusalem as fast as possible. The two men went to where the rest of the disciples were meeting and told them what had happened. Just as they were recounting the day's events, Yeshua appeared in the midst of the group. The apostle John also tells us of this event in his account of that Sabbath day:

JOHN 20:19 **It being, therefore, evening, on that day, the first of the Sabbaths**, and the doors having been shut where the disciples were assembled, through fear of the Jews, Jesus came and stood in the midst, and saith to them, 'Peace to you;' (*YLT*)

JOHN 20:19 **It being, then, the evening of that day, one of the Sabbaths**, and the doors having been locked where the disciples were gathered together, because of fear of the Jews, Jesus came and stood in the midst and is saying to them, "Peace to you!" (*CLNT*)

JOHN 20:19 Οὔσης [it being] οὖν [Then] ὀψίας [evening] τῇ [the] ἡμέρᾳ [on day] ἐκείνῃ [that] τῇ [the] μιᾷ [one] τῶν [of the] σαββάτων [Sabbaths], καὶ [and] τῶν [the] θυρῶν [doors] κεκλεισμένων [having been closed] ὅπου [where] ἦσαν [were] οἱ [the] μαθηταὶ [disciples] συνηγμένοι [assembled] διὰ [because of] τὸν [the] φόβον [fear] τῶν [of the] Ἰουδαίων [Jews], ἦλθεν [came] ὁ [-] Ἰησοῦς [Yeshua] καὶ [and] ἔστη [stood] εἰς [in] τὸ [the] μέσον [midst], καὶ [and] λέγει [said] αὐτοῖς [to them], Εἰρήνη [Peace] ὑμῖν [to you].

John shows us that it was evening (late afternoon) on the First Sabbath when Yeshua appeared to the fearful disciples, who were gathered together in a closed room. Combined with Luke's account, we see that just as Cleopas and Simon had arrived to tell of their encounter on the road to Emmaus, Yeshua himself appeared to confirm their testimony and prove his resurrection. An examination of each of the Gospels proves that all resurrection events took place on the first weekly Sabbath between Passover and Pentecost, not Sunday. There is no justification, other than tradition, for believing in a Good Friday/Easter Sunday resurrection scenario.

In fact, a strong case can be made from the Greek text that Sunday, the first day of the week, is **never** mentioned in the New Testament. Let's look at the remaining two Scriptures where "first *day* of the week" normally appears in the English translations to see the evidence for this claim.

We'll start with the account of Paul's trip from Philippi to Troas. First, let's look at the text as it's normally translated, followed by a literal translation:

ACTS 20:6 But we sailed away from Philippi **after the Days of Unleavened Bread**, and in five days joined them at Troas, where we stayed seven days. 7 Now on the first *day* of the week, when the disciples came together to break bread, Paul, ready to depart the next day, spoke to them and continued his message until midnight. (*NKJV*)

Verse 6 tells us that these events took place immediately after the Feast of Unleavened Bread. A literal translation of verse 7 is somewhat different than what most English versions record:

ACTS 20:7 Now on **one of the Sabbaths**, at our having gathered to break bread, Paul argued with them, being about to be off on the morrow. Besides, he prolonged the word unto midnight. (*CLNT*)

ACTS 20:7 Ἐν ˙on˙ δὲ [And] τῇ [the] μιᾷ [one] τῶν [of the] σαββάτων [Sabbaths] συνηγμένων [being assembled] τῶν [of the] μαθητῶν [disciples] κλάσαι ˙to break] ἄρτον [bread], ὁ [-] Παῦλος ˙Paul] διελέγετο [was discussing] αὐτοῖς [with them], μέλλων [being about to] ἐξιέναι [depart] τῇ [the] ἐπαύριον [next day], παρέτεινέ [he extended] τε [and] τὸν [the] λόγον [message] μέχρι [until] μεσονυκτίου [midnight].

When we examine verse 7 in the Greek, we see that the text again literally says "one of the Sabbaths," not "first *day* of the week."

Luke tells us that Paul and his colleagues arrived in Troas at least five days after the Feast of Unleavened Bread, and that they stayed in Troas for seven days. Paul was on his way to Jerusalem to observe the feast of Pentecost (Acts 20:16). With an understanding of the Sabbath count to Pentecost (Lev.

23:15-16), it's clear that μιᾷ τῶν σαββάτων here indicates that Paul spent one of the seven weekly Sabbaths between Passover and Pentecost with the brethren in Troas. Once again, there is no significance to be found for Sunday in this passage.

Now let's examine the final instance where the "first *day* of the week" is mentioned in most English Bibles. It is found in the 16th chapter of Paul's first letter to the Corinthians:

I CORINTHIANS 16:1 Now concerning the collection for the saints, as I have given orders to the churches of Galatia, so you must do also: 2 **On the first *day* of the week** let each one of you lay something aside, storing up as he may prosper, that there be no collections when I come. (***NKJV***)

Is Paul speaking of a weekly collection to be set aside by the Corinthians every Sunday so a sufficient amount would be available when he arrived? Or is it possible that Paul had something else in mind?

The key to understanding this whole passage is the Greek word κατὰ

which begins verse 2. Thayer says κατὰ is: "a preposition denoting motion or diffusion or direction from the higher to the lower . . ."

This word is frequently rendered "after" by Greek translators ("down from" = "after"). Let's look at the difference it would make to translate this word as "after" instead of "on" in this verse, as well as rendering

μιᾷ τῶν σαββάτων as "one of the Sabbaths":

"On the first *day* of the week" → ***becomes*** → "After one of the Sabbaths"

Here is a literal rendering of the first two verses of I Corinthians 16:

I CORINTHIANS 16:1 Now concerning the collection that is for the saints, as I directed to the churches of Galatia, so also you do. 2 **After one of the Sabbaths**, let each one of you beside himself put something aside, storing up whatever he may have prospered, in order that when I come then collections may not be made; (*literal translation*)

1 CORINTHIANS 16:1 Περὶ [concerning] δὲ [Now] τῆς [the] λογίας [collection] τῆς [the *one*] εἰς [for] τοὺς [the] ἁγίους [saints], ὥσπερ [as] διέταξα [I directed] ταῖς [to the] ἐκκλησίαις [churches] τῆς [the *ones*] Γαλατίας [of Galatia], οὕτω [so] καὶ [also] ὑμεῖς [you] ποιήσατε [do]. 2 κατὰ [After] μίαν [one of] σαββάτων [*the* Sabbaths] ἕκαστος [each] ὑμῶν [of you] παρ' [beside] ἑαυτῷ [himself] τιθέτω [let put *something*] θησαυρίζων [storing up] ὅ [what] τι [something] ἂν [—] εὐοδῶται [he may prosper], ἵνα [in order that] μὴ [not] ὅταν [when] ἔλθω [I come], τότε [then] λογίαι [collections] γίνωνται [*there* may be].

We know that Passover and the Feast of Unleavened Bread were important to the context of Paul's instructions to the Corinthians (I Cor. 5:7-8). It is likely that Paul wrote this epistle during this spring festival. If that was indeed the time frame of the letter, then Paul's encouragement to begin gathering a collection "after one of the Sabbaths" would have been intended to clearly tell the Corinthians WHEN to begin their offering so they would have it completed by the time Paul arrived. Once again, the most logical view of this Scripture does **not** include a recognition of Sunday.

CONCLUSION:

Almost the entire Christian world celebrates Sunday as their day of worship in place of the 7th-day Sabbath God instituted at creation (Gen. 2:2-3). They

justify doing this because they believe that Jesus Christ was raised from the dead on this day. However, as our study of the burial and resurrection has shown, the Greek text overwhelmingly supports another set of facts.
Yeshua was buried late on a Wednesday afternoon, just before the Passover high Sabbath, and he was resurrected very early on the morning of the weekly Sabbath. This particular weekly Sabbath was one of the seven Sabbaths counted to Pentecost. It was known to the Jews as the "First Sabbath" because it was the first weekly Sabbath between Passover and Pentecost. Furthermore, it's likely that the "first day of the week," Sunday, is NEVER even mentioned in the Greek New Testament. May God help us to put away the traditions of men and obey His *Torah*!

Bryan T. Huie
May 10, 1999
Revised: April 11, 2009

The Role of Women
in Church Services

This chapter studies what the Scriptures reveal regarding women's role in church services. While both men and women are heirs of God, the Scriptures reveal that they have different roles assigned by God.

In 21st-century western culture, we see many things practiced in worship and religion that were absent from the 1st-century church. Things taken for granted in some of today's Christian denominations would have been rejected as heresy by the early church. One of the innovations of the past century is the increased participation of women in formal worship services. In today's society, it is considered intolerant to restrict the participation of woman based solely on gender.

However, if we claim to be followers of Yeshua the Messiah and seek to live our lives as he did, what should be our guidance in this matter? Should we follow today's cultural norms without question in order to be "politically correct," or should we look to the Bible to see what God would have us do?

Let's allow Yeshua's own words to answer this question:

MATTHEW 4:4 But he answered and said, "It is written, 'Man shall not live by bread alone, but by every word that proceeds from the mouth of God.' " (*NKJV*)

Moses also addressed what God expects of His people:

DEUTERONOMY 12:32 "Whatever I command you, be careful to observe it; you shall not add to it nor take away from it." (*NKJV*)

Additionally, the book of Proverbs speaks of the value in heeding God's words:

PROVERBS 30:5 Every word of God is pure; He is a shield to those who put their trust in Him. 6 Do not add to His words, lest He rebuke you, and you be found a liar. (*NKJV*)

If we truly are going to live "by every word that proceeds from the mouth of God," we have to put aside what **we** think and what **we** want, and see what GOD thinks and what HE wants. Today's world is in rebellion against God and His commands. Paul's exhortation and warning to Timothy in his final letter to him is very relevant to the time we live in now:

II TIMOTHY 4:1 I charge you in the presence of God and of Christ Jesus, who is to judge the living and the dead, and by his appearing and his kingdom: 2 preach the word; be ready in season and out of season; reprove, rebuke, and exhort, with complete patience and teaching. 3 For **the time is coming when people will not endure sound teaching, but having itching ears they will accumulate for themselves teachers to suit their own passions**, 4 and will turn away from listening to the truth and wander off into myths. (*ESV*)

Certainly today we have a majority of believers who have rejected sound scriptural doctrine. They have turned away from following the truth (God's word-John 17:17) and have instead crafted rationalized fiction to accommodate their own desires and lusts.

In this article, we're going to look at what the Bible says about the role of women in a formal church service. The following information is not MY opinion; it's what the Bible teaches.

In researching this topic, I read dozens of articles by people with a variety of different views. I encountered an incredible amount of rationalization regarding current practices. Some argued that Paul's instructions were cultural and specific to the situations of his day. Some said that Paul was a male chauvinist and should be ignored because his words contradict the teachings of Yeshua. Some said that the Scriptures addressing this topic were not originally part of the Bible, but were instead added later. Some said that Paul was writing only about unconverted or unlearned women who attended worship services. Some stated that just two passages of relevant Scripture weren't enough to establish church doctrine. Some went so far as to claim that the Bible clearly shows women were leaders, teachers and apostles in the early church, and only later did a male-dominated leadership restrict them from these positions.

Most of the world does not understand or accept what the Bible plainly teaches about men and women. The difference between what most people think today and what Paul taught nearly 2,000 years ago is rooted in the fundamental difference in the modern view regarding the composition of the human race.

To Paul, mankind was made up of families. The family was the basic organizational structure for human relationships. Within families, there was an order prescribed by God. This order was instituted by God at the very beginning.

But for those living in today's western feminist societies, the human race is no longer made up of families, but rather of individuals. A woman is just another person like a man. Therefore, most people in today's world don't see any reason for dealing differently with men and women.

Many believers today feel that what the Bible teaches about male and female relationships is irrelevant in our modern society. When we ignore the Bible, as well as the inherent physical, mental, and emotional differences between men and women, there does not seem to be any reason why we should NOT view the sexes as equivalent.

But if we are going to be honest with ourselves about God's word, we have to consider objectively what is written there about the relationship of men and women. This article is going to examine what the Bible teaches regarding the roles God ordained for men and women. In the end, it all comes back to the authority of the Bible in our lives. Are we really willing to live by every word of God?

The best place to begin this study is at the beginning:

GENESIS 2:4 This is the history of the heavens and the earth when they were created, in the day that the LORD God made the earth and the heavens, 5 before any plant of the field was in the earth and before any herb of the field had grown. For the LORD God had not caused it to rain on the earth, and there was no man to till the ground; 6 but a mist went up from the earth and watered the whole face of the ground. 7 And the LORD God formed man of the dust of the ground, and breathed into his nostrils the breath of life; and man became a living being. 8 The LORD God planted a garden eastward in Eden, and there He put the man whom He had formed. 9 And out of the ground the LORD God made every tree grow that is pleasant to the sight and good for food. The tree of life was also in the midst of the garden, and the tree of the knowledge of good and evil. . . . 15 Then the LORD God took the man and put him in the garden of Eden to tend and keep it. 16 And the LORD God commanded the man, saying, "Of every tree of the garden you may freely eat; 17 but of the tree of the knowledge of good and evil you shall not eat, for in the day that you eat of it you shall surely die." 18 And the LORD God said, "**It is not good that man should be alone; I will make him a HELPER** ['ezer] **comparable to him**." 19 Out of the ground the LORD God formed every beast of the field and every bird of the air, and brought them to Adam to see what he would call them. And whatever Adam called each living creature, that was its name. 20 So Adam gave names to all cattle, to the birds of the air, and to every beast of the field. But for Adam there was not found a **helper** ['ezer] comparable to him. 21 And the LORD God caused a deep sleep to fall on Adam, and he slept; and He took one of his **ribs** [tzal'otayv], and closed up the flesh in its place. 22 Then the **rib** [tzela'] which the LORD God had taken from man He made into a woman, and He brought her to the man. 23 And Adam said: "This is now bone of my bones and flesh of my flesh; she shall be called Woman, because she was taken out of Man." 24 Therefore a man shall leave his father and mother and be joined to his wife, and they shall become one flesh. 25 And they were both naked, the man and his wife, and were not ashamed. (**NKJV**)

Very soon after the creation, God saw that Adam was in need of someone comparable to himself to help him with the duties that had been assigned to him. So God took a rib (Heb. *tzela'*) from Adam, and used it to create woman to be his helper.

The fact that God took a rib, and not another part of Adam's body, is very significant. The *The Theological Wordbook of the Old Testament* (*TWOT*) says of *tzela'* that "elsewhere it is an architectural term. It refers to the sides of an object" (p. 768, vol. II). The use of man's rib in the creation of woman clearly shows that she was not to be over the man, nor was she to be trodden under his foot. Rather, she was to be his supporter, working with him at his side.

This view of the role of woman is also confirmed by the use of the word *'ezer* ("helper") in regard to her. *TWOT* states that while the word *'ezer* ">designates assistance, it is more frequently used in a concrete sense to designate the assistant" (p. 661, vol. II). The woman, Eve, was intended by God to be Adam's assistant, helping him with his responsibilities and subject to his authority.

GENESIS 3:1 Now the serpent was more cunning than any beast of the field which the LORD God had made. And he said to the woman, "Has God indeed said, 'You shall not eat of every tree of the garden'?" 2 And the woman said to the serpent, "We may eat the fruit of the trees of the garden; 3 but of the fruit of the tree which is in the midst of the garden, God has said, 'You shall not eat it, nor shall you touch it, lest you die.' " 4 Then the serpent said to the woman, "You will not surely die. 5 For God knows that in the day you eat of it your eyes will be opened, and you will be like God, knowing good and evil." (**NKJV**)

Notice the tactic of Satan the serpent (Rev. 12:9; 20:2). He approached Eve while Adam was absent. He asked her a question regarding instructions Adam alone had received **before** she was created (Gen. 2:16-17). Therefore, the only way she would have known what God had instructed regarding the fruit of the tree of the knowledge was if Adam had relayed it to her accurately. Besides clearly calling God's trustworthiness into question, it is likely that Satan was also subtly tempting Eve to doubt that Adam had told her the full story. While disparaging the motive of God regarding the warning, Satan also tried to cause Eve to distrust Adam.

GENESIS 3:6 So when the woman saw that the tree was good for food, that it was pleasant to the eyes, and a tree desirable to make one wise, she took of its fruit and ate. She also gave to her husband with her, and he ate. 7 Then the eyes of both of them were opened, and they knew that they were naked; and they sewed fig leaves together and made themselves coverings. 8 And they heard the sound of the LORD God walking in the garden in the cool of the day, and Adam and his wife hid themselves from the presence of the LORD God among the trees of the garden. 9 Then the LORD God called to Adam and said to him, "Where are you?" 10 So he said, "I heard Your voice in the garden, and I was afraid because I was naked; and I hid myself." 11 And He said, "Who told you that you were naked? Have you eaten from the tree of which I commanded you that you should not eat?" 12 Then the man said, "The woman whom You gave to be with me, she gave me of the tree, and I ate." 13 And the LORD God said to the woman, "What is this you have done?" The woman said, "The serpent deceived me, and I ate." 14 So the LORD God said to the serpent: "Because you have done this, you are cursed more than all cattle, and more than every beast of the field; on your belly you shall go, and you shall eat dust all the days of your life. 15 And I will put enmity between you and the woman, and between your seed and her Seed; He shall bruise your head, and you shall bruise His heel." 16 To the woman He said: "I will greatly multiply your sorrow and your conception; in pain you shall bring forth children; **your desire shall be for your husband, and he shall rule over you."** 17 Then to Adam He said, "Because you have heeded the voice of your wife, and have eaten from the tree of which I commanded you, saying, 'You shall not eat of it': "Cursed is the ground for your sake; in toil you shall eat of it all the days of your life. 18 Both thorns and thistles it shall bring forth for you, and you shall eat the herb of the field. 19 In the sweat of your face you shall eat bread till you return to the ground, for out of it you were taken; for dust you are, and to dust you shall return." (*NKJV*)

The sin of Adam and Eve led to curses being placed on both men and women. Likewise, the sin of Satan brought a curse upon him and those angels who joined him in rebellion against God. The curses on women are specifically listed in Genesis 3:16.

The book of Genesis provides us with an understanding of God's original intent and purpose (Matt. 19:8). As we'll see when we review the apostle Paul's comments on the role of women in the church, he appeals not to the culture of the day, but rather to the teaching of the *Torah*. He uses chapters Genesis 2 and 3 to support his position.

The Genesis 2 account emphasizes the relationships of the man with his Creator, plants, animals, and the woman. Genesis 2 highlights the three features which differentiate the man and the woman:

1. God created woman at a different time; she was made **AFTER** man. His priority in time has implications, as Paul points out (I Tim. 2:12-13). In the divine order, a firstborn carries responsibility for, and authority over, those who come afterward.

2. God created woman from a different material; she was made **FROM** man. Paul uses this fact to support the headship of the man (I Cor. 11:8).

3. God created woman for a different purpose; she was made **FOR** man. The reverse is not true (I Cor. 11:9). Woman's primary function is in relation to man, but man was created first without reference to her (Gen. 2:15).

All three of these distinctions are mentioned in the New Testament as being significant to the divinely defined roles of men and women. However, this does **NOT** in any way mean that women are inferior to men. As Paul tells us in Galatians 3:28, all who accept the Messiah become heirs to the promise of Abraham:

GALATIANS 3:26 For you are all sons of God through faith in Christ Jesus. 27 For as many of you as were baptized into Christ have put on Christ. 28 There is neither Jew nor Greek, there is neither slave nor free, there is neither male nor female; for you are all one in Christ Jesus. 29 And if you are Christ's, then you are Abraham's seed, and heirs according to the promise. (*NKJV*)

In this passage, Paul shows the potential for the salvation for ALL of humanity. Both men and women will be in the kingdom of God. However, Paul does not mean that NOW there are no longer defined roles and lines of authority. Even though Jews, Greeks, slaves, men and women can all be saved, there are still roles that each will play in God's plan during this age. And these roles are different.

In the the book of Acts, we are told that Paul went from Athens to the Grecian city of Corinth (Acts 18:1). He taught in the synagogue at first, and then at the house of Justus, who lived next door to the synagogue (Acts 18:4-7). In a vision, Yeshua told Paul to stay there because he had many people in the city (Acts 18:9-10). So Paul spent "a good while" longer than a year and half in Corinth, teaching the word of God to many former pagans (Acts 18:11-18).

However, some time after Paul had moved on, he heard from members of the Corinthian church that disputes and heresies had arisen there within the congregation. From the letter Paul subsequently wrote to address these problems, it is clear that the practices of the Corinthian assembly had begun to significantly deviate from those of other messianic congregations.

Much of Paul's first letter to the Corinthians deals with proper conduct of believers during informal and formal worship. As part of his correction and instruction, Paul outlined the divinely established order to the Corinthian congregation in the 11th chapter of his first letter:

I CORINTHIANS 11:1 Imitate me, just as I also imitate Christ. 2 Now I praise you, brethren, that you remember me in all things and keep the traditions just as I delivered them to you. 3 But I want you to know that the **head** [kephale] of every **man** [andros] is Christ, the **head** [kephale] of **woman** [gunaikos] is **man** [aner], and the **head** [kephale] of Christ is God. (*NKJV*)

Paul starts this section of his letter by exhorting the Corinthians to follow his example ONLY as he followed the example of Messiah (v. 1). He begins his correction with a quick acknowledgement that the Corinthians were still adhering to the instructions he had given them while there (v. 2). However, Paul then immediately lays the groundwork for his ensuing guidance by listing the line of authority established by God (v. 3).

God is not the author of confusion (I Cor. 14:33). In the church, as in families, there must be some defined structure of authority for all things to work properly. The Greek word *kephale* is used metaphorically in verse 3 to signify one (or a group) who is superior in authority. According to Paul, the line of authority in the church is as follows:

God the Father
↓
Yeshua the Messiah
↓
Men
↓
Women

The Greek noun *andros*, and its variants (including *aner*), can refer generally to males or specifically to husbands, depending on the context. Alternately, the noun *gune* and its various forms can be translated either as "woman" or "wife" based on context.

However, it is evident in this passage that the broader meaning is intended. Messiah's authority over the church does not extend **just** to husbands and wives. He is over the ENTIRE church (all men and women).

Paul begins his discussion of the wearing of a headcovering by telling the Corinthians that God the Father is the ultimate authority. Under Him is Messiah Yeshua, then males, and finally, females. This seems like a strange way to begin this topic, but it is actually very relevant, as we shall see.

I CORINTHIANS 11:4 Every **man** [aner] praying or prophesying, having his **head** [kephales] **covered** [kata], dishonors his **head** [kephalen]. (*NKJV*)

After outlining the authorities in the church, Paul starts his corrective instructions. He tells the Corinthian men that if they pray or prophesy with their physical head "covered," they dishonor their spiritual head, Yeshua the Messiah (v. 3). The Greek preposition *kata*, which is translated "covered" here, denotes direction and literally means "down from."

Many take the discussion of the headcovering in this passage to be referring specifically to hair. As we shall see shortly, verse 6 absolutely eliminates that possibility. Paul is actually referring to the wearing of a fabric veil or covering on the head.

Paul starts out by addressing the practice the Corinthian men had adopted of praying or prophesying with a veil or covering hanging down from their head. A similar custom is currently practiced by some Jews and messianics, where a tallit ("prayer shawl") is draped over a man's head during prayer. This custom is supposed to represent the man creating a personal "prayer closet" to ensure privacy during the act of praying. It appears that it was the Corinthian's adoption of this custom (or one similar to it) that prompted Paul's instructions here.

I CORINTHIANS 11:5 But every **woman** [gune] who prays or prophesies with her **head** [kephale] **uncovered** [akatakalupto] dishonors her **head** [kephalen], for that is one and the same as if her head were **shaved** [exuremene]. (*NKJV*)

Paul now addresses the reverse situation which was occurring among the Corinthian women. The Greek compound word *akatakalupto* ("uncovered") is made up of three parts: the negative particle *a*, *kata*, and *kalupto*, which means "to cover" or "to veil." Literally, this word means "not veiled" or "not covered" (with a garment that hangs "down from" the head).

Here, Paul notifies the women in the Corinthian church that if they pray or prophesy with their physical head "unveiled" or "uncovered," they dishonor the men in the congregation, who are their spiritual head (v. 3). At the end of this verse, Paul states that the practice of a woman praying or prophesying without a veil covering her head was as scandalous as if her head were shaved (Gr. root *xurao*).

At that time, shaving a woman's head was one of the punishments decreed for convicted adultresses. Additionally, it appears that some of the sacred prostitutes from the pagan temples shaved their heads. Properly understood, this statement was designed to show the Corinthian women how shameful it was to abandon wearing a headcovering.

I CORINTHIANS 11:6 For if a **woman** [gune] is **not covered** [ou katakaluptetai], let her also be **shorn** [keirastho]. But if it is **shameful** [aischron] for a woman [gunaiki] to be **shorn** [keirasthai] or **shaved** [xurasthai], let her be **covered** [katakaluptesthe]. (**NKJV**)

Paul here greatly strengthens his condemnation from the preceding verse. He goes so far as to command that if any woman in the Corinthian assembly refused to wear a headcovering during prayer or prophecy, she should have her hair cut short (Gr. root *keiro*), or shaved off altogether, to make her shame evident to all. He then reverses his statement by saying that if it was considered shameful for a woman to have her hair cut short or shaved off (and it WAS), then she should avoid that fate by covering her head (with a fabric headcovering).

This verse destroys the argument that Paul is speaking of a woman's long hair as her covering. To illustrate the absurdity of that position, let's look at part of this verse using that assumption:

For if a woman is not covered (by long hair), let her hair be cut short.

To take the position that Paul is speaking here of long hair as a woman's covering, we have to believe that his command was that if a woman had short hair, she needed to have her hair cut short as punishment. As you can see, this view doesn't make any sense. Obviously, the covering Paul is speaking of has to be something other than hair.

I CORINTHIANS 11:7 For a **man** [aner] indeed ought not to **cover** [katakaluptesthai] his **head** [*kephalen*], since he is the image and glory of God; but **woman** [gune] is the glory of **man** [*andros*]. 8 For **man** [aner] is not from **woman** [gunaikos], but **woman** [gune] from **man** [andros]. 9 Nor was **man** [aner] created for the **woman** [gunaika], but **woman** [gune] for the **man** [andra]. (**NKJV**)

Contrary to the claims of some, Paul is not basing his teaching on the headcovering on 1st-century culture or circumstances unique to the Corinthians. As he does elsewhere in his writings (cf. I Tim. 2:13), Paul refers back to the creation story to support his position. The order established at the beginning by God is the basis for his teaching. Man was created first. Woman was created afterward **from** man and **for** man.

I CORINTHIANS 11:10 **For this reason** [dia touto] the **woman** [gune] ought to have a **symbol of authority** [exousian] on her **head** [kephales], because of the angels.(*NKJV*)

To most people, this is one of the most enigmatic verses within Paul's writings. However, the beginning of the sentence ("for this reason" - *dia touto*) shows us that Paul's conclusion in this verse is directly tied to his observations in the previous verses. Woman was created **for man**; THAT IS WHY (*dia touto*) a woman should wear a headcovering. This veil is a powerful symbol which shows the angelic realm (Gen. 6:1-4) that the woman wearing it has accepted the divine order established at creation.

As a side note, in his work *Against Heresies*, Catholic church father Irenaeus (120 -202 C.E.) rendered this verse as follows: "A woman ought to have a **veil** [*kalumma*] upon her head, because of the angels" (sec. 2, ch. 8, bk. 1). Irenaeus understood the "power" (*exousia*) on a woman's head to be a cloth covering of some kind and not a woman's hair.

I CORINTHIANS 11:11 Nevertheless, neither is **man** [aner] independent of **woman** [gunaikos], nor **woman** [gune] independent of **man** [andros], in the Lord. 12 For as **woman** [gune] came from **man** [andros], even so **man** [aner] also comes through **woman** [gunaikos]; but all things are from God. (*NKJV*)

Paul now seeks to balance his exposition of scriptural authority with a proper understanding of how that authority should be viewed. In the Lord, men and women are not independent of each other. Just as woman was initially created from the man, now man comes through woman via the birth process. Man was placed in charge by God because order is necessary to the proper functioning of the family, not because man is somehow "better" than woman.

I CORINTHIANS 11:13 Judge among yourselves. Is it proper for a **woman** [gunaika] to pray to God with her head **uncovered** [akatakalupton]? 14 Does not even nature itself teach you that if a **man** [aner] has long hair, it is a dishonor to him? 15 But if a **woman** [gune] has long hair, it is a glory to her; for her hair is given to her for a **covering** [peribolaiou].(*NKJV*)

Paul concludes his teaching on the headcovering by drawing an analogy between nature and the requirement for a woman to be veiled during prayer. Just as nature shows that a woman should have long hair (and conversely, a man should **not**), Paul states that during prayer, a woman should be veiled (and a man should **not**).

It's interesting to note that the Greek word translated "covering" at the end of verse 15 is *peribolaiou*. This word appears only one other time in the New Testament (Heb. 1:12), where it is rendered "cloak." The Greek word for "veil" (*kalumma* - II Cor. 3:13-16) is purposely not used here, because a woman's hair was not the covering or veil Paul was speaking about.

Historical sources from the early centuries of the church agree that the headcovering mentioned in I Corinthians 11:4-13 was a fabric covering worn by the women in worship. These sources sometimes differ about the application of the headcovering, but they are solidly in agreement that Paul's reference to women being covered in worship was to a cloth headcovering and not to the hair of a woman.

I CORINTHIANS 11:16 But if anyone seems to be contentious, we have no such custom, nor do the churches of God. (*NKJV*)

Here Paul wraps up his teaching on the headcovering by stating that no custom such as that which had been instituted at Corinth (men praying with their head veiled, women praying without a veil) existed anywhere else. What he had just explained to them was standard practice throughout all the messianic assemblies, and they were bound to follow it.

Moving on to the 14th chapter of I Corinthians, Paul addresses another issue where the congregation was having problems: Speaking in formal worship services. Because of disorderly **speaking** practices, confusion reigned during the Corinthian worship services.

From the comments made in this chapter by Paul, we see that there were essentially **three** speaking problems that had arisen:

1. Speaking in tongues during services;

2. Prophets speaking during services; and

3. Women speaking during services.

Most of Paul's instruction in this chapter deals with speaking in tongues. To summarize his teaching on tongues, Paul states that he who speaks in a tongue speaks to God, not men (I Cor. 14:2). He says that speaking in tongues is a sign to unbelievers (I Cor. 14:22). Therefore, it does not benefit the congregation for someone to speak in tongues unless there is an interpreter present, and then only two or three should speak (I Cor. 14:27). But if no one is there to interpret, then the one speaking in tongues should remain silent (I Cor. 14:28). To do otherwise would not build up the assembly, and edification is the primary reason to desire such spiritual gifts (I Cor. 14:12).

Paul also explains how and when prophets should address the assembled congregation. He says prophecy is a more important spiritual gift than speaking in tongues (I Cor. 14:1-5). Prophecy is a sign to believers (I Cor. 14:22-24); it shows that God is present in the congregation (I Cor. 14:25). Only two or three prophets were to speak (I Cor. 14:29), and then only one at a time (I Cor. 14:31). The purpose for Paul to outline these instructions was to reign in the chaos that was ensuing from everyone trying to speak at the same time. As he bluntly states, "God is not the author of confusion" (I Cor. 14:33). Only if things were done in an orderly manner could the congregation benefit from these spiritual gifts.

The final section of I Corinthians 14 deals with women speaking in formal worship services:

I CORINTHIANS 14:33b As in all the churches of the saints, 34 the **women** [gunaikes] should keep **silent** [sigatosan] in the churches. For they are not permitted to **speak** [lalein], but should be in **submission** [hupotassesthai], as the Law also says. (*ESV*)

Paul starts off in verse 33 by saying that what he was teaching was common practice in all the messianic congregations. Earlier in his first letter to the Corinthians, Paul stated that his preaching was consistent everywhere (I Cor. 4:17). Therefore, the ensuing instructions were not just for the women of the Corinthian congregation, but for women in all the "churches of the saints." Those who propose that only the Corinthian women were effected by this teaching must ignore other Scriptures which are equally clear on the subject (e.g., I Tim. 2:11-15).

In verse 34, Paul commands that women remain silent and not speak "in the assembly." Some have tried to weaken Paul's teaching by suggesting that the term "speak" here refers simply to idle chitchat or gossip by women during the worship service rather than to serious public participation in the study of Scripture. This position is not supportable based on the original text, however. The Greek root verb *laleo* is used 24 times in this chapter (I Cor. 14:2-6, 9, 11, 13, 18, 19, 21, 23, 27-29, 34, 35, 39). It simply means to audibly speak, whether that speech be in another tongue, from a prophet, or from a woman.

Still others have attempted to paint Paul's teaching as a cultural issue, based on conditions unique to Corinth and unrelated to modern believers. But Paul's command was not based on special circumstances in the Corinthian culture. It was based on the biblical principle of humble submission to divinely-ordained authority (in this case, the authority man has over woman based on creation).

This is the reason for the citation of "the Law" as the basis for his instructions at the end of verse 34. Many try to argue that since there is no **specific** law in the *Torah* forbidding women to speak, Paul must have been referring to some unbiblical law that is not binding on modern believers. However, Paul's use of "the Law" here is a reference back to the creation account we examined previously (Gen. 2-3). "The Law" is simply another name for the *Torah*, the first five books of Moses (cf. Matt. 5:17; 7:12; 22:40; Luke 24:44; Acts 13:15).

It is fashionable now to reject Paul's teaching on women speaking as though it was some chauvinistic doctrine that only he taught, some personal bias that is inconsistent with other biblical revelation. Yet the silence of women in the churches was not a new innovation given only to the Corinthians. The practice Paul required in formal church services was based on the scriptural principle of submission found in Genesis. Peter speaks of this same principle in his first general epistle in relation to marriage (I Pet. 3:1-6).

I CORINTHIANS 14:35 If there is anything they desire to learn, let them ask their husbands at home. For it is **shameful** [aischron] for a woman to **speak** [lalein] in church. (*ESV*)

If verse 34 is difficult for many to accept, verse 35 is even more so. Just as a woman having a shorn or shaved head was said to be "shameful" (*aischron* - I Cor. 11:6), so too is a woman speaking in formal worship services disgraceful. It would almost seem that Paul is "rubbing salt in the wound" here. A woman cannot faith, love, and holiness, with self-control. (*NKJV*)

We may like what Paul says, or we may not like it. In the end, we are either willing to do what he commands, or we are not willing to do it. But there is no room for doubt about what he says.

Some attempt to use the NT example of Aquila and Priscilla to say that women can teach men. But let's look at this scriptural example a little more closely, because it's very instructive if properly understood.

We're introduced to Aquila and his wife Priscilla in Corinth:

ACTS 18:1 After these things Paul departed from Athens and went to Corinth. 2 And he found a certain Jew named Aquila, born in Pontus, who had recently come from Italy with his wife Priscilla (because Claudius had commanded all the Jews to depart from Rome); and he came to them. 3 So, because he was of the same trade, he stayed with them and worked; for by occupation they were tentmakers. (*NKJV*)

They obviously became good friends with the Apostle Paul, because when he left Corinth, they traveled with him for a while:

ACTS 18:18 So Paul still remained a good while. Then he took leave of the brethren and sailed for Syria, and Priscilla and Aquila were with him. He had his hair cut off at Cenchrea, for he had taken a vow. 19 And he came to Ephesus, and left them there . . . (*NKJV*)

After stopping at Ephesus, we see Aquila and Priscilla meet with the Jewish teacher Apollos:

ACTS 18:24 Now a certain Jew named Apollos, born at Alexandria, an eloquent man and mighty in the Scriptures, came to Ephesus. 25 This man had been instructed in the way of the Lord; and being fervent in spirit, he spoke and taught accurately the things of the Lord, though he knew only the baptism of John. 26 So he began to speak boldly in the synagogue. When Aquila and Priscilla heard him, they took him aside and explained to him the way of God more accurately. (*NKJV*)

An attempt is made, based on verse 26, to show that women are allowed to teach men because Priscilla taught Apollos. However, the text clearly shows that she did so **only** in conjunction with and under the authority of her husband, Aquila. Additionally, they did not do so in the synagogue, but rather they "took him aside" and explained "the way of God" to him.

ROMANS 16:3 Greet Priscilla and Aquila, my fellow workers in Christ Jesus, (*NKJV*)

I CORINTHIANS 16:19 The churches of Asia greet you. Aquila and Priscilla greet you heartily in the Lord, with the church that is in their house.

(*NKJV*)

II TIMOTHY 4:19 Greet Prisca [a shortened form of Priscilla] and Aquila, and the household of Onesiphorus. (*NKJV*)

Bryan T. Huie
March 1, 2005

Revised: April 9, 2009

What is Death?

This article reviews the biblical definition of death, being cut off from God spiritually. Satan, the father of all lies, has deceived Adam and his successors, mankind, for thousands of years. However, God has left us His word to discern the truth regarding spiritual separation from Him. How does death affect what we know as hell, the lake of fire and brimstone, Hades, or Tartarus? Call it what you will, but there is a way for ALL of mankind to be saved. Is it universalism? Read the article to find out more.

If asked to define death, most of us would likely answer by saying "death is the cessation of physical life" or something along those lines. Yet is this really what death is? What does the Bible, God's inspired revelation to mankind, have to say about death?

Death appears very early in the Bible. Let's look at Genesis 2:15-17 to see the first mention of death:

GENESIS 2:15 Then **the LORD God** [YHVH 'elohim] took the man and put him in the garden of Eden to tend and keep it. 16 And **the LORD God** [YHVH 'elohim] commanded the man, saying, "Of every tree of the garden you may freely eat; 17 but of the tree of the knowledge of good and evil you shall not eat, for **in the day that you eat of it you shall surely die**." (*NKJV*)

YHVH 'elohim, the "Word of God" (the preincarnate Messiah) plainly told Adam that he would **die** the **very day** that he ate of the tree of the knowledge of good and evil. Just one chapter later, we see Adam and Eve eating of that forbidden fruit (Gen. 3:6). Yet they did not physically die that day. Had the Messiah lied to Adam about dying, as the "serpent" implied to Eve in the Garden (Gen. 3:4)? Or did the Messiah literally mean that Adam would DIE the day he ate of the fruit?

In pronouncing the curse on Adam for eating of the forbidden fruit, the Messiah told him that he would have to work the ground to produce food to eat for the rest of his life. He cursed the soil so that it would produce thorns and thistles and make Adam's job of farming much more difficult. In Genesis 3:19, the Messiah tells Adam his physical fate:

GENESIS 3:19 "In the sweat of your face you shall eat bread **till you return to the ground**, for out of it you were taken; for **dust you are, and to dust you shall return**." (*NKJV*)

But is this fate to return to dust what the Word of God was talking about when He told Adam that he would **die** in the day he ate of the forbidden fruit? No. Genesis 3:23-24 pictures the death the Messiah was referring to:

GENESIS 3:23 Therefore the LORD God **sent him out from the garden of Eden**, to cultivate the ground from which he was taken. 24 So **He drove the man out**; and at the east of the garden of Eden He stationed the cherubim and the flaming sword which turned every direction to guard the way to the tree of life. (*NASU*)

Clearly Adam was banished from the Garden of Eden because of his disobedience. But how does this equate to dying, you might ask?

The answer to that question reveals God's definition of death. The Bible doesn't tell us how long Adam was in the Garden before his expulsion, but we can see from Genesis 2 and 3 that Adam had a personal relationship with the Messiah there. He was in close contact with Him, and certainly the Messiah spent time teaching him many things, including the fundamental concepts of right and wrong. But after his exile, the Scriptures never again mention the Messiah talking to or interacting with Adam. His relationship with **YHVH 'elohim** was cut off at that moment.

Because the Eternal thinks in a way that is fundamentally foreign to mankind (Isa. 55:8), many have failed to realize how He views life and death. The Bible shows that God considers those who are spiritually separated from Him to be dead. Indeed, alienation from God and His ways is more certainly death than the physical cessation of life (Matt. 22:31-32; Mark 12:26-27; Luke 20:37-38). In this article, we're going to examine Scriptures which prove this point.

Let's start in I Timothy 5:5-6. We'll break into the middle of instructions Paul was giving Timothy about the proper care for widows in the Church. Notice what Paul says about their conduct:

I TIMOTHY 5:5 Now she who is really a widow, and left alone, trusts in God and continues in supplications and prayers night and day. 6 But **she who lives in pleasure is dead while she lives**. (*NKJV*)

Here, Paul states that a widow who lives in pleasure is **dead** even while she continues to live physically. What does he mean by this statement? How can one be dead while still alive? In Colossians 2:13, Paul gives us a hint at the answer:

COLOSSIANS 2:13 When **you were dead in your transgressions** and the uncircumcision of your flesh, He [the Father] **made you alive** together with him [Christ], having forgiven us all our transgressions, (*NASU*)

Here, Paul states that a person who transgresses God's law, one who is a sinner, is **dead** in that state. Although physical death is one consequence of sin, clearly Paul isn't speaking of physical death in this verse. In Ephesians 2:1-5, he expands on this concept:

EPHESIANS 2:1 And **you He made alive, who were dead in trespasses and sins**, 2 in which you once walked according to the course of this world, according to the prince of the power of the air, the spirit who now works in the sons of disobedience, 3 among whom also we all once conducted ourselves in the lusts of our flesh, fulfilling the desires of the flesh and of the mind, and were by nature children of wrath, just as the others. 4 But God, who is rich in mercy, because of His great love with which He loved us, 5 even **when we were dead in trespasses, made us alive together with Christ** (by grace you have been saved), (*NKJV*)

Whoever breaks God's law commits sin, for sin is the transgression of His holy law (I John 3:4). Sin separates us from God, and keeps us from knowing Him and having a personal relationship with Him. The Bible tells us that those who keep His commandments have a good understanding (Psa. 111:10). The Scriptures show that without understanding and knowing God, we cannot have eternal life:

JOHN 17:3 "**This is eternal life, that they may know You** [the Father], **the only true God**, and Jesus Christ whom You have sent." (*NASU*)

I JOHN 5:20 We know too that the Son of God has come, and has given us the power to **know the true God** [the Father]. We are in the true God [the Father], as we are in His Son, Jesus Christ. This [the Father] is the true God, **this is eternal life**. (*Jerusalem Bible*)

Knowing the true God is the key to eternal life. However, this knowledge goes beyond simply comprehending who God is. One must obey God to truly know Him. The demons know who God is (Jam. 2:19), but they do not have life because they do not submit to God's law.

In God's view, those who do not live according to His commandments are dead, because their sins cut them off from Him. Unrepentant sinners can have no true relationship with God. Yet through the Father's wonderful grace, we can be made alive when we repent and accept the sacrifice of His Son, Yeshua.

ROMANS 6:11 Likewise you also, reckon yourselves to be dead indeed to sin, but alive to God in Christ Jesus our Lord. 12 Therefore do not let sin reign in your mortal body, that you should obey it in its lusts. 13 And do not present your members as instruments of unrighteousness to sin, but present yourselves to God **as being alive from the dead**, and your members as instruments of righteousness to God. (*NKJV*)

We have been made spiritually alive through repentance and the acceptance of Christ's atoning sacrifice. We have now been reconciled to the Father; we are now to be dead to sin. John tells us one way we can know we have progressed from death to life:

I JOHN 3:14 We know that **we have passed from death to life**, because we love the brethren. He who does not love his brother abides in **death**. (*NKJV*)

Jesus Christ had many things to say about death. Much of what he said was misunderstood by those he spoke to, and remains perplexing to this day. For instance, let's look at what he told one of his disciples after the death of his father:

LUKE 9:59 Then he said to another, "Follow Me." But he said, "Lord, let me first go and bury my father." 60 Jesus said to him, "**Let the dead bury their own dead**, but you go and preach the kingdom of God." (*NKJV*)

What did Yeshua mean when he said "let the dead bury their own dead"? Clearly he was using two different meanings for the word "dead" in this passage. Surely Christ did not intend to downplay the obvious emotional trauma the man had undergone with the recent death of his father. Instead, his comment was meant to draw a distinction between the disciple, who was called to preach the gospel, and those who had not received the call of God. The calling of that disciple by God separated him from those who were spiritually dead.

Regarding life, death, and the call of God, the Messiah told the Jews the following:

JOHN 6:44 "**No one can come to me unless the Father who sent me draws him**; and **I will raise him up at the last day**. 45 It is written in the prophets, 'And they shall all be taught by God.' Therefore everyone who has heard and learned from the Father comes to me. 46 Not that anyone has seen the Father, except he who is from God; he has seen the Father. 47 Most assuredly, I say to you, **he who believes in me has everlasting life**. 48 I am the bread of life. 49 Your fathers ate the manna in the wilderness, and are dead. 50 This is the bread which comes down from heaven, that **one may eat of it and not die**. 51 I am the living bread which came down from heaven. If anyone eats of this bread, **he will live forever**; and the bread that I shall give is my flesh, which I shall give for the **life of the world**." (*NKJV*)

As Yeshua said, when we "eat of the bread which came down from heaven," we will not die in the spiritual sense. We will not be separated from God, even though we may for a time "sleep" because of physical death (I Kings 2:10; 11:21, 43; Job 3:11-15; Psa. 13:1; Dan. 12:2; John 11:11-14; I Cor. 11:30; 15:51), awaiting the resurrection. The Jews totally missed the spiritual point Yeshua was making here, as the ensuing verses show:

JOHN 6:52 The Jews therefore quarreled among themselves, saying, "How can this man give us his flesh to eat?" 53 Then Jesus said to them, "Most assuredly, I say to you, unless you eat the flesh of the Son of Man and drink his blood, **you have no life in you**. 54 **Whoever eats my flesh and drinks my blood has eternal life**, and **I will raise him up at the last day**. 55 For my flesh is food indeed, and my blood is drink indeed. 56 **He who eats my flesh and drinks my blood abides in me, and I in him**. 57 As the living Father sent me, and I live because of the Father, so **he who feeds on me will live because of me**. 58 This is the bread which came down from heaven -- not as your fathers ate the manna, and are dead. **He who eats this bread will live forever**." (*NKJV*)

Christ is not talking about physical death in the verses above; his statement "I will raise him up at the last day" clearly alludes to the future resurrection of believers. To understand this Scripture, we must properly understand God's view of death. Eating the flesh and drinking the blood of our Messiah is symbolic of adopting his very nature and making it an integral part of our being. It is not merely a profession of belief, but a way of life. It is living in complete obedience to God and His laws, the same way of life that Yeshua himself lived while on the earth. This concept is succinctly expressed by the apostle John in his first general epistle:

I JOHN 2:3 Now by this we know that we know him, if we keep his commandments. 4 **He who says, "I know him," and does not keep his command-ments, is a liar**, and the truth is not in him. 5 But whoever keeps his word, truly the love of God is perfected in him. By this we know that we are in him. 6 He who says he abides in him ought himself also to walk just as he walked. (*NKJV*)

John 8:51-53 is another example of the Jews' misunderstanding the true nature of death:

JOHN 8:51 "Most assuredly, I say to you, if anyone keeps my word **he shall never see death**." 52 Then the Jews said to Him, "Now we know that you have a demon! Abraham is dead, and the prophets; and you say, 'If anyone keeps my word he shall never taste death.' 53 Are you greater than our father Abraham, who is dead? And the prophets are dead. Whom do you make yourself out to be?" (*NKJV*)

In the above passage, Yeshua plainly states that those who keep his word (the Father's word-John 12:49) would never see death. It's obvious that he didn't mean fleshly death, because the Jews correctly pointed out that both Abraham and the prophets had died physically. The Messiah was clearly speaking here of spiritual death, or separation from God.

When talking to the Sadducees about the resurrection (Matt. 22:23-32; Mark 12:18-27; Luke 20:27-38), Yeshua again speaks of the living and the dead:

MATTHEW 22:29 Jesus answered and said to them, "You are mistaken, not knowing the Scriptures nor the power of God. 30 For in the resurrection they neither marry nor are given in marriage, but are like angels of God in heaven. 31 But concerning the resurrection of the dead, have you not read what was spoken to you by God, saying, 32 'I am the God of Abraham, the God of Isaac, and the God of Jacob'? **God is not the God of the dead, but of the living**." (*NKJV*)

Some have attempted to use Matthew 22:32 to prove that Abraham, Isaac, and Jacob are now alive in heaven. Yet this belief contradicts numerous clear Scriptures which show that believers are currently asleep in their graves (Job 3:11-19; Psa. 6:5; 115:17; Ecc. 9:5, 10; I Cor. 15:20; Isa. 57:1-2; Dan. 12:2; Acts 2:29, 34; 13:36). God "calls those things which do not exist as though they did" (Rom. 4:17). Christ could confidently tell the Sadducees that Abraham, Isaac, and Jacob were alive, because their resurrection to eternal life is sure due to their faithful obedience. Yeshua's statement does **not** mean that these three men had already been resurrected and were then alive somewhere (Heb. 11:13, 39-40). In fact, Paul specifically labels this teaching as heresy in his second letter to Timothy (II Tim. 2:18). As Paul tells us (I Cor. 15:23), there is an order to God's plan. That order specifies that believers will receive eternal life at the second coming of Christ (Matt. 24:30-31; I Cor. 15:51-52; I The. 4:15-17; Rev. 11:15-18). For additional information on the status of the dead, see my article

"Are the Dead Conscious?"

The glorified Messiah makes it clear that even Christians can return to a state of being spiritually "dead" in the prophetic book of Revelation:

REVELATION 3:1 "To the angel of the church in Sardis write: He who has the seven Spirits of God and the seven stars, says this: 'I know your deeds, that you have a name that you are alive, but **you are dead**. (*NASU*)

With an understanding of the true nature of death, the meaning of a generally misunderstood passage in Peter's first epistle becomes evident:

I PETER 4:3 For we have spent enough of our past lifetime in doing the will of the Gentiles -- when we walked in lewdness, lusts, drunkenness, revelries, drinking parties, and abominable idolatries. 4 In regard to these, they think it strange that you do not run with them in the same flood of dissipation, speaking evil of you. 5 They will give an account to Him who is ready to judge the living and the dead. 6 For this reason the gospel was preached also to **those who are dead**, that they might be judged according to men in the flesh, but live according to God in the spirit. (*NKJV*)

One of the most widely quoted passages regarding death is from Paul's letter to the Roman assembly:

ROMANS 6:23 For **the wages of sin is death**, but the free gift of God is eternal life in Christ Jesus our Lord. (*NASU*)

Although physical death is definitely a consequence of sin, Paul's primary focus here is on spiritual death. He tells us that God's free gift is eternal (Gr. *aionios*) life in Christ. This free gift is available to us because Yeshua offered himself as a sacrifice for our sins:

I CORINTHIANS 15:3 For I delivered to you first of all that which I also received: that **Christ died for our sins** according to the Scriptures, (*NKJV*)

The Scriptures clearly show that the wages of sin is **death**, and that Christ **died** for our sins. Most of the Christian world believes this "death" to be everlasting torment in the fires of hell. Still others claim that this is eternal "death," a death where the sinner is annihilated and ceases to exist.

However, simple logic should tell us that neither of these scenarios are correct. If the Messiah paid for sin in our stead, he had to suffer the penalty that we should have suffered because of our sins. According to Romans 6:23, that penalty is **death**. Yet this "death" cannot be "everlasting torment," because Christ is not now suffering endlessly in an everburning hell. Likewise, it cannot be annihilation, because Christ was not destroyed for eternity. Instead, God resurrected him from death after three days and three nights in the grave.

The **death** spoken of here is the same death referred to in the Scriptures we've looked at previously. This death is simply separation from God. The Scriptures teach that by sinning, mankind has earned separation from God. But God, in His infinite mercy and grace, sent Christ to pay the penalty for our sins on the cross. As Yeshua hung there beaten and bleeding, the sins of the world were imputed to him and he suffered the penalty for sin, death.

MATTHEW 27:46 And about the ninth hour Jesus cried out with a loud voice, saying, "Eli, Eli, lama sabachthani?" that is, "**My God, my God, why have You forsaken me**?" (*NKJV*)

When he who knew no sin was made to be sin for us (II Cor. 5:21), Yeshua felt forsaken by God. For the first time in his existence, he was separated and cut off from the Eternal Father. That separation lasted from the time the sins of the world were laid upon him on the cross until he was resurrected by God after spending three days and three nights in the garden tomb. At that time Christ became the "firstborn from the dead" (Col. 1:18; Rev. 1:5), the first human raised from corruption to incorruption, the first man changed from flesh to spirit, the first person to overcome the sting of sin.

This brings us to a fundamental truth of God's plan that is misunderstood by most. Paul explains part of this truth in his letter to the Romans:

ROMANS 5:12 Therefore, just as **through one man sin entered into the world, and** [spiritual] **death through sin**, and so [spiritual] **death spread to all men, because all sinned** -- 13 for until the Law sin was in the world, but sin is not imputed when there is no law. 14 Nevertheless [spiritual] death reigned from Adam until Moses, even over those who had not sinned in the likeness of the offense of **Adam**, **who is a type of him who was to come**. (*NASU*)

We know sin cuts us off from God and causes us to be spiritually dead even though we may be physically alive. Paul traces this spiritual death back to one man, Adam. As we saw at the beginning of this article, Adam's sin cut him off from God. Yet it did more than that; his sin effectively separated the entire human race from God. But there is hope for humanity, as Paul tells us in his first epistle to the Corinthian Church:

I CORINTHIANS 15:22 For as in Adam **all die**, even so in Christ **all shall be made alive**. (*NKJV*)

The magnitude of meaning in this one small verse is incredible; unfortunately, it has been hidden to most believers. Paul tells us that even as ALL mankind has spiritually died because of Adam's sin, the same ALL will be made spiritually alive because of Christ's sacrifice.

ROMANS 5:18 Therefore, as through one man's offense judgment came to all men, resulting in condemnation, even so through one man's righteous act **the free gift came to all men**, resulting in justification of life. (*NKJV*)

The spiritual resuscitation of all humanity is also called "reconciliation" in the

Bible, and the Scriptures speak of the eventual reconciliation of all mankind to God:

COLOSSIANS 1:19 For it pleased the Father that in him [Yeshua] all the fullness should dwell, 20 and **by him** [Yeshua] **to reconcile all things to Himself, by him** [Yeshua], **whether things on earth or things in heaven**, having made peace through the blood of his cross. (*NKJV*)

II CORINTHIANS 5:18 Now all things are of God, who has **reconciled** us to Himself through Jesus Christ, and has given us **the ministry of reconciliation,** 19 that is, that **God was in Christ reconciling the world to Himself**, not imputing their trespasses to them, and has committed to us **the word of reconciliation.** (*NKJV*)

Most cannot accept that God will eventually reconcile ALL of His creation to Himself through the Messiah. It just seems too unbelievable, too far-fetched. The weight of century upon century of false teachings and faulty translations has obscured the true revelation of the Bible regarding the ultimate fate of God's creation. The numerous Scriptures about hell, the doom of the wicked, the "second death," etc. *seem* to preclude a universal restoration of all of God's self-aware entities. In the remainder of this article, we will examine the true teaching of the Bible on this topic.

One overriding principle in understanding the Bible is the concept of "here a little, there a little" (Isa. 28:9-13). To truly discern God's plan as revealed in the Bible, one must look at **all** the Scriptures on a topic. Since there are so many Scriptures on this subject, I'm going to select a portion that seem to contradict the idea of universal restoration. But when viewed in totality, we will see that the Bible does not contradict itself on this topic; all the relevant Scriptures are in perfect harmony.

Let's start by looking at what the Bible has to say about "hell" (Gr. *geenna*). This term has come to mean the place of eternal fiery torment to most Christians. It is also often equated to "the lake of fire" mentioned in Revelation (Rev. 19:20; 20:10, 14, 15; 21:8). The *New Bible Dictionary* tells us about the origin and meaning of the Greek word *geenna*:

HINNOM, VALLEY OF. A valley to the S of Jerusalem, also styled 'the valley of the son (or sons) of Hinnom'. It was associated in Jeremiah's time with the worship of Molech. Josiah defiled this shrine, and put an end to the sacrifices offered there. Later the valley seems to have been used for burning the corpses of criminals and animals, and indeed refuse of any sort. Hence the name came to be used as a synonym for hell, the Hebrew phrase *ge* ('valley of') *hinnom* becoming *geenna* in Greek, whence Gehenna in Latin and English (p. 484).

The word *geenna* or a variation is used only 12 times in the New Testament. Let's look at each of those occurrences:

MATTHEW 5:22 "But I say to you that whoever is angry with his brother without a cause shall be in danger of the judgment. And whoever says to his brother, 'Raca!' shall be in danger of the council. But whoever says, 'You fool!' shall be in danger of **hell** [geennan] fire." (*NKJV*)

MATTHEW 5:29 "If your right eye causes you to sin, pluck it out and cast it from you; for it is more profitable for you that one of your members perish, than for your whole body to be cast into **hell** [geennan]. 30 And if your right hand causes you to sin, cut it off and cast it from you; for it is more profitable for you that one of your members perish, than for your whole body to be cast into **hell** [geennan]." (*NKJV*)

MATTHEW 10:28 "And do not fear those who kill the body but cannot kill the soul. But rather fear Him who is able to destroy both soul and body in **hell** [geenne]." (*NKJV*)

LUKE 12:5 "But I will show you whom you should fear: Fear Him who, after He has killed, has power to cast into **hell** [geennan]; yes, I say to you, fear Him!" (*NKJV*)

MATTHEW 18:8 "If your hand or foot causes you to sin, cut it off and cast it from you. It is better for you to enter into life lame or maimed, rather than having two hands or two feet, to be cast into the **everlasting** [aionion] fire. 9 And if your eye causes you to sin, pluck it out and cast it from you. It is better for you to enter into life with one eye, rather than having two eyes, to be cast into **hell** [geennan] fire." (*NKJV*)

MARK 9:43 "If your hand causes you to sin, cut it off. It is better for you to enter into life maimed, rather than having two hands, to go to **hell** [geennan], into the fire that shall never be quenched - 44 where 'Their worm does not die, and the fire is not quenched.' 45 And if your foot causes you to sin, cut it off. It is better for you to enter life lame, rather than having two feet, to be cast into **hell** [geennan], into the fire that shall never be quenched - 46 where 'Their worm does not die, and the fire is not quenched.' 47 And if your eye causes you to sin, pluck it out. It is better for you to enter the kingdom of God with one eye, rather than having two eyes, to be cast into **hell** [geennan] fire - 48 where 'Their worm does not die, and the fire is not quenched.' 49 For everyone will be seasoned with fire, and every sacrifice will be seasoned with salt." (*NKJV*)

MATTHEW 23:15 "Woe to you, scribes and Pharisees, hypocrites! For you travel land and sea to win one proselyte, and when he is won, you make him twice as much a son of **hell** [geennes] as yourselves." (*NKJV*)

MATTHEW 23:33 "You snakes! You brood of vipers! How will you escape being condemned to **hell** [geennes]?" (*NIV*)

JAMES 3:6 And the tongue is a fire, a world of iniquity. The tongue is so set among our members that it defiles the whole body, and sets on fire the course of nature; and it is set on fire by **hell** [geennes]. (*NKJV*)

Clearly, *geenna* is often used in conjunction with "fire." Yet it is interesting to examine how the Jews viewed Gehenna at about the time of Christ. In the *Theological Dictionary of the New Testament*, Joachim Jeremias writes:

It is significant that the oldest Rabbinic reference to Gehenna (T. Sanh., 13, 3 and par.) tells us that the disciples of Shammai, as distinct from those of Hillel, ascribe to Gehenna a purgatorial as well as penal character, namely, in the case of . . . those whose merits and transgressions balance one another. It may be that this conception of a purificatory character of the final fire of judgment underlies such passages as Mk. 9:49; 1 C. 3:13-15; cf. 2 Pt. 3:10 (p. 658, vol. I).

Similarly, *The New International Dictionary of New Testament Theology* says:

The word *gehenna* does not appear in the LXX or in Gk. literature. . . . Jewish apocalyptic assumed that this valley would become, after the final judgment, the hell of fire . . . At the end of the 1st cent. A.D. or the beginning of the 2nd the doctrine of a fiery purgatory arose among the Rabbis. All those in whose cases merit and guilt are equally balanced go to *gehenna*. There they are purified and, if they do penance, inherit paradise. Alongside this we find the concept of an eschatological Gehinnom judgment, limited in time, after the last judgment . . . (p. 208, vol. 2).

From the fact that this word does not appear in any Greek literature outside of the New Testament, we can see that the concept of *geenna* was purely Jewish in origin and nature. Apparently, around the time of Christ the Jewish understanding of *geenna* was that it was a place of purification for a **limited** amount of time after the judgment.

But how does this understanding fit with the scriptural discussion of the "everlasting fire" of Gehenna (Matt. 18:8-9), you may ask? The word translated "everlasting" in this verse is the word *aionion*, a variation of the Greek adjective *aionios*. This adjective and its variations are usually translated "everlasting" or "eternal" in the New Testament. The noun from which it is derived (*aion*) is generally translated "ever," "forever," "evermore," or "eternity." Interestingly, however, it is also translated "world" and "age" in numerous places. To fully understand the biblical teaching on this topic, we must understand what these words **really** mean.

Dr. Marvin Vincent, a noted New Testament scholar who taught at the Union Theological Seminary in New York, wrote the following regarding the words *aion*, *aionios*, and their variations:

Άιών, transliterated *aeon*, is a period of time of longer or shorter duration, having a beginning and an end, and complete in itself. Aristotle (περι ουρανου, i. 9, 15) says: "The period which includes the whole time of each one's life is called the *aeon* of each one." Hence, it often means *the life* of a man, as in

Homer, where one's life (αιών) is said to leave him or consume away (*Il.* v. 685; *Od.* v. 160). It is not, however, limited to human life; it signifies any period in the course of events, as the period or age before Christ; the period of the millennium; the mythological period before the beginnings of history. . . . The word always carries the notion of *time*, and not of *eternity*. It always means a period of time. Otherwise it would be impossible to account for the plural, or for such qualifying expressions as *this* age, or the age *to come*. It does not mean something endless or everlasting. . . . The adjective αιώνιος in like manner carries the idea of time. Neither the noun nor the adjective, in themselves, carry the sense of *endless* or *everlasting*. (pp. 58, 59, vol. IV,*Vincent's Word Studies of the New Testament*)

The consistent mistranslation of *aion* and *aionios* as "eternity," "forever," "eternal," "everlasting," etc., is the primary reason why there is such a grave misunderstanding of God's plan for mankind among those who consider themselves to be His people. As Dr. Vincent clearly states, these words do NOT imply "eternity" or "endlessness" as we understand them.

In his detailed study of *aion* and *aionios*, Louis Abbot wrote of how these words were used in secular Greek literature:

Ancient writings, other than the Scriptures, show how *aion* and *aionios* were used in the ordinary affairs of that time period. Long ago in Rome, periodic games were held. These were referred to as "secular" games. Herodian, who wrote in Greek about the end of the second century A.D., called these *aionios*, "eonian," games. In no sense could those games have been eternal.

Adolph Deissman gives this account: "Upon a lead tablet found in the Necropolis at Adrumetum in the Roman province of Africa, near Carthage, the following inscription, belonging to the early third century, is scratched in Greek: 'I am adjuring Thee, the great God, the eonian, and more than eonian (*epaionion*) and almighty . . .' If by eonian, endless time were meant, then what could be more than endless time?" . . .

Dr. Mangey, a translator of the writings of Philo, says Philo did not use *aionios* to express endless duration.

Josephus shows that *aionios* did not mean endlessness, for he uses it of the period between the giving of the law to Moses and that of his own writing; to the period of the imprisonment of the tyrant John by the Romans; and to the period during which Herod's temple stood. The temple had already been destroyed by the time Josephus was writing.

St. Gregory of Nyssa speaks of *aionios diastema*, "an eonian interval." It would be absurd to call an interval "endless."

St. Chrysostum, in his homily on Eph. 2:1-3, says that "Satan's kingdom is æonian; that is, it will cease with the present world."

St. Justin Martyr repeatedly used the word *aionios* as in the Apol. (p. 57), *aionion kolasin . . . all ouchi chiliontaetee periodon*, "eonian chastening . . . but a period, not a thousand years." Or, as some translate the last clause: "but a period of a thousand years only." He limits the eonian chastening to a period of a thousand years, rather than to endlessness.

In 1 Enoch 10:10 there is an interesting statement using the Greek words: *zoen aionion*, "life eonian," or, as in the KJV, "everlasting life" (at John 3:16 and elsewhere). The whole sentence in Enoch is, *hoti elpizousi zesai zoen aionion, kai hoti zesetai hekastos auton ete pentakosia*, "For they hope to live an eonian life, and that each one of them will live five hundred years." Here, eonian life is limited to five hundred years! (ch. 9, *An Analytical Study of Words*)

The following information on the use, meaning, and origin of the word *aionios* comes from Greek language experts J.H. Milligan and G. Moulton:

Without pronouncing any opinion on the special meaning which theologians have found for this word, we must note that outside the NT, in the vernacular as in the classical Greek . . . it never loses the sense of *perpetuus* [Lat., "unbroken," "perpetual," "lasting," "continuous," "uninterrupted"] . . .

In the Sanskrit *ayu* and its Zend equivalent the idea of *life*, and especially *long life*, predominates. So with the Germanic cognates (Gothic *aiws*). The word, whose root it is of course futile to dig for, is a primitive inheritance from Indo-Germanic days, when it may have meant "long life" or "old age" . . . (p. 16, *Vocabulary of the Greek Testament*)

Let's look at one more piece of evidence about the true meaning of *aion* and *aionios*. It comes from a study of these words by John Wesley Hanson published in 1875:

The oldest lexicographer, *Hesychius*, (A.D. 400-600,) defines *aion* thus: "The life of man, the time of life." At this early date no theologian had yet imported into the word the meaning of endless duration. It retained only the sense it had in the classics, and in the Bible. . . .

John of Damascus (A.D. 750) says, "1, The life of every man is called *aion*. . . . 3, The whole duration or *life of this world* is called *aion*. 4, The life after the resurrection is called 'the *aion* to come.' "

But in the sixteenth century *Phavorinus* was compelled to notice an addition, which subsequently to the time of the famous Council of 544 had been grafted on the word. He says: "*Aion*, time, also life, also habit, or way of life. *Aion is also the eternal and endless AS IT SEEMS TO THE THEOLOGIAN."* Theologians had succeeded in using the word in the sense of endless, and Phavorinus was forced to recognize their usage of it and his phraseology shows conclusively enough that he attributed to theologians the authorship of that use of the word. . . .

The second definition by *Phavorinus* is extracted literally from the "Etymologicon Magnum" of the ninth or tenth century. This gives us the usage from the fourth to the sixteenth century, and shows us that, if the word meant endless at the time of Christ, it must have changed from limited duration in the classics, to unlimited duration, and then back again, at the dates above specified!

From the sixteenth century onward, the word has been defined as used to denote all lengths of duration from brief to endless. . . . (ch. II, *The Greek Word Aion -- Aionios, Translated Everlasting -- Eternal in the Holy Bible*)

As the quotations above show, the idea of "eternity" or "endlessness" was **not** conveyed by these related Greek words until theologians assigned such meanings to them centuries after the New Testament was written. Once we understand that *aion* denotes an "age" or "ages," and that *aionios* means "age-lasting," we can begin to see how the doctrines of eternal punishment/death are erroneous and not taught by the Bible.

As stated earlier, many equate the "lake of fire" spoken of in Revelation with *geenna*. From the descriptions given in the Bible, it appears likely that these two are the same place/thing. Let's look at the lake of fire as it is described in Revelation:

REVELATION 19:20 And the beast was seized, and with him the false prophet who performed the signs in his presence, by which he deceived those who had received the mark of the beast and those who worshiped his image; these two were thrown alive into the **lake of fire** which burns with **brimstone** [theio]. (*NASU*)

REVELATION 20:10 And the devil who deceived them was thrown into the **lake of fire** and **brimstone** [theiou], where the beast and the false prophet are also; and **they will be tormented** [basanisthesontai] day and night **forever and ever** [eis tous aionas ton aionon]. (*NASU*)

REVELATION 20:14 Then death and Hades were thrown into the **lake of fire.** This is the second death, the **lake of fire.** 15 And if anyone's name was not found written in the book of life, he was thrown into the **lake of fire.** (*NASU*)

REVELATION 21:8 "But for the cowardly and unbelieving and abominable and murderers and immoral persons and sorcerers and idolaters and all liars, their part will be in the **lake that burns with fire** and **brimstone** [theio],

which is the second death." (*NASU*)

In these Scriptures we see several concepts presented, with the main one being the lake of fire. Revelation 14:9-11 is an additional related passage which also refers to this "lake of fire":

REVELATION 14:9 Then another angel, a third one, followed them, saying with a loud voice, "If anyone worships the beast and his image, and receives a mark on his forehead or on his hand, 10 he also will drink of the wine of the wrath of God, which is mixed in full strength in the cup of His anger; and he will be **tormented** [basanisthesetai] with fire and **brimstone** [theio] in the presence of the holy angels and in the presence of the Lamb. 11 And the smoke of their **torment** [basanismou] goes up **forever and ever** [eis aionas aionon]; they have no rest day and night, those who worship the beast and his image, and whoever receives the mark of his name." (*NASU*)

Let's examine these passages in detail to discover what the "lake of fire" really is. For in understanding this mystery, we can begin to comprehend God's plan for His creation. To do so, we must grasp the true meaning of some of the key words used in the passage above.

First, notice that Satan, as well as the beast, false prophet, and all who worshiped the beast, are to be "tormented." This "torment" is said to be "forever and ever." On the surface, it sounds like God has provided for the eternal torture of those who opposed Him. But is that really what these Scriptures are teaching?

The words "torment" and "tormented" in Revelation 14:10, 11 and 20:10 come from the Greek root words *basanizo* and the related *basanismos*. Understanding the true meaning of these words is one of the major keys to accurately interpreting these verses.

Friberg's Analytical Lexicon says that *basanisthesontai* means "strictly, *rub upon the touchstone* (βάσανος), a Lydian stone used to test the genuineness of metals; hence, *test or make proof of anything . . .*"

Understanding the original connotation of these words and seeing how they evolved over time is very helpful in correctly understanding the meaning of these verses. The ***Theological Dictionary of the New Testament*** gives us the history of these words:

. . . The βάσανος originally belongs to the calling of the inspector of coins. It is linked with the Heb. root (") בחן to test") . . . βάσανος is generally accepted to be a loan word . . . The testing of gold and silver as media of exchange by the proving stone, was first developed by the Babylonians, then came to the Aramaeans and Hebrews by way of Lydia . . . and from them to the Gks. In non-biblical Gk. βάσανος is a commercial expression, or is used in relation to government. It then acquires the meaning of the checking of calculations, which develops naturally out of the basic sense of βάσανος, βασανίζειν . . . In the spiritual sphere it has the figur. sense, which is closely related to the original concrete meaning, of a means of testing . . .

The word then undergoes a change in meaning. The original sense fades into the background. βάσανος now comes to denote "torture" or "the rack," espec. used with slaves . . . βάσανος occurs in the sense of "torment" . . .

The change in meaning is best explained if we begin with the object of treatment. If we put men instead of metal or a coin, the stone of testing become[s] torture or the rack. The metal which has survived the testing stone is subjected to harsher treatment. Man is in the same position when severely tested by torture. In the testing of metal an essential role was played by the thought of **testing and proving genuineness**. The rack is a means of showing the true state of affairs. **In its proper sense it is a means of testing and proving, though also of punishment**. Finally, even this special meaning was weakened and only the general element of torture remained (pp. 561, 562, vol. I).

So we can see that the true meaning of "torment" in these passages is really "to test" or "prove." This change in meaning will be significant to our overall understanding of God's plan.

Now we must look at the phrases *eis aionas aionon* ("to ages of ages") and *eis tous aionas ton aionon* ("to the ages of the ages") which refer to the length of the testing ("torment"). As we have already seen above, *aion* and its variations speak of periods of time, not eternity. So we must come to the conclusion that these phrases do not mean "forever and ever," but rather "for indefinite periods of time."

One additional word we need to define is "brimstone" (*theio*), also known as sulfur. *Friberg's Analytical Lexicon* tells us that the root word *theion*, which is the neuter form of the Greek *theios* ("divine"), was "anciently regarded as divine incense to purify and prevent contagion." *Thayer's Greek-English Lexicon of the New Testament* agrees, saying that "burning brimstone was regarded as having power to purify . . ." (p. 284).

Now that we have the correct understanding of the terms used, let's look at Revelation 14:10-11 again. When we read that those people who accept the mark of the beast will be "**tormented** with fire and **brimstone** in the presence of the holy angels and in the presence of the Lamb," and that "the smoke of their **torment** goes up **forever and ever**," we can understand this Scripture as follows: Those who accept the mark of the beast will be tested and tried for genuineness (*basanisthesetai*) with fire and divine incense that purifies (*theio*) in the presence of the holy angels and Christ. The smoke of their testing and trying (*basanismou*) will go up for a long, indefinite time (*eis aionas aionon*).

It is disturbing to think that Yeshua the Messiah, who gave his life as a ransom for ALL mankind (I Tim. 2:6), would, along with the holy angels, watch these people being tortured forever in fire. However, this is NOT what is being described in this passage. Eternal punishment is not the goal of the testing depicted here. Paul tells us that God "will have **all men** to be saved, and to come to the knowledge of the truth" (I Tim. 2:4). Clearly the Eternal's intent is the eventual purifying of the ones being tested and tried in the lake of fire.

Indeed, refinement and purification through trials is how God has always prepared people for citizenship in His Kingdom (Psa. 34:19; 66:10-12; Pro. 17:3; Isa. 48:10; Jer. 9:7; Dan. 11:35; 12:10; Zec. 13:9; Mal. 3:1-3; II Cor. 4:17; I The. 3:2-4; Heb. 12:10; Jam. 1:2-4; I Pet. 1:6-7; 4:12-13). It is logical and scriptural (Isa. 30:19-21) to assume that He will continue to use this pattern in the future. This fiery testing and purifying in the lake of fire will, in the end, produce the results God has planned for all His creation (Col. 1:20).

The punishment of Sodom and Gomorrah by "**eternal** (*aioniou*) fire" is instructive, when understood correctly. These cities and their inhabitants were destroyed for their sinfulness by fire and brimstone (Gen. 19:24). Jude says that they were an example of those who suffered the judgment (Gr. *diken*) of "eternal fire" (Jude 7). However, Yeshua clearly indicated that the inhabitants of Sodom and Gomorrah would be raised up in the resurrection and be shown more tolerance than the inhabitants of cities which rejected his ministry (Matt. 10:15; Mark 6:11; Luke 10:12). Here, the adjective *aioniou* plainly indicates that this judgment God pronounced upon Sodom and Gomorrah was to last for only a certain amount of time (until the resurrection to judgment).

So when we arrive at the proper understanding of *aion*, *aionios*, and *geenna*, it becomes evident that the idea of a fiery hell where sinners are tortured for all eternity or annihilated is NOT taught in the Bible. Using the meanings of those words at the time of Yeshua, we see a picture of corrective (not destructive or retributive) punishment of sinners for a limited time in "hell."

Intricately tied to "the lake of fire" in these passages in Revelation is "the second death." What is this second death?

REVELATION 2:11 'He who has an ear, let him hear what the Spirit says to the churches. He who overcomes will not be **hurt** [adikethe] by the **second death**.' (*NASU*)

REVELATION 20:6 Blessed and holy is the one who has a part in the first resurrection; over these the **second death** has no **power** [exousian], but they will be priests of God and of Christ and will reign with Him for a thousand years. (*NASU*)

REVELATION 20:14 Then death and Hades were thrown into the lake of fire. **This is the second death, the lake of fire.** (*NASU*)

REVELATION 21:8 "But for the cowardly and unbelieving and abominable and murderers and immoral persons and sorcerers and idolaters and all liars, their part will be in **the lake that burns with fire and brimstone, which is**

the second death." (*NASU*)

First, we see that even those who are members of the Church can be "hurt" by the second death unless they overcome. The word "hurt" here is a form of the Greek verb *adikeo*; it is defined in ***Vine's Expository Dictionary of New Testament Words*** as either "to do wrong, do hurt, act unjustly" or "to wrong, hurt or injure a person" (p. 315). A variant of *adikeo* is used in Revelation 9:10 to refer to the pain inflicted on men by the demons released from the Abyss. Significantly, these demons are not allowed to kill those they are inflicting pain upon (Rev. 9:5).

Next, we see in Revelation 20:6 that the second death will have no "power" over the believers who experience the resurrection at the return of Yeshua. The word translated "power" is a form of the Greek "*exousia*"; it literally means "authority." From the use of this word, we can see that resurrected believers will not be subject to the power or authority of the second death.

Revelation 20:14 and 21:8 clearly states that "the second death" and "the lake of fire" are one and the same. Many have defined the second death to mean either everlasting separation from God in the lake of fire or eternal destruction in the lake of fire. But do the Scriptures support this conclusion?

In order to understand the second death, we must again fix in our minds what the "first" death really is and why it exists. The Scriptures tell us that "it is appointed for men to **die** ONCE, and after that comes judgment" (Heb. 9:27). Yet Paul tells us that those believers who are alive and remain until the second coming of Christ will not physically die, but instead will be changed to spirit in "the twinkling of an eye" (I Cor. 15:50-53; I The. 4:15-17).

Clearly, the Scriptures teach that not all will have to die a **physical** death. So what is the "first" death that all men are appointed to experience, after which comes judgment? Undoubtedly, it's the death Paul referred to in Romans 5:12, the death that was introduced into the world through the sin of Adam:

ROMANS 5:12 Therefore, just as through one man sin entered the world, and **death through sin,** and thus **death spread to all men, because all sinned** - (*NKJV*)

From the point that Adam disobeyed God, all mankind has been cut off from the Eternal Father by sin, because all have sinned and fallen short of the glory of God (Rom. 3:23). As we've already seen from the Scriptures, God views this state of separation as death. So the author of Hebrews is speaking of this alienation from God in Hebrews 9:27. As Paul tells us, the death brought about by Adam's disobedience can and will be reversed by the obedient sacrifice of Yeshua:

ROMANS 5:18 So then as **through one transgression there resulted condemnation to all men,** even so **through one act of righteousness there resulted justification of life to all men.** (*NASU*)

Clearly understanding how the first Adam's sin is offset by the second Adam's obedience is vital for comprehending how the separation of the first death will be neutralized by the reconciliation eventually brought by the second death. Indeed, the Scriptures tell us that the second death will consume the first death (Rev. 20:14).

Through sin, the first man (Heb. *'adam*) died to God and righteousness, bringing death to all mankind. Through obedience, the second man, Yeshua, died to sin and lived his life to God, bringing an acquittal that leads to life for all mankind. The first made all men sinners, the second will make all men righteous. Thus we can see that the lives and the deaths of the two Adams are a contrast to one another.

In like manner, the first and second deaths are also opposite and antagonistic. The second death will undo all the work of the first death in the precisely the same fashion as the last Adam is reversing all the work of the first Adam. Paul tells us that the creation has been subjected to futility (Rom. 8:20), but that futility has an ultimate purpose! Sin has been allowed by God because it accomplishes a goal of His plan; but when that purpose has been achieved, sin will cease to exist.

The first death initiated by Adam (which thereafter spread to all mankind) was a transition from knowing God to being separated from Him by sin. The second death will be a purifying change in the lake of fire from a state of sinfulness to righteousness. The second death is designed to purge, refine, and burn away all sin and its results. In the process, all of God's universe will be cleansed.

Let's look closely at what the book of Revelation really tells us about those who suffer the second death by being cast into the lake of fire. Keep in mind that Revelation is primarily a chronological record of events that will come to pass starting at the end of this age.

In Revelation 20:11, what is commonly called the "great white throne" judgment period is introduced. All those who are still dead come before this throne. The Book of Life is opened, as well as books recording what the dead had done during their lives. They are judged by their deeds as recorded in the books (Rev. 20:12). Anyone whose name isn't found in the Book of Life is cast into the lake of fire (Rev. 20:15).

But the story doesn't end there. In the beginning of Revelation 21, we see the new heaven and the new earth, as well as the New Jerusalem coming down from heaven. At this point, God the Father comes down from heaven and makes His home with mankind (Rev. 21:3). The first death ceases to exist (Rev. 21:4). God then declares "Behold, I make all things new" (Rev. 21:5) and "he who conquers shall have this heritage, and I will be his God and he shall be my son" (Rev. 21:7). But notice, some still exist who aren't accounted as God's sons **yet**:

REVELATION 21:8 But as for the cowardly, the faithless, the polluted, as for murderers, fornicators, sorcerers, idolaters, and all liars, their lot shall be in **the lake that burns with fire and sulphur, which is the second death**." (*RSV*)

Immediately afterward we are given a glorious description of the New Jerusalem that is to come down out of heaven to earth (Rev. 21:9-22:5). But in this passage is a verse which must seem out of place to those who believe that the second death will annihilate all sinners:

REVELATION 21:27 But nothing unclean shall enter it [the New Jerusalem], nor any one who practices abomination or falsehood, but only those who are written in the Lamb's book of life. (*RSV*)

Why, if the lake of fire has already consumed all the wicked at the end of the "great white throne" judgment, is it necessary for John to write that no one "unclean" will be able to enter the New Jerusalem? But an even greater question arises from Revelation 22:14-15:

REVELATION 22:14 **Blessed are those who do His commandments**, that **they may have the right to the tree of life**, and **may enter through the gates into the city**. 15 But **outside** are dogs and sorcerers and sexually immoral and murderers and idolaters, and whoever loves and practices a lie. (*NKJV*)

Here we are told that there are still sinners outside the city who do not **yet** have the right to enter New Jerusalem and eat from the tree of life. But it is also revealed that those who **do** obey God's commandments merit the right to enter into the New Jerusalem and partake of the tree of life. The amazing implication here is that those on the outside, the same sorry lot earlier consigned to "the lake of fire" (Rev. 21:8), can enter the city when they start keeping the commandments of God!

Eventually, after indefinite ages in the "lake of fire," the sinners who are outside New Jerusalem **will** repent and obey God. Then the time Paul speaks of in his letter to the church at Philippi will come about.

PHILIPPIANS 2:9 Therefore God has highly exalted him and bestowed on him the name which is above every name, 10 that **at the name of Jesus every knee should bow**, in heaven and on earth and under the earth, 11 **and every tongue confess that Jesus Christ is Lord**, to the glory of God the Father. (*RSV*)

Yes, the Scriptures clearly tell us that the time is coming when all of God's creation will repent and be reconciled to God the Father through His Son, Yeshua the Messiah:

COLOSSIANS 1:19 For it pleased the Father that in him [Yeshua] all the fullness should dwell, 20 and **by him** [Yeshua] **to reconcile all things to Himself**, by him [Yeshua], whether things on earth or things in heaven, having made peace through the blood of his cross. (*NKJV*)

EPHESIANS 1:7 In him [Yeshua] we have redemption through his blood, the forgiveness of sins, according to the riches of His [the Father's] grace 8 which He made to abound toward us in all wisdom and prudence, 9 having made known to us the mystery of His will, according to His good pleasure which He purposed in Himself, 10 **that in the dispensation of the fullness of the times He might gather together in one all things in Christ**, both which are in heaven and which are on earth -- in Him. (*NKJV*)

When every one of God's sentient creatures bows before Yeshua and confesses that he is their Lord, the second death will no longer be necessary. Death, the separation from God, will have been destroyed. Then will come the time when Christ will hand the entire creation over to his Father, that God may be all in all:

I CORINTHIANS 15:24 Then comes the end, when he [Yeshua] delivers the kingdom to God the Father, when He puts an end to all rule and all authority and power. 25 For he [Yeshua] must reign till He has put all enemies under his feet. 26 **The last enemy that will be destroyed is death**. 27 For "He has put all things under his [Yeshua's] feet." But when He says "all things are put under him [Yeshua]," it is evident that He who put all things under him [Yeshua] is excepted. 28 Now when all things are made subject to him [Yeshua], then the Son himself will also be subject to Him who put all things under him, that God may be **all in all**. (*NKJV*)

This is the true revelation of the mystery of God which was kept secret for long ages (Rom. 16:25), the mystery which was hidden from ages and from generations but now has been revealed to His saints (Col. 1:24), which God ordained before the ages for our glory (I Cor. 2:7). May God be praised for His infinite mercy and kindness!

Bryan T. Huie
February 5, 1999

Revised: April 7, 2009

What Was the Colossian Heresy?

This article unveils the purpose of Paul's letter to the Colossians. The Colossian church was being attacked by Gnostics who were promoting asceticism and angel worship. This commentary reviews the first two chapters of Paul's letter and highlights clues in the text to identify who his foes were.

The first half of Paul's letter to the Colossians, especially the second chapter, is an effort to combat false teachings that were being promoted to the Church there. This epistle is generally dated to the period of 58-60 CE, and is commonly thought to have been written by Paul while he was imprisoned in Rome. In recent years, many scholars have concluded that the internal evidence within the epistle indicates an early form of Gnosticism was the culprit in Colosse.

In order to grasp some of the points Paul makes in his letter, a rudimentary understanding of the basic tenets of Gnosticism is required. Gnosticism wasn't a separate religion; rather, it was a philosophy that was blended with components of existing religions. Apparently, elements of Judaism/Christianity were combined with Gnostic beliefs soon after the Church began, creating the heretical teachings that Paul combats in his letter to the Colossians.

The term "Gnostic" comes from the Greek word *gnosis*, which means knowledge. Gnosticism was a complex religious philosophy which taught that salvation could only be achieved through secret knowledge. Although there were many different types of Gnosticism, they had several common features. *The International Standard Bible Encyclopedia* (*ISBE*) records the following general characteristics found within most varieties of Gnosticism:

The following may be regarded as the chief points in the Gnostic systems:

(1) a claim on the part of the initiated to a special knowledge of the truth; a tendency to regard knowledge as superior to faith and as the special possession of the more enlightened, for ordinary Christians did not possess this secret and higher doctrine;

(2) the essential separation of matter and spirit, matter being intrinsically evil and the source from which all evil has arisen;

(3) an attempt to solve the problems of creation and the origin of evil by postulating a demiurge, i.e., a creator or artificer of the world distinct from the deity, and emanations extending between God and the visible universe (the demiurge for the Gnostics being the God of the OT, an inferior being infinitely remote from the Supreme Being who can have nothing to do with anything material);

(4) a denial of the true humanity of Christ; a docetic Christology which considered the earthly life of Christ and especially His sufferings on the cross to be unreal;

(5) the denial of the personality of the Supreme God, and also the denial of the free will of mankind;

(6) the teaching, on the one hand, of asceticism as the means of attaining spiritual communion with God, and, on the other hand, of an indifference that led directly to licentiousness;

(7) a syncretistic tendency that combined certain more or less misunderstood Christian doctrines and various elements from oriental, Jewish, Greek, and other sources;

(8) ascription of the OT to the demiurge or inferior creator of the world. Some of these ideas are more obvious in one and some of them in another of the Gnostic systems. (pp. 486-487, vol. 2, "Gnosticism")

As we will see when we examine the first two chapters of Paul's letter, the Colossian form of Gnosticism incorporated many of these beliefs. Paul alludes to several Gnostic doctrines and restrictions in his epistle, in addition to specifically listing some of their teachings at the end of chapter two.

We're going to look closely at these two chapters to identify the group Paul is combating. We'll go through each verse, pulling out the clues that Paul gives us. Let's start at the beginning of the letter:

COLOSSIANS 1:1 Paul, an apostle of Jesus Christ by the will of God, and Timothy our brother, 2 to the saints and faithful brethren in Christ who are in Colosse: Grace to you and peace from God our Father and the Lord Jesus Christ. (**NKJV**)

This is Paul's usual form of introduction in his letters. He identifies himself and his companion (Timothy), and then names the Church he is writing to (Colosse). Colosse was situated close to the River Lycus, about 15 miles southeast of Laodicea and a little over 100 miles east of Ephesus, in what is now Turkey.

COLOSSIANS 1:3 We give thanks to the God and Father of our Lord Jesus Christ, praying always for you, 4 since we heard of your faith in Christ Jesus and of your love for all the saints; 5 because of the hope which is laid up for you in heaven, of which you heard before in the word of the truth of the gospel, 6 which has come to you, as it has also in all the world, and is bringing forth fruit, as it is also among you since the day you heard and knew the grace of God in truth; 7 as you also learned from Epaphras, our dear fellow servant, who is a faithful minister of Christ on your behalf, 8 who also declared to us your love in the Spirit. (**NKJV**)

Neither Paul nor Timothy had seen the Colossian church. But they had heard of their faith and love from Epaphras, who ministered to the Colossians. Indeed, it's very likely that Epaphras had carried the gospel to Colosse after hearing Paul preach it elsewhere (probably at Ephesus).

COLOSSIANS 1:9 For this reason we also, since the day we heard it, do not cease to pray for you, and to ask that you may be filled with the **knowledge** [epignosin] of His will in all wisdom and spiritual understanding; 10 that you may walk worthy of the Lord, fully pleasing Him, being fruitful in every good work and increasing in the **knowledge** [epignosin] **of God**; 11 strengthened with all might, according to His glorious power, for all patience and longsuffering with joy; 12 giving thanks to the Father who has qualified us to be partakers of the inheritance of the saints in the light. (**NKJV**)

In this passage, Paul begins his attack on the Gnostic beliefs being promulgated to the Colossians. He does so with a few subtle statements that are easily overlooked if the context isn't recognized. Paul states that he and Timothy have been praying for the Colossians, asking God to fill them with knowledge, that they may be fruitful in every good work. In verses 9 and 10, the word "knowledge" comes from the Greek word *epignosin*. Of this word, Kenneth S. Wuest writes:

The word is an advance upon *gnosis* (knowledge) in that it denotes a larger and more thorough knowledge. It is a knowledge which grasps and penetrates into an object. It was a favorite word of the Gnostics who used it to designate the superior knowledge which they claimed as their exclusive possession. Paul prays that all the saints might become possessors of this knowledge, indicating that it was open for all to appropriate, not a secret mystery into which only a favored few could be initiated. (p. 175, vol. I, *Word Studies in the Greek New Testament*, "Ephesians and Colossians")

Paul uses *epignosin* to emphasize the true and full knowledge of God that he wanted the Colossians to attain. The implication is that the knowledge of the Gnostics was neither true nor full.

COLOSSIANS 1:13 He has delivered us from the power of darkness and conveyed us into the kingdom of the Son of His love, 14 in whom **we have redemption through his blood**, the forgiveness of sins. (**NKJV**)

Paul continues his indirect discourse against Gnosticism in verses 13 and 14. The Gnostics denied that the Messiah had come in the flesh. They taught that one did not need the atoning sacrifice of his blood for salvation, because he had never really lived as a human being. Rather, the Gnostics emphasized that salvation could be attained only through the secret knowledge that Christ had given his disciples.

The Eerdmans Bible Dictionary (*Eerdmans*) states: "Increasingly, scholars recognize that Christianity's proclamation of a divine savior provided the catalyst for the Gnostic movement. Many Gnostics traced their teaching back to him and the secret teaching he purportedly revealed after the resurrection. Gnostic christologies offer a savior without the incarnation (a Christ-spirit) who gives knowledge instead of calling for faith . . ." (p. 422, "Gnosticism"). This is a theme we'll see Paul combat again later in his letter.

COLOSSIANS 1:15 Who is the image of the invisible God, **the firstborn of every creature**: (**KJV**) 16 for **in him all things were created**, in heaven and on earth, visible and invisible, whether thrones or dominions or principalities or authorities — **all things were created through him** and for him. 17 He is before all things, and in him all things hold together. 18 He is the head of the body, the church; he is the **beginning** [arche], the first-born from the dead, that in everything he might be pre-eminent. (*RSV*)

In verses 15 through 18, Paul contradicts the Gnostic view of creation and the structure of the Godhead. Regarding the Gnostic belief about the composition of the Godhead, *Eerdmans* says, "Between God and matter lie a host of spiritual powers, collectively termed the fullness (*pleroma*) of God. From its lowest rank comes the creator, a demiurge identified with the Old Testament Yahweh. Fallen spiritual powers, often linked with astral referents, now rule the world" (p. 421, "Gnosticism").

The Gnostics believed that angels were emanations from the Most High God. They were all imperfect, with the highest and most ancient of them being more ethereal and inviolate than those in the next level down, and so on through the ranks. To discredit this Gnostic teaching on the"fullness of the Godhead," Paul specifically states in verse 15 that Christ is the "firstborn of every creature," thereby establishing his preeminence in the order of creation. For additional information on this topic, see my article "The Lord Our God, The Lord Is One."

The Gnostics taught that the demiurge was the creator of the earth and of mankind. Yet in verse 16, Paul says that the entire creation, both material and spiritual, was accomplished by God through Christ. This would place Christ, the instrument of creation, second only to God the Father in the spiritual order. Obviously, this teaching contradicted the Gnostic view of the spiritual hierarchy.

In verse 18, Paul again emphasizes that Christ is the "beginning" (Gr. *arche*). This is the same word found in Revelation 3:14, where Christ states that he is "the beginning of God's creation." Once more Paul is highlighting the primacy of Christ's position in the order of created things.

COLOSSIANS 1:19 For it pleased the Father that in him all the **fullness** [pleroma] should dwell, 20 and by him to reconcile all things to Himself, by him, whether things on earth or things in heaven, having made peace through the blood of his cross. 21 And you, who once were alienated and enemies in your mind by wicked works, yet now he has reconciled 22 in the body of his flesh through death, to present you holy, and blameless, and above reproach in his sight — 23 if indeed you continue in the faith, grounded and steadfast, and are not moved away from the hope of the gospel which you heard, which was preached to every creature under heaven, of which I, Paul, became a **minister** [diakonos]. (*NKJV*)

In verse 19, Paul first introduces the term *pleroma* in his epistle. An understanding of the Gnostic view of the "fullness of the Godhead" will aid in ascertaining why Paul brings up this concept several times in his letter to the Colossians.

In the *Jewish New Testament Commentary* (*JNTC*), David H. Stern writes: "*'Pleroma'* was a technical term used by the Gnostics and their antecedents to refer to the totality of the various spiritual 'levels' and the beings or entities presumed to exist there . . ." (p. 605).

Of the "*pleroma*," *ISBE* states:

For the Gnostics God is the ultimate, nameless, unknowable being called the 'Abyss.' He is perfect, but the material world is alien to the divine nature. How, then, does it come to exist at all? What is the source of its imperfections and evils? The Gnostic answer is that the FULNESS (Gr. *pleroma*) of the diety could flow out in no other way than in emanations or aeons or angels, all of which are necessarily imperfect, the highest of them being more spiritual than the grade immediately below. Of these aeons there is a gradation so numerous that at length the lowest of them is almost wholly corporeal, the spiritual element having been gradually diminished or eliminated until at last the world of mankind and of matter is reached, the abode of evil. In this way the gulf is bridged between God and mankind. The highest aeons approximate closely the divine nature, so spiritual are they and so free from matter. These form the highest hierarchy of angels, and these with many other grades of angelic hosts are to be worshiped. (p. 488, vol. 2, "Gnosticism")

We see this Gnostic belief in the need to worship the angelic host specifically referred to later in the letter (Col. 2:18). Paul's argument for the primacy of Christ, which began in verse 15, rebuts the Gnostic teaching on the nature of the Godhead. It is not through the hierarchy of angels (aeons) that Christians are reconciled to God, but rather through His son, Yeshua the Messiah.

Paul states that this reconcilement is through the body of the Messiah's flesh. Again he is contrasting the false Gnostic beliefs about Christ not actually coming in the flesh with the truth of the gospel, which shows that the Messiah **did** live on earth as a human. Paul says that Christ's death on the cross will reconcile the Colossians to the Most High God, as long as they faithfully hold fast to the original gospel that was preached to them.

COLOSSIANS 1:24 I now rejoice in my sufferings for you, and fill up in my flesh what is lacking in the afflictions of Christ, for the sake of his body, which is the church, 25 of which I became a **minister** [diakonos] according to the stewardship from God which was given to me for you, to fulfill the word of God, 26 the **mystery** [musterion] which has been **hidden** from ages and from generations, but now has been revealed to His saints. 27 To them God willed to make known what are the riches of the glory of this **mystery** [musteriou] among the Gentiles: which is

Christ in you, the hope of glory. 28 Him we preach, warning every man and teaching every man in all wisdom, that we may present every man perfect in Christ Jesus. 29 To this end I also labor, striving according to his working which works in me mightily. (*NKJV*)

Here, Paul mentions another aspect of the Gnostic teaching, that of the divine "mystery" (Gr. *musterion*). In the religious cults of the Graeco-Roman world, this word literally referred to a religious secret that was confided only to the initiated, a secret rite. By his use of *musterion*, Paul is emphasizing that the teaching the Colossians had received about Christ was the true revealing of the long-hidden mystery of God. Conversely, Paul implies that the mystery the Gnostics wished to reveal to them was false.

When Paul calls himself a "minister" (Gr. *diakonos*) in verses 23 and 25, most assume that to be an office within the hierarchy of the early church. However, in Greek *diakonos* really only means "one who renders service," or "a servant." This same word or a variation of it is translated in the *NKJV* as "servant" (Matt. 20:26; 23:11; Mark 9:35; 10:43; John 12:26), and "deacon" (Phi. 1:1; I Tim. 3:8, 10, 12, 13), as well as "minister" (Rom. 13:4; Gal. 2:17; Eph. 3:7; 6:21; Col. 1:7; 1:23; 1:25; 4:7; I Tim. 4:6). The different translations of this word from Greek into English come more from the traditional hierarchical view of church government than from the actual meaning of the word itself.

COLOSSIANS 2:1 For I want you to know what a great conflict I have for you and those in Laodicea, and for as many as have not seen my face in the flesh, 2 that their hearts may be encouraged, being knit together in love, and attaining to all riches of the full assurance of understanding, to the **knowledge** [epignosin] of the **mystery** [musteriou] of God, both of the Father and of Christ, 3 in whom are **hidden** [apokruphoi] all the treasures of wisdom and **knowledge** [gnoseos]. (*NKJV*)

The second chapter begins with Paul telling the Colossians that although he had not been to their city, he was aware that they were having problems and was concerned about them. Verse 2, which emphasizes knowledge (Gr. *epignosin*) and understanding, is another clue to the source of the problem the Colossians are experiencing. The Greek word *apokruphoi*, which is translated "hidden" in verse 3, literally means "a hidden thing, a secret." Paul here takes another subtle shot at the Gnostics, saying that all the "secret knowledge" the Colossians need is found in God the Father and the Messiah.

COLOSSIANS 2:4 **Now this** [touto de] I say lest anyone should deceive you with persuasive words. (*NKJV*)

The words "now this" (Gr. *touto de*) indicate that verse 4 is Paul's summation of everything he's written up to this point in his letter. According to Friberg's ***Analytical Lexicon to the Greek New Testament (Friberg)***, the pronoun *touto* ("this") is "used to call attention to a designated person or object, often with special emphasis . . ." *Friberg* says that the conjunction *de* ("now") is used "most commonly to denote continuation and further thought development . . ." This shows that Paul's prior statements were written to set the stage for his attack on the false teachings being presented to the Christians in Colosse.

COLOSSIANS 2:5 For though I am absent in the flesh, yet I am with you in spirit, rejoicing to see your good order and the steadfastness of your faith in Christ. 6 As you have therefore received Christ Jesus the Lord, so walk in him, 7 rooted and built up in him and established in the faith, as you have been taught, abounding in it with thanksgiving. (*NKJV*)

In verse 5 Paul launches into the second part of his letter by praising the Colossians' faith, which was most likely reported to him by Epaphras. Evidently, the Gnostic teachers had not yet made any significant headway in the community of believers. Before Paul begins his rebuttal of the Gnostics, he exhorts the Colossians in verses 6 and 7 to remain faithful to the teachings initially brought to them.

COLOSSIANS 2:8 See to it that no one takes you captive through **philosophy** and **empty deceit**, according to **human tradition**, according to **the elemental spirits of the universe** [ta stoicheia tou kosmou], and not according to Christ. (*NRSV*)

Paul gets to the heart of the problem in verse 8. He warns the Colossians of the devious philosophy the Gnostics were promoting and labels their doctrines the traditions of men (see Matt. 15:1-9; Mark 7:1-13), as well as the teaching of demons.

The Greek phrase *ta stoicheia tou kosmou*, translated as "the elemental spirits of the universe" above, has been interpreted in several ways. However, *The New International Dictionary of New Testament Theology* states: "In the case of Gal. 4:3, 9 and Col. 2:8, 20 it is a disputed question whether or not the *stoicheia tou kosmou*, the "elements of the world", are angels, demons, gods, i.e., personified forces as taught by a certain gnostic heresy. Most commentators hold this to be the case . . ." (p. 452, vol. 2).

Of the Greek phrase *stoicheia tou kosmou* used by Paul, *JNTC* says, "**Elemental spirits of the universe** . . . both Jews and Gentiles, **were slaves** to them. Gentiles served these demonic spirits as gods. Jews, though knowing the one true God, were sometimes led astray by demonic spirits . . ." (p. 556). Clearly, this "philosophy" Paul refers to in verse 8 was contrary to Christ, being derived from human tradition and demonic influence.

COLOSSIANS 2:9 For in him the whole **fullness** [pleroma] of deity dwells bodily, 10 and you have come to **fullness** [pepleromenoi] in him, who is the head of **every ruler and authority**. (*NRSV*)

In verse 9 Paul reemphasizes Christ's spiritual position by using the term *pleroma* again. In verse 10, he uses a related Greek word for "fullness" (*pepleromenoi*) to show the Colossians that they have no need of anything other than Christ. In the last half of verse 10, Paul clearly states that Christ is above all spiritual rulers and powers (cf. Eph. 6:12). Therefore, there is no reason for the Colossians to worship angels (Col. 2:18) in order to reach God. As Paul later wrote in his first epistle to Timothy, "there is one God, and there is **one mediator** between God and men, the man Christ Jesus" (I Tim. 2:5).

COLOSSIANS 2:11 In him you were **also** [kai] circumcised with the circumcision made without hands, by putting off the body of the sins of the flesh, by the circumcision of Christ, 12 buried with him in baptism, in which you **also** [kai] were raised with him through faith in the working of God, who raised him from the dead. (*NKJV*)

Theologians have long believed that Paul's mention here of circumcision is directly related to the heresy being promoted in Colosse. Yet an objective look at the context of this statement does **not** indicate that Paul was combating false teachers who wished to have the Gentile Colossians physically circumcised. Rather, he was using the symbolism of spiritual circumcision and baptism to illustrate to the Colossians how they had come to fullness in Christ (Col. 2:10) because he had purified them from sin.

Paul's use of the Greek particle *kai* ("also") demonstrates that his intent with this line of reasoning was not to counter teachers promoting physical circumcision. In verse 10, Paul stated that the Colossians had been made complete in Christ ("in him"). Paul uses *kai* in verse 11 to reinforce and connect this statement with his assertion about spiritual circumcision. The same usage of *kai* is also found in verse 12. The entire passage from verse 9 through 15 advances the theme of Christ's preeminence and sufficiency in atoning for sin.

COLOSSIANS 2:13 And when you were dead in trespasses and the uncircumcision of your flesh, God made you alive together with him, when he forgave us all our trespasses, 14 erasing the **record** [cheirographon] that stood against us with its legal demands. He set this aside, nailing it to the cross. (*NRSV*)

Paul states in verse 13 that the Colossians had previously been considered "dead" because they were uncircumcised (i.e., Gentile) sinners. However, once they accepted Christ and were spiritually circumcised and baptized, their sins were forgiven because of Yeshua's sacrifice on the cross. Taken as a whole, verses 11 through 14 emphasize the redemption the Colossians had through the Messiah.

Many denominations teach that the phrase "handwriting of requirements that was against us" (*NKJV*) in verse 14 refers to God's Law. Because of this interpretation, they hold the antinomian position that Christ's death abolished the Law. Yet that interpretation doesn't fit the context here, because verses 11 through 14 talk of sins being wiped out. The abolishment of the Law would not make humans sinless, because sin was in the world before the Law was given (Rom. 5:13), and death reigned from Adam to Moses because of sin (Rom. 5:12, 14).

So what is Paul saying in verse 14? The term "handwriting of requirements" comes from the Greek phrase *cheirographon tois dogmasin*. In recent years scholars have found where the word *cheirographon* was used by other writers in the same time period to refer to a signed bill of indebtedness. Such bonds were handwritten by the debtor so they could not be disputed later on. The word implies a sense of awareness of one's sins and the consequent indebtedness to God. *Friberg* defines *cheirographon* as "strictly, *a handwritten document*; in legal matters *a promissory note, a record of indebtedness, bond*; fig [uratively] in CO 2.14, not as the law itself, but as the *record of charges* (for breaking God's law), which stood against us and which God symbolically removed by 'nailing it to the cross,' *handwritten account, record of debts*."

Romans 6:23 tells us that the penalty for sin is death, because under the Law there can be no forgiveness of sins without the shedding of blood (Heb. 9:22, Lev. 17:11). Clearly, Paul is saying in verse 14 that when the Colossians repented and accepted Christ's sacrifice on the cross, God allowed His death to pay their debt in satisfaction of the strict standards of the Law.

COLOSSIANS 2:15 Having disarmed principalities and powers, he made a public spectacle of them, triumphing over them in it. (*NKJV*)

In verse 15, Paul says that Christ, through his sacrifice, has disarmed the spiritual principalities and powers that rule over this world (for more information on these spiritual rulers, see my article "The Heavenly Divine Council"). The Messiah has taken away the fallen angels' ability to accuse Christians of sin (Rev. 12:10) and lobby for their punishment according to the law, since their debt to the law was nailed to the cross.

COLOSSIANS 2:16 Therefore let no one judge you in food or in drink [en brosei kai en posei], or regarding a festival or a new moon or Sabbaths, 17 which are [esti] a shadow of things to come, but the substance is [soma] of Christ. (*NKJV*)

In verse 16, Paul comes to the primary point he wants to make. He tells the Colossians **not** to let anyone (including the Gnostics) **judge** them in eating or drinking, or in the observance of festivals, new moons, or Sabbaths.

This passage is widely misunderstood because most scholars begin with the assumption that the Sabbath, new moons, and Holy Days mentioned in verse 16 are among the false teachings Paul is combating. They assume that the Gentile Colossians were not keeping these days, but the heretics (who are usually labeled "Jewish Gnostics") were trying to force them to observe them. Two points discredit this theory.

First, Paul calls the Gnostic teachings the "tradition of men" (Col. 2:8) and the "commandments and doctrines of men" (Col. 2:22). Regardless of how Paul felt about the observances he lists in verse 16, being a Pharisee trained in the Law (Acts 22:3; 23:6; 26:5; Phi. 3:4-6), he would **not** have called them the "traditions of men." They are clearly defined in the *Torah* (Exo. 16, 20; Lev. 23; Deu. 16) as **divine** commands the Israelites were to obey.

Furthermore, it's clear that the heretics' teaching involved strict ascetic regulations (Col. 2:21-23). Yet asceticism is the **opposite** of feasting. You don't promote asceticism by **encouraging** the observance of feast days. Instead, you elevate asceticism by **criticizing** the way someone is keeping a feast, or by **condemning** the fact that they are celebrating a feast at all.

Because of an anti-Jewish bias which can be traced back to the early Catholic church, almost all scholars have misunderstood the meaning of Paul's statement in these verses. For the Gnostics to be judging the Colossians regarding the manner of observance of the Sabbath, new moons, and Holy Days, they obviously had to be **keeping** them!

The phrase "in food or in drink" does not accurately convey the meaning of the original text. The Greek reads "*en brosei kai en posei*" and refers to the **acts** of eating and drinking. The strict Gnostics were substituting an ascetic philosophy (Col. 2:8, "human tradition") and "doctrines of demons" (see I Tim. 4:1-3) for the truth that had previously been taught to the Colossians. They were evidently quick to find fault with anyone did not follow their teaching of denying oneself food and drink.

The text shows that the Gnostic teachers were also condemning the Colossian Christians for their observance of the Sabbath, new moons, and Holy Days. The Gnostics' reason for judging the Colossians in these matters goes hand in hand with their criticism of "eating and drinking." Jews in the 1st century (as well as early Christians) treated the Sabbath as a weekly feast day, and fasting was forbidden on the Sabbath. In his book *From Sabbath To Sunday*, Dr. Samuele Bacchiocchi writes:

. . . For the Jews the Sabbath was anything but a day of fast or of mourning. Even the strictest Jewish sects objected to fasting on the Sabbath . . . That the early Christians adopted this Jewish custom is implied, for instance, by Augustine's rhetorical remark, when referring to the Sabbath, he says: "Did not the tradition of the elders prohibit fasting on the one hand, and command rest on the other?" Further support can be seen in the opposition to the Sabbath fast by Christians in the East and in some important Western areas, such as Milan at the time of Ambrose (d. A.D. 397), and in certain churches and regions of North Africa. (pp. 187, 188)

Furthermore, during most of the annual festivals (with the exception of Atonement), God commanded his people to rejoice and enjoy food and strong drink (Deu. 14:23-26, Neh. 8:10,12). This most certainly would have conflicted with the Gnostics' ascetic outlook.

Because of the view that Paul was condemning the observance of the Sabbath, new moons, and Holy Days in verse 16, nearly all scholars have misunderstood verse 17. Most try to connect the first part of the verse ("which are a shadow of things to come") with the last part ("but the substance is of Christ") to form a complete thought. To accomplish this, they translate the last part of the verse *to* ("the") *de* ("but") *soma* ("substance is," "substance belongs to," "reality is") *tou* ("the") *Christou* ("of Christ").

As you can see above, the phrase "substance is" comes from the single Greek word *soma*. This word is used 74 times in the *Textus Receptus* version of the New Testament; 72 times the *NKJV* translates it as "body" and once it is represented as "bodies." Nowhere else is it rendered "substance is," "substance belongs to," or "reality is," as most modern versions of the Bible translate it in verse 17. In reality, these renderings of *soma* are unjustified **interpretations**, not translations.

The literal translation of the Greek in the last part of verse 17 is "but the body of Christ." In Greek, verses 16 and 17 say: "**Consequently, let no one judge you in eating or in drinking with respect to a festival or a new moon or sabbaths (which are a shadow of things to come) but the body of Christ.**" The phrase "body of Christ" should not be confusing, for Paul uses it several other times in the letter to the Colossians (1:18; 1:24; 2:19; 3:15), as well as in some of his other epistles (Rom., I Cor., and Eph.). In these instances it is a figurative reference to the Church.

Therefore, the phrase "which are a shadow of things to come" was intended by Paul to be a parenthetical statement. It was added to give the Colossians additional insight into the festivals, new moons, and Sabbaths. However, it was not necessary to complete the thought. Even if Paul had left that phrase out, his admonition would have been understandable: "**Let no one judge you regarding eating and drinking (at these times) . . . but the body of Christ.**"

Paul is plainly saying here that the Church was to be the Colossians' only guide on eating and drinking, as these things related to Sabbath, new moon, and festival observances. They were not to let the Gnostics force ascetic practices on them, especially during these holy times (which are a shadow of the good things coming in the future - cf. Heb. 9:11, 10:1).

This grant of power to the Church is not unique in the writings of Paul. While he clearly condemns Christians who judge one another in questionable matters (Rom. 14), Paul gave the Corinthian Church the power to judge and expel those brethren who were openly sinning (I Cor. 5, 6). When combined with the earlier admonitions to hold fast to the teachings they had received previously (Col. 1:23; 2:6, 7), verses 16 and 17 clearly show that Paul expected the Colossian Church as a whole to enforce the original **true** teachings brought to them by Epaphras. Evidently those true teachings included the observance of the weekly and annual Sabbaths, new moons, and annual festivals.

One last point about verse 17; the word translated "are" is the Greek verb *esti*. This verb is in the present tense; Paul is saying the annual Holy Days and the Sabbath **ARE** currently shadows of things to come. Paul does **not** say that they **were** shadows that were fulfilled at the coming of Christ. From this we know that the events they foreshadow have not been completed yet; therefore, the shadows still have relevance. Instead of doing away with God's Sabbath and the Holy Days, this passage of Scripture, when understood correctly, affirms them and shows that the Colossian Church was actually keeping them. COLOSSIANS 2:18 Let no one defraud you of your reward, taking delight in **false humility** and **worship of angels, intruding** [embateuon] into those things which he has not seen, vainly puffed up by his fleshly mind, 19 and not holding fast to the head, from whom all the **body** [soma], nourished and knit together by joints and ligaments, grows with the increase which is from God. (**NKJV**)

Now in verse 18, Paul warns the Colossians of two **specific** false doctrines being taught by the Gnostics: "false humility" as manifested in ascetic practices, and the worship of the angelic host. These teachings were probably the ones most emphasized by the Gnostics. In verse 19 Paul warns the congregation that these doctrines take one away from Christ, the head of the Church. Again, as in verse 17, we see the Church symbolically depicted as a "body."

Regarding Paul's use of the Greek word *embateuon* above, **Friberg** states, ". . . A second century inscription leads some to see it as a relig[ious] t [echnical] t[erm] for the second step of an initiate into a mystery relig[ion] as he entered an inner sanctuary; *enter* into mysteries." Kittel's **Theological Dictionary of the New Testament** tells us that *embateuon* ". . . is used inversely to signify the action of those who have just received the mysteries (p. 535, vol. II)." Given the nature of Paul's argument to this point in the epistle, such a use of *embateuon* fits the context and appears reasonable.

COLOSSIANS 2:20 If with Christ you died to **the elemental spirits of the universe** [ton stoicheion tou kosmou], why do you live as if you still belonged to the world? Why do you submit to regulations, 21 "**Do not handle, Do not taste, Do not touch**" 22 (referring to things which all perish as they are used), **according to human precepts and doctrines**? 23 These have indeed an appearance of wisdom in promoting rigor of devotion and self-abasement and severity to the body, but they are of no value in checking the indulgence of the flesh. (**RSV**)

The Bible consistently teaches that angelic beings currently rule over the world. Since the Colossians had symbolically died to the world at baptism (Col. 2:12; Rom. 6:4) and were considered "citizens of heaven" (Phi. 3:20), they were no longer under the authority of fallen angels. Now that they knew the one true God and were in His son Yeshua, the demons had no further dominion over them and no right to their obedience or worship. If they submitted to angelic powers as the Gnostics advocated, the Colossians would have been denying their salvation in Christ. Part of that submission consisted of ascetic regulations which prohibited sensory pleasures: "do not handle, do not taste, do not touch."

Verse 22 makes it clear that these prohibitions were human institutions. Every indication is that Paul is **not** referring to the Law in this chapter. Indeed, the word "law" is never used in the Colossian epistle. Evidently these false teachings were human traditions derived from demonic precepts (Col. 2:8; I Tim. 4:1-3).

In verse 23, Paul says that these doctrines might seem on the surface to promote wisdom and spiritual growth through the abuse of the physical body. Yet he concludes that they're really of no value in curtailing fleshly indulgence. Paul shifts gears in the third chapter and begins to exhort the Colossians to seek heavenly things, not the things which pertain to this world (Col. 3:1-2).

CONCLUSION

The first two chapters of Paul's letter to the Colossians were intended to combat false teachings being advocated to the Christians in Colosse. These teachings apparently were a form of early Gnosticism, and they threatened to lead the Colossians away from the truth that had originally been given to them. Both subtly and explicitly, Paul counters these false doctrines and explains why Christ is the only valid mediator between God and mankind. He encourages the Colossians to hold fast to Christ, who is the head of his body, the Church. Paul ends by exposing the Gnostic doctrines for what they are: the demonically-inspired traditions of men.

Bryan T. Huie

October 25, 1997

Revised: June 27, 2009

Synchronizing Calendars

WHERE ARE WE IN THE HISTORY OF THE WORLD?

Determining where we are in the biblical time line from creation is not easy. However, it can be done if we look at ALL the relevant Scriptures before arriving at a conclusion. To get started, let's establish the beginning of our time line based on the chronology given in Genesis:

EVENT	TIME	SCRIPTURE	DATE
Adam's creation to Seth's birth	130 years	Gen. 5:3	130 AM
Seth's birth to Enosh's birth	105 years	Gen. 5:6	235 AM
Enosh's birth to Cainan's birth	90 years	Gen. 5:9	325 AM
Cainan's birth to Mahalaleel's birth	70 years	Gen. 5:12	395 AM
Mahalaleel's birth to Jared's birth	65 years	Gen. 5:15	460 AM
Jared's birth to Enoch's birth	162 years	Gen. 5:18	622 AM
Enoch's birth to Methuselah's birth	65 years	Gen. 5:21	687 AM
Methuselah's birth to Lamech's birth	187 years	Gen. 5:25	874 AM
Lamech's birth to Noah's birth	182 years	Gen. 5:28-29	1056 AM
Noah's birth to the Flood	600 years	Gen. 7:6	1656 AM
Flood to Arphaxad's birth	2 years	Gen. 11:10	1658 AM
Arphaxad's birth to Salah's birth	35 years	Gen. 11:12	1693 AM
Salah's birth to Eber's birth	30 years	Gen. 11:14	1723 AM
Eber's birth to Peleg's birth	34 years	Gen. 11:16	1757 AM
Peleg's birth to Reu's birth	30 years	Gen. 11:18	1787 AM
Reu's birth to Serug's birth	32 years	Gen. 11:20	1819 AM
Serug's birth to Nahor's birth	30 years	Gen. 11:22	1849 AM
Nahor's birth to Terah's birth	29 years	Gen. 11:24	1878 AM
Terah's birth to Abram's birth	70 years	Gen. 11:26	1948 AM
Abram's birth to Isaac's birth	100 years	Gen. 21:5	2048 AM

AM = *Anno Mundi* - Year of the Earth (from creation)

As you can see from the chart above, Abram was born in the year 1948 AM (not coincidentally, the modern nation of Israel, composed of Abraham's descendants, was reborn in the year 1948 CE).

GALATIANS 3:16 Now to Abraham and his Seed were the promises made. He does not say, "And to seeds," as of many, but as of one, "And to your Seed," who is Christ. 17 And this I say, that **the law, which was four hundred and thirty years later**, cannot annul the covenant that was confirmed before by God in Christ, that it should make the promise of no effect. (*NKJV*)

In Galatians 3:17, Paul tells us that from the establishment of God's covenant with Abraham until the giving of the Law on Mount Sinai, 430 years elapsed. Genesis 12:1-3 shows us this initial covenant:

GENESIS 12:1 Now the LORD had said to Abram: "Get out of your country, from your family and from your father's house, to a land that I will show you. 2 I will make you a great nation; I will bless you And make your name great; and you shall be a blessing. 3 I will bless those who bless you, and I will curse him who curses you; and in you all the families of the earth shall be blessed." 4 So Abram departed as the LORD had spoken to him, and Lot went with him. And **Abram was seventy-five years old when he departed from Haran**. (*NKJV*)

When was this covenant established? Most would answer that it was established when Abram was 75 years old. This would be an incorrect deduction, however. Elsewhere the Scriptures show that God brought Abram out of Ur of the Chaldees BEFORE he brought him out of Haran (Gen. 11:31; 15:7; Neh. 9:7).

Stephen confirms this fact in his discourse before the Sanhedrin:

ACTS 7:2 And he said, "Brethren and fathers, listen: **The God of glory appeared to our father Abraham when he was in Mesopotamia, BEFORE he dwelt in Haran**, 3 and said to him, 'Get out of your country and from your relatives, and come to a land that I will show you.'" (*NKJV*)

So how do we determine how long Abram was in Haran after God made the covenant with him? Genesis 15 gives us the answer:

GENESIS 15:13 Then He said to Abram: "Know certainly that **your descendants will be strangers in a land that is not theirs, and will serve them, and they will afflict them four hundred years**. 14 And also the nation whom they serve I will judge; afterward they shall come out with great possessions. 15 Now as for you, you shall go to your fathers in peace; you shall be buried at a good old age." (*NKJV*)

According to the cantillation signs placed in the Hebrew text of Genesis 15:13 by the scribes, the phrase "400 years" refers back to the words, "your descendants will be strangers in a land that is not theirs." The years of Abraham's offspring being strangers in a strange land BEGAN with the birth of Isaac (2048 AM), NOT with the Egyptian enslavement. Therefore the text ought to be understood as follows: "Know certainly that your descendants will be strangers in a land that is not theirs . . . 400 years." Adding 400 years to the date of Isaac's birth brings us to 2448 AM, which is the year of the Exodus and the giving of the Law at Mount Sinai.

The 30-year difference in the number of years mentioned by Paul in Galatians 3:17 and the number of years specified to Abram by God is due to two different starting points for the same ending point. God's first recorded covenant with Abram (Gen. 12:1-3) was instituted 430 years before the Law was given on Mount Sinai, while Genesis 15:13 refers to 400 years between the birth of Abraham's chosen offspring, Isaac, and the Exodus from Egypt. This means that God made that first covenant with Abram in 2018 AM, 30 years before Isaac was born. Genesis 12:4 tells us that Abram left Haran at the age of 75, which would have been in 2023 AM. The covenant of the pieces (Gen. 15) was probably made ten years later in the year 2033 AM, just before the birth of Ishmael in 2034 AM.

However, because of a statement made by Stephen, many think that Abram didn't leave Haran until after his father died:

ACTS 7:4 "Then he came out of the land of the Chaldeans and dwelt in Haran. And from there, **when his father was dead**, He moved him to this land in which you now dwell." (*NKJV*)

Based on the biblical chronology shown above, we know that Terah was born in 1878 AM. Genesis 11:32 tells us that Terah lived 205 years. So simple math establishes that Terah didn't physically die until **2083 AM** (35 years AFTER the birth of Isaac). There is no way to reconcile Stephen's statement if we apply it to Terah's physical death. Therefore, unless we assume (incorrectly) that Stephen was mistaken, we have to realize that he was referring to Terah's **spiritual** death, not his physical death.

Many times the Scriptures speak of the living as being dead because of **sin** (Rom. 6:13; Col. 2:13; Eph. 2:1, 5; I Tim. 5:6; I John 3:14; I Pet. 4:6; Rev. 3:1). We know that Terah worshiped other gods (Jos. 24:2). Clearly Stephen was referring to Terah's spiritual state, not his physical state, when he mentioned his death.

Exodus 12:40-41 tells us the very day that God first made His covenant with Abram:

EXODUS 12:40 Now the **sojourn** of the children of Israel who lived in Egypt was **four hundred and thirty years**. 41 And it came to pass at the end of the **four hundred and thirty years – ON THAT VERY SAME DAY** – it came to pass that all the armies of the LORD went out from the land of Egypt. (*NKJV*)

The Bible tells us that the Israelites started their trek out of Egypt on the 15th of the month of Abib (Num. 33:3). Therefore, we know that 430 years earlier, on 15 Abib (or Nisan), God first told Abraham to leave Ur of the Chaldees and promised to bless him if he did.

Some argue that Exodus 12:40-41 shows conclusively that the Israelites were slaves in Egypt for 430 years. However, the focus of these verses is the SO-

JOURN of the children of Israel. Literally, this sojourn began when Abraham left Ur at the age of 70.

It is easy to prove from the Bible itself that the period of time that the Israelites dwelt in Egypt was not 400 or 430 years:

GENESIS 46:2 Then God spoke to Israel in the visions of the night, and said, "Jacob, Jacob!" And he said, "Here I am." 3 So He said, "I am God, the God of your father; do not fear to go down to Egypt, for I will make of you a great nation there. 4 I will go down with you to Egypt, and I will also surely bring you up again; and Joseph will put his hand on your eyes." 5 Then Jacob arose from Beersheba; and the sons of Israel carried their father Jacob, their little ones, and their wives, in the carts which Pharaoh had sent to carry him. 6 So they took their livestock and their goods, which they had acquired in the land of Canaan, and **went to Egypt**, Jacob and all his descendants with him. 7 His sons and his sons' sons, his daughters and his sons' daughters, and **all his descendants he brought with him to Egypt**. 8 Now **these were the names of the children of Israel, Jacob and his sons, who went to Egypt**: Reuben was Jacob's firstborn. . . . 11 The sons of **Levi** were Gershon, **KOHATH**, and Merari. (*NKJV*)

We see that when Jacob and his descendants left Canaan to move to Egypt, his son Levi and his grandson Kohath were among those who made the journey. After arriving in Egypt, Kohath had a son named Amram (Exo. 6:18). In turn, Amram had a son named Moses (Exo. 6:20). Moses was 80 years old when the Exodus took place (Exo. 7:7).

To find the MAXIMUM possible time between the Israelites move to Egypt and the Exodus, we will make some assumptions. We are told that Kohath lived to be 133 years old (Exo. 6:18), and Amram lived to be 137 years old (Exo. 6:20). Let's assume that Kohath had just been born when Jacob and Levi his father moved to Egypt. We will also assume that Amram had Moses in the last year of his life. To these two life spans, we will add Moses' age at the Exodus (80):

Kohath lived **133** years (Exo. 6:18)

Amram lived **137** years (Exo. 6:20)

Age of Moses at the Exodus was **80** years (Exo. 7:7)

TOTAL – 133 + 137 + 80 = **350**

The **maximum** possible time for the sojourn is only **350 years**. We see that the biblical chronology does not allow for 430 or 400 years in Egypt. Therefore, the 400 years of Genesis 15:13 must be a reference to something else. As demonstrated above, it is referring to the period of time between the birth of Isaac and the Exodus from Egypt. Now let's go back to the year of Isaac's birth and work our way forward on the time line.

An interesting thing happened after Solomon completed the Temple in seven years (1 Kings 6:38) and then his own house in 13 years (1 Kings 7:1). God once again appeared to him and told him the penalty for future disobedience:

EVENT	TIME	SCRIPTURE	DATE
Abram's birth to Isaac's birth	100 years	Gen. 21:5	**2048 AM**
Isaac's birth to the Exodus	400 years	Gen. 15:13; Acts 7:6	**2448 AM**
Exodus to the beginning of Solomon's Temple	480 years	1 Kings 6:1	**2928 AM**
Beginning of Solomon's Temple to the completion of his house	20 years	1 Kings 9:10; 2 Chr. 8:1	**2948 AM**

1 KINGS 9:1 And it came to pass, when Solomon had finished building the house of the LORD and the king's house, and all Solomon's desire which he wanted to do, 2 that **the LORD appeared to Solomon the second time**, as He had appeared to him at Gibeon. 3 And the LORD said to him: "I have heard your prayer and your supplication that you have made before Me; I have consecrated this house which you have built to put My name there forever, and My eyes and My heart will be there perpetually. 4 Now if you walk before Me as your father David walked, in integrity of heart and in uprightness, to do according to all that I have commanded you, and if you keep My statutes and My judgments, 5 then I will establish the throne of your kingdom over Israel forever, as I promised David your father, saying, 'You shall not fail to have a man on the throne of Israel.' 6 But if you or your sons at all turn from following Me, and do not keep My commandments and My statutes which I have set before you, but go and serve other gods and worship them, 7 then **I will cut off Israel from the land which I have given them; and this house which I have consecrated for My name I will cast out of My sight**. Israel will be a proverb and a byword among all peoples. 8 And **as for this house, which is exalted, everyone who passes by it will be astonished and will hiss, and say, 'Why has the LORD done thus to this land and to this house?'** 9 Then they will answer, 'Because they forsook the LORD their God, who brought their fathers out of the land of Egypt, and have embraced other gods, and worshiped them and served them; therefore the LORD has brought all this calamity on them.' " (*NKJV*)

In the Ezekiel, we see a prophecy which speaks of the destruction of both the first Temple and second Temple in Jerusalem:

EZEKIEL 4:1 "You also, son of man, take a clay tablet and lay it before you, and portray on it a city, Jerusalem. 2 Lay siege against it, build a siege wall against it, and heap up a mound against it; set camps against it also, and place battering rams against it all around. 3 Moreover take for yourself an iron plate, and set it as an iron wall between you and the city. Set your face against it, and it shall be besieged, and you shall lay siege against it. This will be a sign to the House of Israel. 4 Lie also on your left side, and lay the iniquity of the House of Israel upon it. According to the number of the days that you lie on it, you shall bear their iniquity. 5 For I have laid on you **the years of their iniquity, according to the number of the days, 390 days**; so you shall bear the iniquity of the House of Israel. 6 And when you have completed them, lie again on your right side; then you shall bear the iniquity of the House of Judah 40 days. I have laid on you a day for each year. 7 Therefore you shall set your face toward the siege of Jerusalem; your arm shall be uncovered, and you shall prophesy against it." (*NKJV*)

What is the meaning of these actions that God commanded Ezekiel to perform? An understanding of the symbolism and the time periods portrayed gives us valuable chronological information related to the biblical time line.

This prophecy was given in the 5th year of the captivity of King Jehoiachin of Judah (Eze. 1:2). The final siege of Jerusalem and destruction of the city (including Solomon's Temple) by the Babylonians was still several years in the future.

First, let's identify the specifics given to us in the prophecy:

- Clay brick (v. 1) = Jerusalem
- Iron plate (v. 3) = walls around Jerusalem
- House of Israel (vv. 3-5) = all the tribes of Israel
- House of Judah (v. 6) = only the southern kingdom of Judah
- 390 days = 390 years of iniquity by all the tribes of Israel (both Samaria & Judah)

40 days = 40 years of iniquity by only the southern kingdom of Judah

The focus of this prophecy given to Ezekiel was two future sieges of the city of Jerusalem. Ezekiel was told to portray through his actions two different periods of time (390 years and 40 years). It was during these time periods that the events which would bring about those sieges of Jerusalem would take place. How do we know what these time periods represent? First, we have to determine a starting point. What better starting point for the countdown to the destruction of Solomon's Temple than God's personal warning to Solomon regarding the future destruction of Jerusalem and the Temple as punishment for disobedience (1 Kings 9:1-9)?

Secular history tells us that the destruction of Jerusalem and the first Temple by Nebuchadnezzar and Babylon took place in 586 BCE (interestingly, the gematria of " ירושלם Jerusalem" in Hebrew equals 586). If we add 390 years to the date of God's warning to Solomon regarding the destruction of Jerusalem and the Temple (2948 AM), we see that Solomon's Temple was destroyed by the

Babylonians in 3338 AM.

In agreement with the creation date we calculated above, rabbinic sources generally place the destruction of the first Temple in the creation year 3338 AM. When synchronized with secular history, it becomes clear that the Jewish calendar in common usage has a period of approximately 163 years omitted.

Having identified the creation year 3338 AM with the Roman year 586 BCE, we now are able to synchronize the creation calendar to our commonly used Roman calendar:

EVENT	DATE (BCE/CE)	DATE (AM)
Babylonian destruction of Jerusalem/the Temple	587/586 BCE	3338 AM
Second Temple completed	517/516 BCE	3408 AM
Artaxerxes' commission to Ezra to rebuild Jerusalem	458/457 BCE	3467 AM
Nehemiah appointed governor of Judah by Artaxerxes	445/444 BCE	3480 AM
Daniel's seven weeks of years completed	410/409 BCE	3515 AM
Antiochus Epiphanes desecrates Second Temple	168/167 BCE	3757 AM
Judas Maccabee recaptures & cleanses Second Temple	165/164 BCE	3760 AM
Yeshua's birth	5/4 BCE	3920 AM
Tiberius begins co-rule with Augustus Caesar	12/13 CE	3936 AM
Yeshua begins his ministry	26/27 CE	3950 AM
Yeshua crucified and resurrected	29/30 CE	3953 AM
Destruction of the Second Temple	69/70 CE	3993 AM
Birth of the modern State of Israel	1947/1948 CE	5871 AM
Six-Day War & Recapture of the Temple Mount	1966/1967 CE	5890 AM
Egyptian-Israeli Peace Treaty	1978/1979 CE	5902 AM
Oslo Peace Accord	1992/1993 CE	5916 AM
Palestinian Al-Aqsa Intifada begins	1999/2000 CE	5923 AM

We are currently in the creation year 5933 AM (2009/2010 CE), which is 5770 on the Jewish calendar.

Bryan T. Huie